..........................................

# THE RISE OF CHINA VS.

# THE LOGIC OF STRATEGY

# THE RISE OF CHINA VS.
# THE LOGIC OF STRATEGY

EDWARD N. LUTTWAK

*The Belknap Press of Harvard University Press*

CAMBRIDGE, MASSACHUSETTS

LONDON, ENGLAND

2012

*Library of Congress Cataloging-in-Publication Data*

Luttwak, Edward.

The Rise of China vs. the Logic of Strategy / Edward N. Luttwak.

pages   cm

Includes bibliographical references and index.

ISBN 978-0-674-06642-7 (alk. paper)

1. China—Strategic aspects.   2. China—Military policy.

3. China—Foreign relations—1976–   4. Geopolitics—China.

I. Title.

UA835.L87   2012

355'.033551—dc23        2012007972

# Contents

CONTENTS

# *Preface*

*It is as a strategist* and not as a Sinologist that I approach the phenomenon of today's China, for the universal logic of strategy applies in perfect equality to every culture in every age.

While my text relies on documents and the works of the scholars here cited, and others too, no doubt, I confess that it is also colored by my own travels in and around China, which started long before its opening to the world, and even then reached its most remote parts.

Since that time, in conditions ever easier, I have continued to travel far and wide in China. For that reason, I am acutely conscious both of the atrocious miseries that persisted while Mao Zedong lived, and of the wonderful transformations that started very soon after his death, that continue still. While recognizing that all manner of abuses and shortcomings still persist, I cannot but rejoice in the very great advances of the peoples of China in both material conditions and personal freedoms—outside the still strictly reserved political realm, which regrettably encompasses national and ethnic self-expression as well. Thus, it is not as a detached observer that

I view China and its peoples, but rather as one thoroughly engaged in their hopes and anxieties, as manifested by those in China who have long ago proven their strong and true friendship, for which I am most grateful.

Hence I cannot rejoice in the sad, even sinister consequences that must ensue if China's rapid advance were to collide with the paradoxical logic of strategy. Indeed, if this book has a further purpose beyond the analysis on which it must stand or fail, it is the hope, howsoever naive and improbable, that China's rulers will disenthrall themselves from the illusion that magnitude of planetary dimensions, very rapid economic growth, and an equally rapid increase in military strength can all coexist in the same world, and simply persist. It is only *un*balanced growth—economic but not military—that the logic of strategy will allow to China in its present condition, and that logic cannot be circumvented by conciliatory words or clever stratagems. Instead, to avert cruel consequences, the logic must be obeyed even when it contradicts common sense and every ordinary human instinct. Rapidly increasing wealth hardly inspires humility or restraint, yet no other course is possible in a world of independent states bound to resist aggrandizement on China's unique scale.

As a nonspecialist, I have benefited greatly from the global expertise on China, much of it from China, constantly offered by the C-Pol network that Professor Richard Baum's serene authority keeps miraculously free of on-line drivel.

This book started as an inquiry commissioned in 2010 by Andrew W. Marshall, head of the Office of Net Assessment of the Department of Defense. To have worked with him more than once over the years has been a privilege, for Andrew Marshall's talent as a strategic thinker is as legendary as his unique longevity in office: born in 1921, he created, in 1973, the office he still directs in 2012. I have also benefited from the advice of his collaborators, and notably David F. Epstein, while Adam S. Lovinger was most helpful from start to finish. Naturally, none of the above is in any way responsible for the text, which is entirely my own.

Because this was not an adversarial investigation of an enemy power, but rather an open-ended attempt to explain the conduct of a great state with which ever-expanding cooperation is at least as likely as intensifying rivalry, and altogether more desirable, I could naturally benefit from conversations with friends in China as well, including senior military officers and prominent governmental advisors. In addition, one of my closest friends, Francesco Sisci, has been a Beijing resident for decades, and although he disagrees with some of my conclusions, he did make my recent visits to China all the more agreeable.

Finally, it is a particular pleasure to thank Michael Aronson of Harvard University Press, who has long been an initiator as well as an editor of my books, never uncritical but always constructive.

·······································

# CHAPTER ONE

# The Fallacy of Unresisted Aggrandizement

*It is now widely believed* that the future of the world will be shaped by the rise of China, that is, by the continuation of its phenomenally rapid economic growth—even if less rapid eventually—and what comes naturally with such an immense growth in economic capacity, from ever-increasing influence in regional and world affairs, to the further strengthening of China's armed forces.

These expectations are certainly consistent with China's economic performance since the death of Mao in September 1976. Its economy started to grow rapidly in the 1980s, recessions since then have been neither long nor severe, and there are no signs of structural deceleration even now, after more than three decades of rapid economic expansion. Recent gross domestic product increases have exceeded 9 percent annually—twice the maximum sustainable growth rate of the economy of the United States, and almost three times as much as the equivalent rate for mature European economies—let alone the dismal growth rates actually experienced in the post-2007 crisis years.

Nor is there any inherent reason why China's economic growth should decelerate greatly in the near future. In rural China, even in patches and pockets not very far from major cities, vast numbers are still grossly underemployed in traditional agriculture, in the lowest rungs of commerce, and in humble personal services. As the rural poor find new employment in manufacturing, even of the most manual kind, in construction, and in modern services, their productivity increases sharply and, with it, China's gross domestic product. In addition, there is of course the organic growth of China's modern economic sectors, several of which remain highly competitive and can therefore grow rapidly even as global markets grow more slowly.

As for China's military expenditures, in recent years they have reportedly increased as rapidly, or almost as rapidly, as the economy as a whole, with estimates of the order of 9 percent per annum in real terms—a phenomenal rate of growth at a time when military expenditures worldwide, including those of the United States, but for immediate war costs, have been mostly stagnant or declining.[1]

The People's Liberation Army, the PLA, has thus received an expanding torrent of resources—and the days are long past when more resources could not yield much new military strength, because they were mostly absorbed by belated remedies for long-neglected basic necessities.

Pay and benefits have now increased to levels sufficiently competitive to recruit men and women in sufficient numbers in spite of expanding civilian employment opportunities,[2] while the rehabilitation or replacement of decrepit barracks, bases, depots, and other installations has been largely accomplished, along with the provision of adequate maintenance facilities, equipment, and tooling.

With past neglect remedied, in spite of a great deal of supplier fraud (even attentive civilians purchasing on a much smaller scale are regularly defrauded by false labeling for substandard products), and outright misappropriation by its own officers,[3] the PLA has been able to acquire new platforms, weapons, munitions, and ancillary equipment in rising numbers for every branch of every service, and to build, enlarge, and upgrade facilities of every kind while concurrently increasing its training and operating tempo.

All this results in rapid and all-round military aggrandizement, of the kind last seen in the United States long ago during the years of the Korean War rearmament, and in the Soviet Union from the later 1960s until the 1980s. In both cases, vigorous qualitative advancement was coupled with numerical increases in the weapons and personnel of every service; and as the Marxists liked to say, large quantitative increases can generate their own qualitative effects, compounding the overall result. That is why, for example, when spending on the U.S. Air Force more than tripled from 1950 to 1960 and both the number and the performance of its aircraft rapidly and concurrently increased, the Air Force's capabilities became not merely greater but altogether different—and disproportionately more powerful.

3

It is the straightforward assumption that China's economic and military growth will persist at a rapid pace, and that China's global influence will also increase in step, that generates the now widespread expectation that China is bound to emerge as the world's predominant power in the foreseeable future, eclipsing the United States.[4] Yet that must be the least likely of outcomes, because it would collide with the very logic of strategy in a world of diverse states, each jealous of its autonomy. Some states, moreover, are culturally predisposed and politically structured to try to influence other states rather than be influenced.

It is true that the three-sided growth of China's economy, military strength, and political standing was perfectly complementary in the 1980s and 1990s (after the 1989 interval), but that was so only because China was not yet rich, or strong, or influential by American standards—or by Japan's, for that matter—and still remained mostly an exotic offstage presence for Europe and Latin America. But adversarial reactions are bound to be evoked as China's economic and military growth continue beyond the levels that can be accepted with equanimity by other powers—that is, beyond the culminating level of unresisted Chinese achievement.

With that natural reaction under way, any further increase in the level of Chinese power could only be accepted unresistingly if there were radical changes inside or outside China—whether by a democratic transformation of China itself and the consequent legitimization of its government, or

4

the emergence of more pressing threats that convert China from a threat to a desirable ally for the country in question. (Pakistan is the exemplary case; as China's power increases, it becomes a yet more valued patron.)

Democratization would not nullify the strategic significance of China's rise and the reactions it must evoke—after all, even the very democratic United States evokes resistance from its own good allies on occasion, simply because it is overwhelmingly powerful. But if democratization did take place and China's policies were no longer formed in total secrecy by a few party chiefs, and if its policies were no longer so largely focused on the maximization of power, there would certainly be less concern over China's rise, and less resistance by neighbors and peers. Democratization would not suspend the logic of strategy that mandates growing resistance to growing power, but it would raise the culminating level of unresisted Chinese aggrandizement.

As it is, China's rise has already passed that level, whether in the economic, military, or political sphere, activating the paradoxical logic of strategy[5] through the reactions of all the other powers large and small that have started to monitor, resist, deflect, or counter Chinese power. No matter at what level, from a knife fight in an alley to the multidimensional and multilateral engagements of grand strategy in peacetime, the logic is always the same: action—in this case the growth of power—evokes reaction, which need not stop the action but which does prohibit its simple, linear progress.

In this case, because of the mounting opposition it is evoking, China's continued and rapid growth in economic capacity *and* military strength *and* regional and global influence cannot simply persist. If Chinese leaders ignore the warning signs and forge ahead, the paradoxical logic will ensure that instead of accumulating more power, they will remain with less as resistance mounts.

Far from being the inevitable result of the simple prolongation of recent trends, China's emergence as the world's predominant power through an uninterrupted and concurrent rise in economic capacity, military strength, and global influence would require the intervention of improbable events.[6] The logic of strategy itself presages the slowing down or even partial reversal of China's rise, with the former more likely if Chinese policies are more conciliatory or downright emollient, and the latter if they are more alarming.

None of the above presumes any form of provocative or threatening behavior by the Chinese. It all derives from the reactions necessarily evoked by the very rapid growth of a power that is very great to begin with. Given China's dimensions, its rapid growth is destabilizing in itself, regardless of its conduct. Recent suggestions that China is in need of an Otto Von Bismarck to direct its foreign policy in less counterproductive ways therefore miss the point: the essential problem is not China's conduct but the growth in its all-around magnitude.

Riders in a crowded elevator cabin into which an extremely fat Mr. China has just stepped in must react self-protectively if

6

he is becoming fatter at a rapid rate, squeezing them against the walls—even if he is entirely unthreatening, and indeed affable. True, the crowded elevator cabin already contained an even fatter, louder, and frequently violent Mr. America, but simply because he had long been a fellow rider, almost everybody had over the decades come to a satisfactory accommodation with his noisy bulk, with the exceptions—Cuba, Iran, North Korea, Syria, Venezuela—themselves an advertisement for Mr. America's respectability. Most important, Mr. America is not rapidly becoming fatter, thereby undermining past accommodations and compromises, and it is also very helpful that no sudden threats are to be feared from him, because of his mostly very open democratic decision processes.

It will be obvious by now that the approach here followed, which is indeed my own way of understanding the workings of power between states modern or ancient, is far different from that of the prevailing "realist" school. It is frankly deterministic. Instead of seeing leaders striving to act pragmatically in pursuit of their goals and preferences within the operative political constraints, I see them as trapped by the paradoxes of the logic of strategy, which imposes its own imperatives, all the more so when they retain the delusion of free choice in the presence of conflict. Were it not so, the history of humanity would not be a record of its crimes and follies.

# CHAPTER TWO

# Premature Assertiveness

*As it happens*, China's recent conduct has been far from affable with a number of countries, and with some it has even been threatening in some degree. In a process disregarded at the time but quite evident in retrospect, the 2008 financial crisis, the seeming downfall of the "Washington consensus" and the seeming vindication of the "Beijing consensus" greatly emboldened the Chinese ruling elite, inducing a veritable behavioral shift that became manifest in 2009–2010. There was a sudden change in the tone and content of Chinese declarations, which became sharply assertive on many different issues, from monetary policy to the relevance of Western democracy. More strikingly, mostly dormant territorial disputes were loudly revived with India, Japan, the Philippines, and Vietnam—and all more or less at the same time, amplifying the effect. Actual incidents duly followed with the vessels or island outposts of Japan, the Philippines, and Vietnam, with successive episodes that have continued till the present writing.

Because no discernible policy objective was served, or could have been served, by verbal outbursts and actual incidents that did nothing to substantively advance China's territorial claims, some expert observers concluded that China's rulers had been unhinged by the sudden rise in their fortunes, with full-blown hubris displacing their earlier preference for prudent conduct presented in a distinctly modest manner. Official statements of no practical effect but of remarkable arrogance can be cited in support of this interpretation. Xi Jinping, by then the designated successor of Hu Jintao (Hú Jǐntāo), was thus recorded in Mexico on February 16, 2009, saying: "There are a few foreigners, with full bellies, who have nothing better to do than try to point fingers at our country."[1] Even a lowly Foreign Ministry spokeswoman, Jiang Yu, was casually dismissive on March 3, 2011, when foreign journalists complained about being attacked and harassed, and asked what law applied to them: "Don't use the law as a shield."[2] The Foreign Ministry in particular seems to cultivate arrogance, with Vice Foreign Minister Fu Ying, an assimilated Mongol of some elegance and perhaps a descendant of Genghis Khan, something of a champion amid much competition from her colleagues.

An alternative explanation is that the various institutional protagonists of assertiveness in general, and of the territorial quarrels specifically, may have their own aims that are purposeful for their own institutions and/or for themselves personally, even if Chinese interests as a whole suffer the consequences. For example, Foreign Minister Yang Jiechi gave arrogance a bad name at the July 2010 17th Regional Forum of the Association of Southeast Asian Nations in Hanoi by declaring that maritime disputes between China and member states (including Vietnam, the host) could not be negotiated multilaterally—and this at an multinational forum (!): "Turning the bilateral issue into an international, or multilateral one would only worsen the situation and add difficulties to solving the issue." Yang Jiechi went on to deny that anything was amiss: "Nobody believes there's anything that is threatening the region's peace and stability."[3] The predictable result was to drive Vietnam as well as the Philippines into the arms of the United States, but it did gain "leftist" (nationalist) praise for the Foreign Ministry, and no doubt for Yang Jiechi personally. In the Chinese system, policy is made by party leaders in conclave, so that the Foreign Ministry is merely an executive organ of scant importance. But it too evidently has enough freedom of action to pursue its own aims, under the rather flexible form of collective leadership that has prevailed in the time of Hu Jintao.

A third explanation is that China's leaders believe that assertive, even threatening language and provocative action can have a beneficial effect by inducing others to negotiate long-unresolved outstanding issues, which they may even be ready to do in a conciliatory manner; this belief, moreover, has deep cultural roots. Both are explored in what follows, but what is certain is that the post-2008 behavioral shift noted by many observers did in fact occur, even as the conciliatory and would-be reassuring official doctrine of "Peaceful Development"

(*Zhōngguó hépíng fāzhǎn*, better known under the original title "Peaceful Rise," *Zhōngguó hépíng juéqǐ*), presented by Hu Jintao's official senior advisor Zheng Bijian[4] was not repudiated or amended.

On the contrary, a strategic and not merely tactical commitment to accommodating and unaggressive policies was officially reaffirmed in a lengthy (7,000-character) article by the appropriate senior official, State Councilor Dai Bingguo.[5] Although this was undoubtedly a conciliatory initiative, the very length of that defense of the official "Peaceful Development" policy raises questions about the magnitude of the "leftist" (nationalist) and military opposition that is publicly calling for even more assertive policies. Finally, on March 31, 2011, Zheng Bijian, with his personal authority newly reinforced by his very prominent role in Hu Jintao's January 2011 Washington visit, issued a declaration to the doyen of foreign correspondents in Beijing, Francesco Sisci, which started by recognizing that China's rise was causing anxieties, requiring a restatement of Peaceful Rise.[6]

By the end of 2010, the earlier behavioral shift had seemingly given way to another in the opposite direction, with fence-mending official visits, charm offensives, soothing declarations, and import and investment promises where Chinese exports had aroused particular resentment.

The two most notable episodes of this phase were the December 15–17, 2010, visit of Premier of the State Council Wen Jiabao (Wēn Jiābao) to India in the company of some

400 businessmen and managers, and President Hu Jintao's visit to the United States that began in Washington on January 19, 2011.

Nothing much went wrong with either visit, but neither achieved anywhere near the intended effect—and a great deal had been expected from Hu Jintao's visit, as this author learned beforehand from its chief architect, Zheng Bijian, who accompanied Hu Jintao to Washington and was second in precedence at the official dinner. In sharing the proposed ten-point agenda with me in a prior Beijing meeting, Zheng Bijian emphatically insisted, although perhaps with more sincerity than confidence, that the Chinese side was ready to do its part in the urgent task of stopping the erosion of China-U.S. cooperation and goodwill.

Chinese expectations for what the two visits could achieve—greatly over-optimistic, because of the anxieties they themselves had caused—were symptomatic of a pronounced insensitivity to foreign sensitivities that I have here labeled "great-state autism." The American and Russian versions are better known, but the Chinese strain of this malady is especially virulent, as befits the most populous of all states, and one moreover anciently formed in isolation from any comparable state.[7]

# CHAPTER THREE

# Great-State Autism Defined

*In all great states* there is so much internal activity that leaders and opinion-makers cannot focus *seriously* on foreign affairs as well, except in particular times of crisis. They do not have the constant situational awareness of the world around them that is natural in small countries of equal advancement. After all, individual sensory and cranial capacities are much the same in smoothly operating states of a few million people, and in mega-states such as the Russian Federation, the United States, India, and China, whose leaders face internal urgencies if not emergencies each day somewhere or other, in addition to their ordinary decision-making sessions and ceremonial obligations.

The result is not mere inattention. On the contrary, it is not only possible but common for great-state leaders and even entire ruling elites to make much of foreign affairs if only as welcome diversion from the harder choices of domestic politics, in which almost any decision that pleases some must displease others—and not mere foreigners whose political support will not be missed.

Great-state autism is worse than inattention because in the absence of the serious and earnest study that domestic urgencies make impossible, decision-makers cannot absorb in-depth information with all its complexities and subtleties, even if it is offered to them (which is unlikely: when intelligence officers adhere to the rule that their highest duty is to tell top leaders what they do not want to hear, their careers suffer). Instead, decisions on foreign affairs are almost always made on the basis of highly simplified, schematic representations of unmanageably complex realities, which are thereby distorted to fit within internally generated categories, expectations, and perspectives. Only thus can a Massachusetts or Michigan politician who would never consider himself qualified to pronounce on the local politics of, say, Mississippi ("too different, do not know the local pols . . .") unhesitatingly state his view of what will work best in Afghanistan, Iraq, or Libya.

That no doubt is how it came to pass that in Beijing highly intelligent people could persuade themselves that a visit to India by Premier Wen Jiabao would offset a whole slew of fresh resentments and anxieties aroused by recent Chinese initiatives,[1] by offering alluring prospects of profitable business dealings with China. In this case, as so often, the schematic representation took the familiar form of utterly misleading mirror-imaging: while for many Chinese, China's business is indeed business, India's business is India, because economic interests within it are not strongly expressed in its foreign policy, which is dominated by the concerns of its professional diplomats and by the stances of the more ideological of its elected politicians (were that not so, U.S.-Indian relations could hardly have been as restricted as they were from 1947 until quite recent years).

The bounties promised by Chinese business executives and entrepreneurs to their Indian counterparts were thus mostly irrelevant to the actual decision-makers, officials focused on geopolitical rather than economic interests, and politicians who might perhaps have been moved by private economic gain, but not by national economic interests. In any case, both Indian officials and politicians know full well that they cannot make any territorial concessions whatsoever without promptly losing their offices, if not more.

That may be hard to understand for Chinese leaders, who have conceded territory, or at least given up long-asserted territorial claims, rather liberally in recent years to settle frontier disputes with neighboring countries. In bilateral negotiations, the Chinese side conceded 100 percent of the Afghan claim, 76 percent of the Laos claim, 66 percent of Kazakhstan's, 65 percent of the Republic of Mongolia's claim, 94 percent of Nepal's, 60 percent of North Korea's, 96 percent of Tajikistan's, and 50 percent of Vietnam's land claim (in sharp contrast to Chinese intransigence over its maritime claims). With the Soviet Union and then the Russian Federation, successive negotiations were also concluded successfully on a roughly 50/50 basis.[2]

Evidently, the territories in question were viewed pragmatically by the Chinese as negotiable assets, and because they were neither large in relative terms nor significantly valuable in themselves, while their populations were either very small or mostly non-Han, or both, the concessions were made. One Chinese aim was to clear the way for transborder trade, which was economically far from important on a national scale, but politically important locally, to enrich and stabilize restive non-Han borderland populations; a parallel aim was to remove an obstacle to security cooperation in regard to those same populations, which mostly extend into the neighboring countries. To ensure that frontier guards on both sides would cooperate to repress dissident non-Hans, it was necessary to define and demarcate the frontier in question amicably, and the Chinese were willing to pay the price.

Businesslike bargaining solved territorial disputes with twelve of China's neighbors by dividing up disputed tracts of land, because they were essentially property transactions from the Chinese point of view, and the lands in question were not economically valuable properties.

For India, on the other hand—the actually existing India as opposed to its schematic perception in Chinese eyes—frontiers have an entirely different meaning that allows no room at all for pragmatic bargaining to divide disputed territory. That must be so because India's borders derive exclusively from a one-time colonial inheritance from the British that lacks any *Indian* historical origin or any other organic legitimacy whatever. Therefore, any subtraction from the original 1947 inheritance would compromise the legitimacy of the whole.[3]

The British had arbitrarily excluded Burma, Ceylon, and Sikkim from the Indian Union before conceding its independence, while including Assam, which was no more Hindi-speaking or "Indian" in any other way than Ceylon or Burma—from which Assam had been taken away.

The object of China's territorial claim, the state of Arunachal Pradesh, was itself cut out from the Assam inheritance, as were the states of Nagaland, Meghalaya, and Mizoram, and if one were to be given up as not belonging to India, as "non-Indian" in effect, so might the others.

This legitimacy nexus has prevented successive Indian governments of different political complexions from offering any territorial solutions for the unending conflict in Jammu-Kashmir; because of it, territory in the particular is inseparable from the legitimacy of Indian sovereignty over the whole. For the same reason, no conceivable Indian government could concede any part of Arunachal Pradesh to China. But evidently Beijing decision-makers are not focusing on India as it actually exists, but instead operate on the basis of a schematic representation of an India that is sufficiently China-like to have a pragmatic attitude toward the disposition of its territory.

Chinese analysts would no doubt point out that Americans are also subject to great-state autism in general, and to mirror-imaging in particular. Moreover, it is arguably the mirror-imaging of a narrow elite of urbane secularists very unrepresentative of Americans as whole. Religious agitations, for example, are routinely interpreted by this elite as opportunistic expressions of political or economic dissatisfactions, rather than as outbursts of religious distress at the intrusions of modernity—even though that is a distress shared by the many churchgoing non-elite Americans.

Russians likewise will almost always interpret the motives of others in almost exclusively Russian terms. The classic example was the post–Cold War enlargement of the North Atlantic Treaty Organization (NATO) through the admission of five ex-Communist satellites and the three ex-Soviet Baltic states. For the Americans, it was the fastest and cheapest way of stabilizing fragile new democracies—European Union admission procedures being necessarily much slower—and the Russians themselves were expected to participate in the process and benefit from it. They had already been invited to cooperate not only with but within NATO, which could no longer be anti-Soviet and had no reason at all to become anti-Russian.

For the Russians, on the other hand—that is, almost all policy-elite Russians known to this author in person or through their writings[4]—NATO's enlargement was a calculatedly hostile American move, a forward deployment toward Moscow fervently desired by "the Pentagon," and of course inherently offensive in intent. It was also perfidious in their view, because the withdrawal of Soviet forces from eastern Europe had been preceded by, and predicated on, unwritten U.S. promises that NATO would not expand eastward. That is perfectly true, but irrelevant in American eyes in the absence of any hostile intent.

Of lesser examples of Russian mirror-imaging of foreign motives there is no end, and it is revealing that within these schematic representations of more complex realities, the essential building block is the attribution of deeply malevolent motives. The common Russian presumption is that foreigners would want a weaker, poorer, less secure, less happy Russia, with all benevolent words, even deeds, mere camouflage. That is the subtext of the daily presentation of international news in Russian media—and not only in those under direct official control. That authoritarian leaders are obviously well served by such misrepresentations does not mean that they themselves see matters differently.

Chinese leaders are necessarily even more Sino-centric, and thus even more autistic, than Russians are Russo-centric or the Americans are U.S.-centric, in the first instance simply because their own internal realities are not only greater but also much more dynamically unstable: on any given day, somewhere in China there is an emergency under way important enough to engage the top leaders, be it an earthquake, a major flood, ethnic rioting, an abrupt economic shift such as a sudden upsurge in food prices, or an actual or imagined internal political threat.

Abundant evidence shows that the leaders of the Chinese Communist Party (CCP) evaluate the gravity of domestic political threats in an extremely prudent manner—if that is the right adjective for the wild exaggeration of mostly very minor threats to the stability of the regime. Or perhaps it is the vast apparatus of state security that habitually inflates internal threats. Either way, the top CCP leaders can easily become absorbed by them—and even more by the chain reactions unleashed by their own exaggerated repressive reactions. In the spring of 2011, for example, extremely feeble attempts to import the North African ("Jasmine") model of popular insurgency triggered by social-media appeals to gather and demonstrate, resulted in major disruptions. While the actual attempts did not go beyond a few social-media communications, large numbers of very belligerent riot police appeared to confront nonexistent demonstrators in the country's most central venues, notably Beijing's Wángfujing, where innocent passersby and entire families of Chinese tourists were brusquely ordered to leave. Nor did the absence of any perceptible demonstrations dissuade arrests of "usual suspects" all over China, known human rights activists, rule-of-law campaigners, free trade-union would-be organizers, and political liberalization advocates. That in turn activated the lawyers who habitually try and mostly fail to defend the usual suspects—and the authorities reacted by arresting many of them as well. On top of that, harsh warnings were issued to all and sundry to keep out of trouble. To reinforce this excess of precautionary intimidation, China's most prominent example of an independent-minded yet establishment artistic figure, Ai Weiwei, was arrested in a totally unnecessary dramatic manner at Beijing's airport as he was about to board a flight to Hong Kong. That in turn triggered Ai Weiwei protests all over the world—one spoiled China's expensive investment in a Biennale pavilion in Venice—adding greatly to the very real political costs of the imaginary "Jasmine" threat.

Thus, when there is no earthquake, flood, major riot, or abrupt economic trouble[5] to divert the attention of China's leaders from the complexities of the outside world, they create their own disturbance by overreacting in extreme degree to very minor political threats, indeed to the mere auto-suggestion of nonexistent threats. This pattern of conduct is highly significant because it reflects a permanent predicament: the structural insecurity of the leaders of the CCP, whose power has neither democratic legitimacy nor the ideological legitimacy that their predecessors could claim, regardless of the objective merits of that ideology. Attempts to revive it with commemorative megafilms and officially organized choral singing have had no perceptible positive effects for the CCP, while they do evoke the ridicule and contempt of the educated.

The leaders evidently realize their predicament: there is visible evidence of their insecurity in the pervasive protective measures visible in and around Beijing. In Moscow and Washington also, security measures have become very visible in recent years—but in Beijing they are plainly intended to counter mass uprisings, as opposed to isolated acts of terrorism as in Moscow and Washington.

Yet more striking is the visible evidence that China's top leaders mistrust their own guardians. It can be found outside the main entrance of the Zhongnanhai, a vast walled compound in the heart of Beijing, just west of the Forbidden City, that houses sundry meeting pavilions, party offices, and leader residences around two large ponds. It is, in effect, China's Kremlin or White House, if very much larger (though the current top leader, Hu Jintao, does not actually live there, reportedly—that too is a state secret, significantly). The evidence is manifest at the traditional curved gate that masks the main entrance on Chang'an boulevard—Beijing's central axis: it is guarded by three entirely separate police forces—the national police in black uniforms, the paramilitary People's Armed Police in green, and the security police in white[6]—each with its chiefs present on the scene, who answer to different offices in different ministries.

Obviously none of the three police forces is fully trusted, and with good reason: those policemen also see luxurious displays of every kind every day of their lives while they themselves must survive on small salaries in the relatively expensive Beijing area. The potential for disaffection is obvious, and there is oblique evidence that it was already actualized at least once. Even though the Zhongnanhai's security guard had been greatly upgraded ever since the vast 1989 demonstrations in Tiananmen Square just down the boulevard, on April 25, 1999, its denizens woke up one morning to find some 10,000 devotees of the Falun Dafa organization, or Falun Gong, holding hands in silent protest—a gathering entirely impossible without police complicity, or at least knowing passivity.

Foreign observers oblivious to the acute political insecurity of CCP leaders overlook an important source of their conduct, and a major reason for their autism toward the outside world.

# CHAPTER FOUR

# *Historical Residues in Chinese Conduct*

*It is unnecessary* to examine in any depth another and far more complex cause of China's great-state autism: its idiosyncratic history as a solitary great presence bordering only on sparsely populated high-altitude plateaus, deserts, semi-deserts, frigid steppes, and tropical jungles. Powerful and at times over-whelming threats could and did emerge, from the steppes especially, but none of the bordering areas contained even remotely comparable states with which the Chinese could ha-bitually interact, thereby acquiring the skills and habits of inter-state relations, as the states of Europe did, starting in the consanguineous and often adjacent states of Italy.

As they dealt with one another over the centuries, peace-fully or otherwise, the Italian states evolved the political hab-its and the diplomatic formalities, rules, and techniques that with subsequent enhancements are now the only global stan-dard. They include the absolute immunity of resident envoys who are legally entitled to observe and report, treaty-making procedures including authoritative language designations and the capitulary format derived from Justinian's codex, and the indispensable legal doctrine that subordinates domestic laws to inter-state treaties.

All this was based on the presumption of formal equality between states of differing power (for example, the equal immunity of all ambassadors)—exactly what was ruled out by the tributary system of foreign relations of imperial China that persisted over more than two millennia. There are now different scholarly views of its actual workings, beyond the generic exchange of imperial forbearance and actively virtuous benevolence, *rén* (仁), symbolized by gifts, for the deference of lesser nations symbolized by tribute. But the formal inequality of the parties is the starting point of all interpretations.

Indeed, the greatest benefit extended by the empire to its subjected tributary neighbors was their inclusion within its ethical as well as political sphere, or rather within the concentric circles of the *Tianxia* (天下), the "all under heaven" that radiated outwardly from the emperor himself, elevating those nations above outer barbarians living in unrelieved savagery. The tributaries in turn confirmed the ethical as well as the political supremacy of the emperor by their deferential obeisance.[1]

The logic of strategy and its manifestations, such as the "balance of power," are inherently universal, but the Tianxia concept and the tributary system that emerged under the Western Han (conventionally 206 BCE–9 CE), after a very protracted and ultimately successful struggle with the Xiongnú horse-nomad warriors,[2] is very characteristically Chinese.

As formidable mounted archers, the Xiongnú greatly troubled the cavalry-poor Han until, after more than 140 years of intermitted warfare, Huhanye, their paramount chief or *Chanyu* (Qagan) at the time,[3] formally submitted to the emperor Han Xuandi in 51 BCE, undertaking to pay homage, to leave a son at court as a hostage, and to deliver tribute, as befits an "outer vassal"—a downfall from the familial status of earlier Chanyus of the epoch of Xiongnú predominance, whose sons and heirs could have imperial daughters in marriage, and who received tribute from the Han instead of the other way around.

An important residue of this historical turning point is the "barbarian-handling" mentality that persists in official China, and even its basic techniques. Although it was enriched by subsequent Han dealings with other non-Han states and tribes over more than two millennia, the "barbarian-handling" tool box was first described and advocated by the celebrated scholar and imperial advisor Liu Ching by 199 BCE. He was active at a time when the Xiongnú were still very strong and the Han were not only tactically inferior (their chariots were of little use in fighting mounted archers) but also beset by political divisions, so much so that a 198 BCE treaty imposed the payment of an annual tribute in kind (silk and grain mostly) and the attestation of equality embodied in a marriage alliance. That was formalized later on by imperial letters that made the equality between emperor and Chanyu fully explicit.[4]

The first tool of barbarian handling recommended by Liu Ching[5] is normally described as "corruption" in English translations, but perhaps "addiction" or, more fully, "induced economic dependence" is more accurate: the originally self-sufficient Xiongnú were to be made economically dependent on Han-produced goods, sophisticated silk and woolen cloths instead of their own rude furs and felt, and all manner of other products beyond their own modest craft skills. At first supplied free as unrequited tribute, they could still be supplied later on when the Han were stronger, but only in exchange for services rendered.

The second tool of barbarian handling is normally translated as "indoctrination"; the Xiongnú were to be persuaded to accept the authoritarian Confucian value system and the collectivistic behavioral norms of the Han, as opposed to the steppe value system that generated voluntary allegiance to heroic (and successful) fighting and migration leaders. One immediate benefit was that once the Chanyu's son and heir married an imperial daughter, he would be ethically subordinated to the emperor as his father-in-law—remaining so when he became Chanyu in turn. The much larger, longer-term benefit of the second tool was to undermine the entire political culture of the Xiongnú, and make them psychologically as well as economically dependent on the imperial radiance, which was willingly extended in brotherly fashion when the Han were weak, and then withdrawn when the Xiongnú were reduced to vassalage.

What happened between the Han and the Xiongnú from the equal treaty of 198 BCE to the vassalage treaty of 51 BCE, remained thereafter, and still remains today, the most hopeful precedent for Han dealings with powerful and violent states—evidently the role of the United States at present, in the CCP worldview.

The derived rules of conduct form a logical sequence:

- Initially, concede all that must be conceded to the superior power, to avoid damage and obtain whatever benefits or at least forbearance that can be had from it.
- Entangle the ruler and ruling class of the superior power in webs of material dependence[6] that reduce its original vitality and strength, while proffering equality in a privileged bipolarity that excludes every other power ("G-2," at present).
- Finally, when the formerly superior power has been weakened enough, withdraw all tokens of equality and impose subordination.

Given its longevity, it would be passing strange if the tributary system, the Tianxia hierarchy, and the manner of its gradual imposition did not leave at least an unconscious remembrance in current Chinese conduct, in spite of radically altered international circumstances.[7] But there is much more than that—there is a conscious predisposition to manipulate foreign powers in that particular manner.

One of its most striking echoes is the great prominence that Chinese officialdom gives to each and every visiting head of government, head of state, minister, and assorted Pooh-Bah from anywhere in the world, including the smallest and least active countries. They arrive in Beijing in an unending stream, with or without anything in particular to actually discuss, beyond mere anodyne conversation.

The absence of any actual business is remedied by an abundance of ceremony and elaborately hosted meals, part of a more generous hospitality, including nicely chosen gifts, than is on offer from most other countries, and certainly by the United States, where the State Department's usual tipple even for multihour sessions is watery coffee unaccompanied by any food at all. (In the U.S. Embassy in Beijing, very scandalously, even prolonged encounters, even if they start at 12 noon, habitually feature no food—inducing intense gastronomic anti-Americanism, which is only intensified when starved visitors who complain are taken to the sordid cafeteria complete with cashier.)

The serious amounts of time that top Chinese leaders, not infrequently including Premier Wen Jiabao or even President Hu Jintao, devote to meetings with their counterparts from the likes of Kiribati, Vanuatu, Uruguay, Latvia, Burundi, and other such—none of whom would be accorded more than a one-minute photo-op by the White House even after years of waiting—further detract from the ability of top Chinese leaders to focus seriously on the less unimportant parts of the outside world. It is not surprising, therefore, that when their own understanding of foreign-power priorities, motivations, and decision processes is probed, it is almost invariably revealed as exceedingly superficial, schematic, or plain wrong. Exchanging polite compliments with hundreds of mostly inarticulate foreigners from different climes does not help to diminish great-state autism.

It is the very extensive media coverage given to these trivial visitations that tells us what is really going on: just as in the tributary system of the emperors, the unending procession of foreign potentates—the more colorfully varied the better—is portrayed as proof positive of the authority of China's rulers, who can be depicted as greatly in demand for their wisdom, sagacity, and benevolent generosity. That is why the sheer multiplicity and exotic variety of visitors is important in itself, regardless of the substantive unimportance of the resulting encounters—the Chinese population at large is to be impressed by how many ostensibly important foreigners travel all the way to Beijing for the privilege of meeting its rulers.

A second and often pleasing echo of the tributary system is the striving to reward visitors with memorable gifts, as if to ensure their eagerness to visit again. To be sure, under the Tianxia concept such visitors should arrive bearing tribute, but one may suppose that China's chronic merchandise trade surpluses with many countries, which deindustrialize them as China continues to industrialize, are tribute enough.

Sometimes it is not only the sheer magnitude but also the modalities of Chinese gift-giving that betray its tributary origins. To cite a recent example, on the very day that Dilma Rousseff, the newly elected president of Brazil, arrived in Beijing for a full-dress state visit on April 12, 2011, two different Chinese airlines announced a total of thirty orders for the Brazilian-made Embraer E-190 regional jet, plus five options.[8] That is not the sort of gift that the U.S. government, or Japan's, could or would give—All Nippon or United would not obediently line up to buy diplomatically preferred aircraft, and announce their purchase exactly on the diplomatically preferred date. The Chinese no doubt hoped that the government of Brazil would reciprocate by continuing to accept passively the undervaluation of China's currency, which has facilitated the exports that have devastated Brazil's light industry. Instead of producing its own apparel, accessories, bar stools, and hundreds of other things, Brazil now imports them from China, thereby becoming even more of a raw-material exporter than it used to be, notwithstanding Embraer. Ironically, it was only after the Rousseff visit that Brazil started to react to the undervaluation of the yuan, energetically depressing its own currency. Moreover, in response to Chinese purchases of vast tracts of farmland, Brazil (as also Argentina) passed new laws barring land sales to foreign owners. There was no such reaction when Americans and Europeans were buying land.

China's tributary gift-giving practices have certainly played a large role in its penetration of Africa. There is nothing sinister about the oil exploration, mining, and land development activities of China's state-owned enterprises; they operate much in the same way as their Euro-American counterparts, give or take a safety practice or two, albeit with much lower expatriate manpower costs, and therefore many more expatriates—including common laborers in many cases.

What is different is the accompanying invitational program for African politicians, the ones who decide which exploration and production licenses are issued, and which ones are denied. Hundreds of African politicians have been ceremoniously welcomed in Beijing in recent years, with all the protocol courtesies and also valuable gifts, including hard cash.

It was an integral part of the tributary system to blithely entertain even the most unwashed barbarians from the steppe and tundra in the silken elegance of the court, if they could render service to the emperor by fighting his enemies. Today's Chinese officials seem just as unfazed in dealing with the eccentricities of their African guests—few of whom have ever been invited to Britain, France, or the United States; those countries also have invitational programs, but they are much smaller, altogether less alluring, and giftless except for trivial souvenirs. Unsurprisingly, Chinese barbarian-handling hospitality techniques are particularly successful with less accomplished official visitors, a large group.

As for the tribute itself, ordinarily it takes the valuable form of government concessions to extract raw materials. Even if they are granted to newly operating Chinese companies on exactly the same terms as those offered to established Western companies, that is still a great boon for the Chinese, who often cannot offer reliable environmental and work-safety guarantees, and who need not employ locals to reduce high expatri-ate manpower costs.

Yet another echo of the tributary system manifest in China's African diplomacy is its cultural dimension. In the original version, the emperor owed the obedience of his subjects and the deference of his tributaries to his superior virtue, actively expressed in his benevolence. The would-be neo-Confucian rulers of today's China strive to project a caring, benevolent image—as soon as there is a natural disaster worthy of his attention, anywhere in China, Premier Wēn Jiābǎo quickly arrives on the scene, all kitted out with studiously informal clothes, ready to go out to embrace victims, commend rescuers, and hurry up local officials to serve the people faster.

It is the second-order effects that are relevant here: with such benevolent rulers, happiness must prevail in the land, and the media must accordingly report the news in positive fashion. The ultra-radiant super-happiness of Maoist propaganda has gone, but it has been replaced by tales of advancement and progress—in spite of sundry acknowledged difficulties.

This dimension of China's public culture—the positive tone of its media but for credibility-enhancing minor criticisms here and there—has great attractions for most African politicians. Mr. Samuel Okudjeto-Ablakwa, Ghana's deputy minister of information, recently explained why, in fully explicit terms: he praised "Xinhua, the China News Agency . . . [for its] high sense of professionalism on information published about

Ghana, . . . unlike some other foreign media which usually portrayed Ghana and other African countries in a bad spotlight [*sic*]."[9] Okudjeto-Ablakwa offered this praise while opening a Xinhua photo gallery at the Department of Linguistics, University of Ghana.

The third echo of the tributary system derives from one of its inherent characteristics: bilateralism. There can only be two protagonists: the tamed barbarian bearing tribute, and the benevolent emperor ready to reward his homage with valuable gifts. If there has been unpleasantness in the borderlands, some severity and a dressing down might be called for; or to the contrary, depending on the balance of power, the emperor might have especially valuable gifts to hand over. But the one thing rigidly prohibited was any ganging-up by the chiefs of different barbarian bands—they might indeed gang up, but the emperor would not receive them as a group; tributary rituals are inherently bilateral.

This specific issue has arisen over the Spratly Islands: the ASEAN countries that claim rights over adjacent South China Sea islands are all threatened by the Chinese claim over the entire archipelago, distant as it is from the nearest coast of China. With multiple parties involved, the ASEAN members in conclave in July 2010 proposed multilateral negotiations, logical enough one might think, but the reaction of China's foreign minister Yang Jiechi was furious, or at least he successfully conveyed that impression.[10] The inherently uneven bilateralism of the tributary system obviously suits China's power position, but it is also the only model for the conduct of its foreign relations that is embedded in the official culture.

China's great-state autism is therefore aggravated not only by the internal absorption caused by its dimensions, but also by the tacit presumptions of centrality and hierarchical superiority that are inherent in the tributary tradition of Han foreign relations.

Incidentally, it was the same presumption of hierarchical superiority that made the Chinese so especially bitter about the "unequal treaties" of the nineteenth century, starting with the 1842 Treaty of Nanjing imposed on the Qing (Qīng) dynasty by the victorious British, which levied obligations only on the Chinese side. It was not the inequality that rankled, but rather the reversal of the usual pattern of inequality, in which it was the emperor who subjected foreigners, and not the other way around.

The claim here advanced that the ancient Tianxia concept informs current Chinese conduct in foreign affairs might be dismissed as an illegitimate, manipulative, and hostile "Orientalist attribution." It is therefore worth noting that the local branch of the Beijing-based Confucius Institutes, funded by the government's Hanban (the Chinese National Office for Teaching Chinese as a Foreign Language, a cultural propaganda arm), co-sponsored a May 2011 event at Stanford University under the title "A *Tianxia* Workshop: Culture, International Relations, and World History. Rethinking Chinese Perceptions of World Order." This sounds like a historiographical exercise, but it was no such thing, as the accompanying description reveals:

> The practical value of the traditional Chinese vision of world order, or *tianxia* . . . [is that] . . . this vision anchors a universal authority in the moral, ritualistic, and aesthetic framework of a *secular* high culture, while providing social and moral criteria for assessing fair, humanitarian governance and proper social relations. Varied discourses indebted to *tianxia* have resurfaced in modern China in quest of moral and cultural ways of relating to and *articulating an international society*. We believe that the Chinese vision may prove productive . . . in the tension-ridden yet interconnected world. [Italics added]

How it could be productive is pointedly explained in the introductory brochure:

> As China is becoming an economic and political power, thinkers and writers are debating the theoretical implications of the traditional Chinese vision of world order. [China's] . . . attempts to be part of the international community and to enter world history *ran counter to the Western temperament steeped in the conflict of nation-states, in geopolitical rivalry, and in economic theory based on possessive individualism and imperialist expansion*. These elements

36

of capitalist modernity have fostered a *divisive* sense of mystified *cultural difference* and *geographical inequality.* [Italics added]

The Hanban certainly got value for its money, for it turns out that it was given the opportunity to attack core Western values to promote a China-centered vision of international relations in a major Western institution, with Stanford itself footing most of the bill.[11]

........................................

# CHAPTER FIVE

# The Coming Geo-Economic Resistance
## to the Rise of China

*The post-2008 outbursts* of provocative behavior certainly accelerated reactions to the rise of China. But those reactions
had not been caused by the provocations, and could not be
ended by conciliatory gestures, fence-mending state visits, or
soothing language, because they reflect perceptions of power
rather than assessments of Chinese conduct.

The weights of those perceptions and those assessments
are very different.

First, power is the reality that will not go away, as opposed
to the variable of conduct.

Second, conduct is assessed in retrospect whereas perceptions of power look forward to the future. Moreover, as opposed
to future money whose present value is discounted, future
power is anticipated and indeed usually magnified. It seems
that in focusing on a rising trend-line there is an inherent tendency to project it further ahead, giving credit in advance, so
to speak, disregarding countervailing factors and possible dis-
turbances unless they are obviously imminent and greatly significant. The "wave of the future" is more impressive than the
standing water of the present.

Reverting to the fundamental contention here presented—the inherent incompatibility between the concurrently rapid growth of China's economic capacity *and* military strength *and* diplomatic influence—what remains to be defined in concrete terms is just how each dimension of China's advancement could impede the others in the proximate future or is already doing so, because of the adversarial reactions of China's neighbors, peers, and indeed other countries that are neither of those things.

Only one of these incompatibilities has an obvious and familiar form—the contradiction between a threatening military posture and diplomatic influence over any state that still retains its autonomy, that has not already passed the tipping point beyond which subordination to overwhelming power is accepted as inevitable. Only then can a rising military threat generate more influence, and very effectively too.

In this regard also, the logic of strategy cannot be linear: a rising military threat normally stiffens resistance against it, leading to a loss of influence; if the threat persists and intensifies, the threatened power will strive to re-arm or seek allies, or do both if it can. But if the threat increases still more, overtaking both rearmament efforts and allied support, a culminating point of resistance will be reached. If no other factors or powers then intervene to interrupt the process, any further increase in the threat will not evoke more resistance in most cases, but to the contrary it will induce more accommodating attitudes that might even evolve toward submission.

As overall balances—economic capacity, military strength, diplomatic influence—continue to shift in China's favor, each of its neighbors and peers must make successive choices between accepting increased measures of Chinese leverage over its own doings, or at least over its allies and clients (which would become China's in due course), and the costs of increasing its powers of resistance, both by internal strengthening and by coalescing with other powers that are also threatened in some way by the rise of China and are thus in the same predicament.

Inevitably, each form of reaction to an excessively risen power has its costs. Internal strengthening may require not only the allocation of scarce resources for military purposes if it comes to that, but also the sacrifice of other weighty interests or even values, or at least ideological constructs such as the American devotion to "free trade." That is so because in our nuclear age, with any significant warfare between nuclear powers largely inhibited, the logic of strategy must find alternative, nonmilitary expressions in "geo-economic" ways.[1]

These contentions require justification, of course, and the first contention is more easily justified than the second.

China has nuclear weapons and sundry means of delivering them, none of very impressive capability but collectively persuasive enough to have dissuaded the Soviet Union at its most hostile (and at a time when Chinese strategic nuclear forces were still embryonic). On the other hand, even the feckless and reckless post-2008 conduct of China's foreign relations, which has made new enemies for China and recruited new friends for the United States, does not begin to approach the degree of chiliastic irrationality that would be required for a large-scale Chinese attack on the United States or major components of its armed forces.

For both sides, that would still leave room for small-scale, strictly localized military actions, as well as for maritime provocations and such.

But no such small-scale or nonlethal actions could be of any use to the United States to contain China's economic growth— the source of the problem, for it supplies the wherewithal for military aggrandizement. As for the Chinese, they have repeatedly tried to use harassing actions to inhibit U.S. intelligence-collection activities at sea and in the air, with one deadly aerial incident and more near-misses at sea. These attempts have been insufficient to diminish U.S. intelligence collection activities, while the Chinese for their part have so far been dissuaded from the use of more effective means by the evident threat of escalation toward general war, whose outcome could in turn impose a choice between regime destruction and nuclear use.

Thus it may be said that although not all forms of combat between nuclear powers are inhibited by the excessive destructive power of nuclear weapons (they overshoot the culminating point of usefully destructive capacity), *effective* forms of combat that could theoretically achieve significantly substantive results are indeed inhibited. That much was proven through all the successive phases of the Cold War, and Soviet leaders were not on the whole more prudent than China's in their use of force.

As for the second contention, that the logic of strategy *must* find alternative, nonmilitary expressions in "geo-economic" ways, it is first necessary to clarify that the logic of strategy remains exactly the same in the geo-economic context as well, in which the same logic is expressed with the means of commerce instead of military means.

It follows that in geo-economics also there can be an escalation all the way up to the level of a full interruption of commercial relations, or near enough, as in the case of U.S. economic nonrelations with Cuba.

Now almost unthinkable at a time of normal U.S.-China relations, such a geo-economic escalation could quickly become a very natural default position in the event of any major Chinese act of aggression against third parties, including Taiwan, even in the absence of formal treaty obligations.

But that undoubted possibility does not in any way prove the validity of the contention here advanced: that because China's continuing rise ultimately threatens the very independence of its neighbors, and even of its present peers, it will *inevitably* be resisted by geo-economic means—that is, by strategically motivated as opposed to merely protectionist trade barriers, investment prohibitions, more extensive technology denials, and even restrictions on raw material exports to China if its misconduct can provide a sufficient excuse for that almost warlike act.

This is a contention about the future, advanced in full recognition of very different current realities, notably the strenuous efforts of many governments to increase all manner of economic relations with China, whether to export more to its expanding markets, produce within them, or to attract Chinese investments, each of which inhibits, if not prohibits, the geo-economic measures that would be useful to slow down China's economic growth.

Strictly speaking, the prediction is justified here only *a priori* by the twin contentions that nuclear weapons constrain the use of force too severely for the purpose, and that China's neighbors and peers will seek to protect their independence nonetheless—inevitably therefore by geo-economic means.

But there is already some scattered evidence of geo-economic actions that can be adduced, mere straws in the wind for now but indicative of what is to come:

- In the United States, the growing resistance to government federal, state, or local procurement of Chinese-made infrastructural or other major products—and much of this resistance is very new. For example, the San Francisco Bay bridge purchased from China is more controversial now (June 2011) than it was when the contract was first awarded under the former governor. As for the Department of Defense, rule FR 45074 of August 2, 2010, prohibited outright the

43

procurement of U.S. Munitions List items from Chinese-controlled sources, and there is now a move under way in Congress to prohibit all procurement of Chinese-made items by the Defense Department.

- Also in the United States, the importation of telecommunication switchgear and other infrastructural equipment from China has been effectively prohibited by the threatened denial of government service contracts to telecommunication providers.

- In India, the same prohibition was imposed by government order in 2010, but with the major difference that while the United States was only a potential market for Chinese telecommunications infrastructural equipment, India was the single largest market worldwide for those Chinese exports.

- In both Argentina and Brazil, the very recent (2011) prohibitions against the sale of farmland or ranch land to "foreigners"—such a measure was never before imposed when it was Europeans and Americans who were buying sometimes huge tracts of land, but it was promptly legislated when Chinese buyers arrived on the scene. Other Latin American countries are enacting similar measures.

- In Brazil also, the belated recognition that the China trade was enriching the country's raw-material exporters while deindustrializing the rest of the country provoked rising demands for tariff barriers against

Chinese imports. The parallel demand is feebly advanced by the U.S. Treasury, the last stronghold of cooperation with China at any cost, including deindustrialization, and ideologically committed to "free trade" no matter what. But Brazil was rapidly regressing into the diminished role of a mere commodity exporter, and its central bank finally acted, by reducing interests rates (at the risk of increasing inflation) to depress the value of its real to offset the undervaluation of the Chinese yuan. Other countries that still have light industries to preserve are likely to follow.

- In Australia, where there are no barriers to Japanese, European, or U.S. acquisitions of operating companies of any sort, including major raw-material producers, any such Chinese acquisitions have been effectively prohibited by administrative injunctions.

- In Mongolia, which has perhaps the world's largest deposits of unexploited low-sulfur coal at Tavan Tolgoi in the Tsogttsetsii sum district of Ömnögovi Province, the government decided in 2011 to build the rail connection northward to the Russian Federation (and ultimately to Port Vostochny in Vrangel Bay) rather than southward, expressly to contain its economic dependence on China.[2]

None of these measures is especially powerful, and they certainly do not amount to any coherent or concerted effort to impede China's economic growth. But each attests to a real sense of threat, and each is an attempt to respond by economic means within the severe constraints of the current international trading regime, which disallows the most effective measures on the presumption that all will follow the same rules. The habit of allowing China to violate them was formed when it was still economically insignificant. This is the now very costly indulgence that China exploits in pursuit of one-sided benefits, notably access to foreign advanced technology without the effective protection of foreign intellectual property in China; unequal trade, as for instance the free export of films while restricting imported films to just twenty per year; the export of infrastructure products as large as complete bridges while foreign companies are barred from competing for Chinese infrastructure contracts; and many more such.

All countries bend the rules of international trade if they can get away with it, but China alone combines such malpractices with its magnitude and rapid economic growth.

So far all has been accepted passively by the United States because of the powerful ideological commitment to "free trade," but it is indicative of what is bound to happen that even a formerly committed free-trader such as the current Republican U.S. presidential contender Mitt Romney declares (June 2011) that the United States would be justified in cutting off *all* trade with China because of China's theft of U.S. intellectual property, among other reasons.[3] More broadly, content analysis would undoubtedly show a sharp increase in the volume of anti-China economic measures proposed during successive electoral seasons since 2008; eventually some action is likely to follow the great number of words.

It remains to be seen if the sum of all geo-economic action by all countries will ever suffice to impede China's economic growth in sufficient degree—say, to reduce its growth rate to 4–5 percent per year from the present 9 percent or so, or the 6 percent or so inherently more likely beyond the medium term. It must be recognized, of course, that a 4 percent annual growth rate may be both incompatible with the stability of the CCP regime and yet essential to preserve the U.S. position in the world. In any case, what the logic of strategy predicts is a geo-economic struggle, though it cannot predict its outcome. For what it is worth, the present writer is confident that China will not ultimately disrupt the equilibrium of world politics, because the Chinese themselves will moderate their conduct as they advance culturally as well as economically (two different translations of *The Iliad* are now on sale). The de-provincialization of a culture at once ancient, exceedingly authoritative, uniquely insular, and also ill-suited for the pursuit of happiness in a world of independent states, will take time, to be sure. Geo-economic containment would find its best application in providing an interim solution to preserve the world's equilibrium without worse forms of conflict.

# CHAPTER SIX

# China's Aggrandizement and Global Reactions

*The Chinese authorities* undoubtedly understand the implications of the nuclear inhibition but evidently—and reasonably—still believe that they can benefit from increasing their military capabilities, not only for the sake of military prestige but also to intimidate or even attack defiant non-nuclear powers unprotected by any ironclad security treaty, such as Vietnam.

Another rational purpose for China's military aggrandizement is to achieve at least localized escalation dominance even against nuclear powers such as India, the United States, and conceivably the Russian Federation—at least in circumscribed confrontations short of any significant use of lethal force. There have already been many incidents of harassment and even more of hostile posturing (instead of returning salutes, PLA Navy warships have been known to switch on their fire-control radars).

Alternatively, enhanced military capabilities can at least reduce the escalation dominance of others, including the United States—initially only in highly favorable circumstances, to be sure—but more broadly as China's relative strength increases.

It follows that China's non-nuclear neighbors also have good reasons to try to keep up their own relative military strength, to dissuade intimidation or even fight off attacks if it comes to that—war is not inhibited in their case.

Given the costs of resisting China's rise, the acceptance of at least a tacit, decently veiled, and certainly unacknowledged subordination has its advocates in some neighboring countries, even Japan.[1] But with the possible exception of the Republic of Korea,[2] policies of accommodation to Chinese preferences, leading to the acceptance of China's hegemony, are unlikely to prevail over policies of resistance—not only for the usual cultural-political and national-identity reasons, but also because of the feared material consequences.

When the United States was extending its influence over East Asia after 1945, it was almost universally perceived as a generous rather than a predatory power, and indeed it provided material help and then greatly favored export-led growth in the region by opening its own markets. Even Marxists, who in accordance to their doctrine had to view the United States as focused on securing overseas markets and access to raw materials, could not plausibly depict the United States as predatory.

But that is exactly how China and the Chinese are persistently viewed in neighboring countries and beyond, even though China has become a considerable investor and to some degree an importer of manufactured goods; at any rate it is no longer only a fiercely competitive exporter and rival to local industries.

Prejudice against local Chinese, especially in Southeast Asia where their capital-creating role is widely misperceived as exploitative in the customary way—they are accused of draining away the very wealth their industriousness and savings create—certainly contributes to negative perceptions of China itself. But while the ethnic factor has remained constant—or if anything has even declined with rising prosperity, as in Indonesia—now it is the rapid rise in China's overall economic capacity and military strength that is inducing increasing anxiety.

One fear is that China will use its rising power to take away valuable maritime resources from its neighbors—not an imaginary threat in the case of the Paracel and Spratly Islands, most notably.

Another fear is that the Chinese will dictate new rules of bilateral commerce to suit themselves—that, for example, they will demand investment access to local telecommunication and other infrastructures while continuing to deny reciprocal access.

So far there are no indications that China's increasing economic capacity is hurting rather than aiding other countries, except for direct industrial competitors, of course. Yet there is solid evidence that the attitudinal shift against China extends beyond its beleaguered competitors.

A recently published multinational opinion survey usefully compares 2005 and 2011 responses.[3] The data shows that in just six years negative views of China's economic role in the world increased not only regionally but globally: from 31 to 53 percent in France, from 37 to 55 percent in Canada, from 44 to 55 percent in Germany, from 47 to 57 percent in Italy, from 45 to 54 percent in the United States. In two countries where there was less than average hostility toward China in 2005, hostility has also increased, from 31 to 41 percent in the United Kingdom, and more sharply from 18 to 43 percent in Mexico. In East Asia, the more significant data in this context concern China's trade practices: they are viewed as "unfair" by 58 percent of South Korean and 70 percent of Japanese respondents, though Pakistanis and Indonesians were more favorable.[4]

These very rapid attitudinal shifts reflect the equally rapid change in China's relative magnitude in the global economy; if that were to change again, but in a different direction—for example, if higher labor costs were to make China less competitive at home and concurrently a greater investor abroad—attitudes toward it would no doubt change as well.

But for now, rightly or wrongly, the path of appeasement and subordination is further dissuaded by fears that China's hegemony would be exploitative and thus materially costly for its subjects—in contrast to China's historical record, for the empire often paid more in "gifts" than it received in tribute from its nominal subjects. (That is not what contemporary Chinese theorists envisage when they commend the tribute system as the basis for a new "Chinese school of international relations.")[5]

The emergence of China as a military power naturally evokes even stronger reactions, according to the cited survey. In smaller neighboring countries, respondents were variously "negative" toward China: 76 percent in South Korea, in whose more recent history Japan was the imperial oppressor, but which experienced Chinese power for much longer (the 21 percent in favor presumably remember Japan too well). In the Philippines, 63 percent were negative; the population has become much more U.S.-oriented than ever before since the emergence of the maritime dispute with China (the 29 percent in favor may conceivably include a Sino-Philippine element); and 76 percent in Australia, which is neither small nor China's neighbor, except subjectively perhaps.

Unsurprisingly, in China itself respondents were very favorable to China's rising military strength, at 94 percent, with only 5 percent opposed (which could also reflect the responses of actively oppressed minority populations); and respondents were also decidedly favorable in Pakistan, at 61 percent, with only 11 percent opposed, evidently reflecting the de facto alliance between the two countries against their common adversary, India.

In India itself only 24 percent of the respondents were negative with fully 44 percent positive, numbers that no doubt reflect the level of information of the Indian population at large—a few among the respondents may in addition have been Maoists and Sinophiles by extension, but many more probably knew nothing of China, given the prevailing level of literacy. (Literacy is even lower in Pakistan, but mosque attendance rates are very high, and many sermons feature the international politics of the perpetual Islamic struggle.)

At the opposite extreme, 88 percent of Japanese respondents expressed a negative view of China's military rise, which is not surprising, especially because the polling took place soon after the September 7, 2010, confrontation near the Senkaku Islands (Diaoyutai to the Chinese) and before the devastations of the March 11, 2011, earthquake and tsunami that diverted Japanese attention from all else.

More remarkably, exactly the same proportion of respondents—88 percent—was negative in Germany, where only 2 percent expressed a favorable view, even though unlike Japan, Germany cannot have territorial disputes with China, and Germans have no reason to feel threatened by any amount of Chinese military strength, so long as the United States and the Russian Federation endure. Yet among respondents worldwide, a higher percentage of Germans expressed a negative view of China's military aggrandizement than Americans (79 percent), Canadians (82 percent), British or Russians (both at 69 percent), though in Russia only 10 percent were favorable, distinctly fewer than the UK's 25 percent; finally, Italians, antagonized by commercial rivalries and more anti-militaristic than most, were 81 percent negative.

Unless the cited data is merely mistaken, there is the interesting possibility that German attitudes to China's rising military power reflect neither hostility nor fear but rather benevolent concern. Germans are inclined to remember their modern history, centered on Germany's meteoric trajectory from overwhelming scholarly, cultural, industrial, and financial success in the late nineteenth century to the disastrous downfall of the First World War, and the three yet more catastrophic decades that followed. Germans may well see parallels in the evolution of contemporary China, whose military strength is also expanding in proportion to the growth of a very successful economy, so that it may simultaneously be viewed as merely commensurate *domestically*, and as dynamically threatening *internationally*. Nor more than that is required to set in motion adversarial forces leading to confrontation and conflict. That the Chinese government (and public opinion too, it seems) views its rapidly increasing military expenditures as merely "reasonable and appropriate," in the words of the 2010 National Defense report,[6] is a perfect example of the great-state autism that is the essential precondition of massive strategic failure, and whose specifically Chinese version is especially acute. Out-of-context quotations can easily mislead, so it is worthwhile to consider the entire paragraph, at the beginning of part VIII, "Defense Expenditure":

> China adheres to the principle of *coordinated development* of national defense and economy. In line with the demands of national defense and economic development, China decides on the size of defense expenditure in an *appropriate way*, and manages and uses its defense funds *in accordance with the law.*
>
> With the development of national economy and society, the increase of China's defense expenditure has

been kept at a *reasonable and appropriate level*. . . . China's defense expenditure was RMB 417.876 billion in 2008 and RMB 495.11 billion in 2009, *up 17.5 percent and 18.5 percent respectively over the previous year.* In recent years, the share of China's annual defense expenditure within its total GDP has *remained relatively steady.* [Italics added]

It often happened in the past that U.S. defense expenditures were excessive according to retrospective analyses, just as they were inadequate at other times by the same standards.

But either way, a U.S. document comparable to *China's National Defense in 2010* would start with a threat assessment, perhaps exaggerated or perhaps not, but either way it would start with at least a representation of the Other or Others, and the change under way in its or their military strength that requires such and such a response, to variously block, absorb, deflect, or counteract different threats.

That is the great absence in *China's National Defense in 2010*, the dog that did not bark in *The Hound of the Baskervilles*, the silent sign of great-state autism.

..........................................

# CHAPTER SEVEN

# The Inevitable Analogy

*Historical analogies* are notoriously false friends and poor teachers—the only true lesson of history is that humans never seem to learn from their history. But perhaps analogies are not always entirely useless.

Now that China has overtaken Japan in gross economic terms and is bent on overtaking the United States in like manner, it is worth recalling that by 1890 Germany had overtaken Britain in industrial innovation, thereby winning global markets, accumulating capital, and funding more innovation to overtake British primacy in one sector after another. In the then-still-fundamental steel industry, the German technological advantage was increasing; in the then-leading-edge chemical industry, it was already absolute. That facilitated Germany's superiority in other forms of manufacturing as well, including the electrical industry (the world's first public electricity supply started in England in 1881, but the alternator was made by Siemens). British entrepreneurs and managers were too uneducated to make much use of science and technology, and in any case it was German and not British universities that were advancing science, technology, and indeed most forms of scholarship. Moreover, in British mines and factories—often the scene of outright class warfare— trade unions strongly resisted labor-saving machinery and techniques, that is, most forms of innovation. With the world's first old-age and disability pensions, as well as health and accident insurance, and with the persistence of widespread industrial paternalism, German workers were much more secure and far more willing to embrace innovation.

The German advantage was therefore systemic—the centralizing "Berlin consensus" was far more effective than the ("muddling through") pragmatism celebrated by the British. Both countries were parliamentary democracies with monarchical heads of state, but the German executive's constitutionally stronger powers were used not only to contain the parliamentary opposition but also to guide investment to innovate on a large scale. One result was the state pension system, destined to be copied worldwide; another was that the newly unified German lands were served by a railway network far more efficient than the chaos of the 120 British railway companies, which left London with multiple unconnected stations, and whose lines sometimes ran parallel for long distances to reach different stations in the same small town. German centralization influenced industry as well, favoring the emergence of powerful amalgamated companies that could finance systematic research and development, as their smaller British competitors could not.

All this meant that the British could not realistically hope to avoid their relative decline. German superiority in all things was only a matter of time, while in scholarship across the board the contest was already over: by 1900 even in British universities it was impossible to study subjects as varied as chemistry or Greek poetry without knowing German first, while English was only essential for . . . English literature. In finance, the more rapid generation of capital of the more dynamic German economy was prevailing over both the expertise and the global connections of the London merchant bankers and their systemic advantage in presiding over the pound sterling, the world's leading reserve currency. The Warburgs of Hamburg were overtaking the Rothschilds of London, and even the largest British banks were already eclipsed by the Deutsche Bank, the world's largest by 1914, and by far the most competent in financing industry (as it still is, by all accounts).

Starting in 1890, under any realistic thirty-year projection, as the beneficiary of the world's most advanced industries, best universities, richest banks, and the most harmonious society thanks to its welfare state, by 1920 Germany should have been altogether superior in every way to an increasingly antiquated Britain. Instead, by 1920 Germany was defeated, ruined, and destined for another quarter century of mounting disasters, with the seemingly realistic expectations of 1890 utterly disappointed. The British paid a high price for their victory, but they did succeed in overturning the future before them and perpetuating Britain's Great Power status for decades to come.

German strategic incompetence, a frequent companion of tactical genius, was the necessary precondition of catastrophic national failure, which necessarily started with hubris—like many Chinese now, many Germans of the time were plainly unhinged by the rapidity of their rise.

But it was the British reaction to Germany's rise that ensured the final outcome.

In 1890, Britain was still locked into a fierce colonial competition with France in Africa and Indochina, and with an advancing Russia in central Asia—France and Russia were enemy number 1 and enemy number 2. That made it impossible to oppose Germany, whose global commerce to the contrary enjoyed all the benefits of British naval protection.

But then the German government came to accept the idea that a risen Germany could not remain merely a Great Power; it had to become a Global Power as well. Hence, it needed an *appropriate, proportionate,* and therefore oceanic navy, instead of the modest coastal and Baltic fleet it had till then. Starting in 1898, a series of naval laws funded the construction of battleships, heavy cruisers, and light cruisers. Because Germany's economy was growing rapidly, so could its fleet: the second German naval law of June 1900 funded the doubling of the Imperial Navy from nineteen to thirty-eight battleships, and it was followed by further naval laws in 1906, 1908, and 1912.

What characterizes the realm of strategy is the impossibility of achieving straightforward results by straightforward action, because others exist and others react in between the two.[1] Accordingly, the German action in building oceanic warships resulted, not in the acquisition of oceanic naval power in an otherwise unchanged world, but in a global strategic trans-formation that ensured the ultimate nullity of German naval power, and then Germany's defeat. For the German action in rapidly building an ever greater number of increasingly power-ful warships was too threatening to evoke a merely imitative British reaction.

One decidedly asymmetrical British response was to intro-duce an all-big-gun vessel of revolutionary design—the *Dread-nought*, launched in 1906, which immediately made earlier mul-ticaliber battleships obsolescent.

But the major British response to Germany's new global and naval ambitions was even more asymmetrical: it amounted to a veritable diplomatic revolution, which reshaped the entire strategic context.

France had been Britain's enemy par excellence over the centuries, lately because of intense colonial rivalries in many different places around the world. But because it was more im-mediately threatened by Germany, if colonial disputes were settled France could become Britain's ally. With the sharp discipline that an effective grand strategy invariably requires, the British set aside both ancient enmities and fresh rivalries to rapidly negotiate many separate agreements with France, over access to Morocco, Newfoundland fishing rights, territo-rial disputes in West and Central Africa and on the borders of Siam, over the Madagascar trade, and the disposition of the New Hebrides (now Vanuatu).

It was all done by April 8, 1904, and from then on Germany's access to the oceans would depend on the conjoint consent of the British and French fleets—automatic so long as Germany remained at peace with both, readily deniable otherwise. Even a superior German battle fleet in the North Sea could only have counterblockaded Britain; it could not have blocked France, with its Mediterranean access and Suez Canal outlet.

To reach an understanding with the Russian Empire was altogether more difficult, not so much because of colonial rivalries over Persia and Central Asia, but rather because of the intense domestic opposition in Britain to any close connection with the repulsively reactionary and anti-Semitic czarist autocracy.

But strategy is stronger than politics (as the 1972 Nixon-Mao understandings also showed, among countless examples), and the more threatened French had overcome their own inhibitions long before, signing a pact with Russia in 1892. Finally in August 1907, the signature of an Anglo-Russian Convention opened the way for staff talks and broader military coordination.

The British-led diplomatic revolution thus accomplished by 1907, encircled Germany with the increasingly coordinated power of the British, French, and Russian Empires. In the Far East, the Russians could have been distracted by Japan, but the British had already preempted any possible German-Japanese alliance with their own 1902 treaty—the first truly equal Euro-Asian alliance, anchored by close naval cooperation. Finally, the British kept all their disputes with the United States under firm control—it was their set diplomatic doctrine to preserve good relations with the Americans at any cost.

That left for Germany only allies more needy than useful: Hapsburg Austria-Hungary with its strengths including an effective Adriatic fleet, but hopelessly fragmented by rival nationalisms; the Kingdom of Italy a treaty ally but wavering, and with a weak army; even weaker Bulgaria besieged by enemies; and the Ottoman Empire, whose secularizing modernizers could not prevail against the countermodern undertow of Islam. Moreover, any alliance with the Ottoman Empire would antagonize Italy—the two fought a war in 1911. Italy was not a useful ally on land, but at sea it could do much by confining the Austro-Hungarian navy in its upper Adriatic anchorages, freeing the British fleet from any serious threat in the Mediterranean. That made Italy strategically important and a focus of patient British diplomacy.

Once the allies on each side of the First World War were arrayed against each other, the outcome was utterly preordained. At sea, the British, French, and Japanese fleets, with their global network of coaling stations, controlled every oceanic passage worldwide, confining the German navy to the futility of its North Sea home waters. On land, the German army won many victories, but none could rescue Germany from blockade, crippling shortages of raw materials, and consequent defeat by cumulative economic exhaustion leading to societal disintegration. Only the arrival of fresh American troops interrupted that economic death spiral with a faster military defeat: instead of having to surrender eventually in 1919 or 1920 because Germany could no longer feed itself, the High Command had to accept the November 11, 1918, armistice because it could no longer resist Allied offensives.

Once the British formed their world alliance, a strategically competent German government would have recognized the irremediable futility of the beautiful ships of the German navy, and the irremediable irrelevance of the formidable German army.

But autism prevailed over strategic thinking, also in part because the Germans were persuaded that strategic thought was their very own specialty, for indeed the founder of modern Western strategy, Carl von Clausewitz, was as German as Sunzi (Sūnzǐ; or Sun Wu, Sun Tzu) was Chinese—thereby confirming the dangers of reading such intoxicating texts.

Tactics are important, but the higher art-of-war operational level dominates tactics; the level of theater strategy governed by geographic factors in turn dominates the operational level—the 34 kilometers of open sea between England and France, the vast geographic depth of Russia, sufficed to neutralize the most dynamic of invaders in the past, and matter still even in the present.

But final outcomes are determined at the still higher level of grand strategy, in which all military factors are in turn dominated by the overall human, economic, and technological capacity that states can harness from their own populations and from their allies—a function of political cohesion and leadership within states, and within alliances. None of the many tactical and operational-level victories of the German army between 1914 and 1918 could break through the higher levels of strategy to reach all the way up to the top level of grand strategy. Hence, all its hard fighting achieved nothing, just as if it were the worst of armies, instead of the best.

A strategically competent, nonautistic government would have recognized that only Germany's *non*military abilities had any value—its banks, factories, and universities could keep rising without limit, advancing the prosperity of the population and expanding German influence all over the world—as was indeed happening until 1914. By contrast, the German army could be useful only defensively and the German navy was actually counterproductive, for it could achieve nothing strategically in spite of its considerable operational-level strength, while its very existence was mobilizing the British to oppose Germany globally.

In theory, Germany could easily have overcome its fatal strategic encirclement by the British, French, and Russian world empires. Jointly they were very powerful, but their alliance was only as strong as their individual fear of Germany. Therefore, the perfect German response to the Anglo-Russian Convention of 1907 that completed the encirclement was simply to renounce oceanic naval power, literally to scrap the better warships or sell them, with Russia as the preferred customer. That would have removed immediately the chief motive for the British alliance strategy against Germany. As for the Franco-Russian alliance, it was kept together only by a common fear of the German army. If its strength had been reduced to ensure "defensive primacy"[2] and nothing more, the pro-German party at the czar's court would have won, even if the French Republic would have persisted in its politically embarrassing alliance with the czarist autocracy.

Nor would these measures have disarmed Germany, for even a reduced army less capable of mounting large-scale offensive operations could have defeated any invasion of Germany and secured all its territory, including its eastern lands with their restless and restive Polish minority, a smaller German Xinjiang.

That only a militarily nonthreatening and diplomatically conciliatory grand strategy could have served Germany well—accelerating its peaceful rise to new heights of cultured prosperity—is perfectly obvious in retrospect. But by 1907, and indeed long before, that best strategy had become simply unthinkable for Germany's political elite, including its trade-unionists and social-democratic parliamentarians. An abrupt reversal from hubris and military aggrandizement had become emotionally impossible after long years of triumphalism.

Politically it was just as impossible, because there was a strong national consensus for a strong army and an expanding navy. Bureaucratically, on the other hand, the Army General Staff and the Imperial Naval Cabinet, vigorously backed by a good part of public opinion, would have resorted to any means, including a coup d'état, to stop demilitarization. Germany was a constitutional monarchy ruled by an elected parliamentary government, but cultural militarism (even world-famous scientists were proud to serve as low-ranking reserve officers) conferred immense authority on the military elite, whose operational skills were indeed admired worldwide. (It was only much later that their utter incompetence at the level of grand strategy was universally recognized. The logic is the same at every level, but the grammar of combat requires sharp choices, whereas the grammar of grand strategy requires compromise.)

But it never came to a coup d'état to stop demilitarization, because the greatest obstacle to the adoption of the correct grand strategy was purely intellectual, as is so often the case.

The paradoxical logic of strategy is directly contrary to common sense: only in strategy can less be better than more. Specifically, a weaker army and navy are better than stronger ones if they exceed the culminating level of *systemically* acceptable strength, evoking more-than-proportionate adversarial reactions, both symmetric and asymmetric.

As the strength of a rising Great Power continues to increase, friendly neighbors become watchful, allies edge toward neutrality, former neutrals become adversaries, and committed adversaries old and new are compelled to overcome their differences to combine against the Great Power rising too quickly. In a world of independent states, even the strongest rising power can be overcome by the gathering of adversaries summoned by the very increase of its own strength.

# CHAPTER EIGHT

# Could China Adopt a Successful Grand Strategy?

*Each historical period* and each state is different, invalidating most analogies. But the paradoxical logic of strategy is always the same.[1] China's rising power necessarily evokes increasing resistance, so that it may well become weaker at the level of grand strategy *because* of its own rising military strength—a paradoxical outcome rather common in the realm of strategy. A mild and yielding diplomacy, free of arrogance and ready to make concessions at every turn, could be a palliative for a while. But if military growth continues, such a remissive foreign policy would be interpreted in a sinister light as deliberately deceptive—mere camouflage for continued military aggrandizement.

It follows that the only correct grand strategy for today's China would have to contradict common sense and go against all normal human instincts by renouncing any but the slowest military growth. In addition, insofar as CCP rule also rests on the support of its military leaders, a contention that is not undisputed, such a grand strategy would also require a drastic political restructuring, to either replace CCP rule with democratic legitimacy—and one sustained by an antimilitarist consensus (a further leap)—or to the contrary, to further elevate the CCP into a position of unquestioned authority over the armed forces. It is a bizarre thought that to construct a non-threatening grand strategy, the CCP might have to become a Stalinist party sustained by secret police terror, rather than military support, with, in Mao-speak, power still growing out of the barrel of the gun, but of very small caliber.

China's failure at the level of grand strategy, absent political leadership of superhuman perspicacity and courage, is therefore overdetermined:

- It would be abnormal to adopt a humble foreign policy *because* China's all-round power is increasing rapidly;
- it would be abnormal to reduce military expenditures *because* China's rapid economic growth allows their rapid increase;
- it would be abnormal for the PLA to overcome universal bureaucratic proclivities to accept its own diminution; and
- it would be abnormal for Chinese public opinion, insofar as it counts, to support the unilateral renunciation of military strength, especially given the humiliating past of military impotence. Indeed, there is strong evidence of public support for more military expenditure, and more ambitious expenditure, notably the acquisition of one or more aircraft carriers.

According to the results of a public opinion poll conducted for *Global Times* that was published in May 2011,[2] "more than 70% of respondents" approved the acquisition of a carrier; 68 percent approved of the building of more than one carrier in the future, with "a quarter" opposed. As to the purposes of that carrier: 77.8 percent chose "safeguarding territorial integrity and fending off invasions," but 81.3 percent chose "making China stronger." Yet "more than half" agreed with the statement that "building a carrier may trigger an arms race in Asia." In regard to the cost, only 41 percent agreed with the statement that "building a carrier is economically viable for China" while 35.5 percent said that it was "worthwhile . . . despite the huge construction costs." And 75.2 percent said that it would "boost China's military technology development and army building [*sic*]."

In that context, Peng Guangqian of the PLA Academy of Military Science was quoted with an adaptation of the standard formula: "China's aircraft carrier, if there is one, is only part of the nation's military equipment advancement under the defense policy principle. It won't serve any strategy of global expansion or contending for supremacy." On the other hand, Song Xiaojun ("a Beijing-based military expert") suggested an economic motive: "China has an increasing demand for resources and energy, some of which have to be imported from abroad. If their transportation and trade are threatened, industrialization and urbanization will be in question."

The "four abnormals," to use a typically Chinese formulation, are already formidable obstacles to the formation of a correctly unthreatening grand strategy. But over and above them, there is China's especially acute form of great-state autism as discussed above, which is further reinforced by the lingering tradition of the tributary system, whose very premise was the formal inequality of states, all being inherently and irremediably inferior to China. A less autistic China, more aware of others' perceptions and feelings, would already have slowed its military growth, given the strong reactions it is already evoking even in this embryonic stage—reactions to which the Chinese political elite has been demonstrably oblivious. One reason for this is the final and most ironical impediment to strategic wisdom, which arises from the very core of Han strategic culture.

# CHAPTER NINE

# The Strategic Unwisdom of the Ancients

*Thus we reach* a specifically Chinese and most peculiar obstacle to the formulation of a successful grand strategy: a stubborn faith in the superior strategic wisdom to be found in ancient texts, and the resulting belief that China will always be able to outmaneuver its adversaries with clever expedients, circumventing the accumulating resistance caused by its rise.

Remarkably undiminished by the actual record of Chinese history, with its repeated subjugations by relatively small numbers of primitive invaders, this great confidence in Chinese strategic abilities reflects the immense prestige of China's ancient writings on statecraft and the art of war, and more particularly seven texts gathered in a set canon by the Song dynasty's sixth emperor, Song Shenzong, in 1080.[1] Much reproduced or anthologized thereafter, albeit in different versions, these texts, which are variously dated from some centuries before the Common Era to the Tang dynasty, also served as examination fodder, further ensuring their survival.

Each of the seven texts[2] has its adepts and its distinctive merits. Some emphasize higher statecraft and some descend all the way down to tactics and stratagems, but the most prominent by far is the *Sūnzǐ Bīngfǎ*, usually translated in English as *The Art of War*, attributed to an author who is variously known as Sunzi (Sūnzǐ), Sun Wu, or Sun Tzu, among other names. Now the star of screen and stage,[3] he has been famous for at least two millennia—a reassuringly familiar edition of his text was recovered from a bamboo scroll found in a Han dynasty tomb in 1972. In translation, *The Art of War* became known even in remote Europe by 1772,[4] and much earlier than that in Japan, where it was the claimed inspiration of the most strategic of Japanese warlords, the celebrated Takeda Shingen, and where it has been published even as a *manga* (comic book).

The undoubted merit of *The Art of War* is its presentation of the universal and unchanging paradoxical logic of strategy in a form less cryptic than that of the coeval epigrams of Heraclitus (the unity of opposites, and so forth), and altogether more succinct than the *On War* of Carl von Clausewitz. To be sure, the latter is altogether superior intellectually because Clausewitz explains his reasoning step by step, starting from first principles in a manner at once systematically philosophical and exhilarating, while *The Art of War* baldly presents its prescriptions in an oracular manner. *On War* therefore offers a systematic methodology lacking in *The Art of War*, but there is no doubt that it too conveys the same (paradoxical) truths, and far more expeditiously.

What makes this excellent text potentially very misleading and even dangerous—along with some of the other Chinese strategic literature of ancient origin[5]—is the *context* of its prescriptions: the two and a half centuries or so of the "Warring States" period, *Zhànguó Shídà*, that ended with the unification of 221 BCE.

That Homeric chariots are the principal instruments of combat in *The Art of War*, even though fully fledged cavalry forces of lancers and mounted archers had by then reached Chinese lands, is not the problem of course, because fundamental strategic concepts can outlast any technology.

What is highly consequential, on the other hand, is that all the protagonists were Han—they were the rulers, generals, and advisors of rival Chinese states, all of whom operated within the same framework of cultural norms, with similar objectives, priorities, and values. Because their inter-state relations were *intra*-cultural, there were exceptionally ample opportunities for diplomacy, espionage, secret operations, and political subversion alike, all of them both facilitated and bounded by a common language, a common mentality, and shared cultural premises.

It was much the same in Renaissance Italy, whose states likewise engaged in intracultural war, diplomacy, and subversion on a continuous basis. The result in both cases was the swift alternation of conflict and cooperation between states that could make and break alliances with equal ease, fighting each other one day only to become allies the next—because there was no accumulation of ethnic, racial, or religious animosity between fellow Italians, or fellow Han Chinese. Moreover, when the Warring States did fight, the essential similarity of their armies and their tactics enhanced the ritualistic element in their combat.[6]

A highly abbreviated account of just one short phase (301–284 BCE) of the Warring States period is sufficient to illustrate the nature and implications of intracultural war, and peace.

In 300 BCE, chief minister Mèngcháng Jūn of the state of Qi formed an alliance with the states of Wei and Han. The state of Qin, weakened by internal strife, submitted to the Qi, Wei, and Han coalition, appointing Mèngcháng as its own chief minister. Two years later, the state of Zhao persuaded Qin to leave the coalition, driving out Mèngcháng. But then Qi, Wei, and Han attacked Qin, and after much fighting gained territory for the states of Han and Wei. Mèncháng's coalition, centered on his own Qi, next defeated the states of Yan and Chu.

In 294 BCE Mèngcháng was defeated in a court intrigue and fled to Wei. Qi and Qin then made a truce, which allowed Qi to attack the state of Song and allowed Qin to attack the reduced Han-Wei coalition. Six years later, Qi and Qin were planning a joint attack on the state of Zhao, when the Qi ruler was persuaded that only Qin would benefit; instead of attacking Zhao, he started forming a coalition against Qin. In danger of isolation, Qin responded by giving back territory it had seized from Wei and Zhao.

In 286 BCE, Qi seized the entire state of Song, alarming the states of Qin, Zhao, Wei, and Yan, which promptly formed a coalition under the guidance of Qi's very own former chief minister Mèngcháng back from his Wei exile. Yan next launched a powerful surprise attack on Qi, which also came under attack by Qin, Zhao, and Wei, losing most of its territory.

Next Zhao and Qin started a long war that allowed Qi to recover—and so it went on, and on, and on, much as in Renaissance Italy.

It is theoretically possible that the propensity of Chinese officials to constantly cite the strategies and stratagems of the Warring States period as exemplary lessons in cunning statecraft, diplomatic finesse, and the art of war, is nothing more than an antiquarian pose, with no effect at all on the actual conduct of today's Chinese rulers and officials. It is theoretically possible that the same is true of the admiration frequently lavished on the most successful Warring States protagonists as great masters of statecraft, intrigue, and war, and also of the worshipful admiration of Sunzi's *Art of War*.

By the same token, it is theoretically possible that their Renaissance origins have no role in shaping contemporary Italian political practices, even though they are characterized by exactly the same propensity for abrupt realignments that transform coalition partners into opposition parties, and sometimes back again in short order (*transformismo* is the term; fittingly, there is no English equivalent). In both cases, the theoretically possible is contradicted by ample empirical evidence.

The first detectable residue of the Warring States/*Art of War* mentality, or rather of the misapplication of intracultural norms to intercultural conflict, is the presumption of unlimited pragmatism in inter-state relations. The Qi, Qin, Zhao,

Wei, and Yan states could be allies one day, enemies the next, and then perhaps allies again, simply because at each remove it was the profitable thing to do. Chinese foreign policy evidently presumes that foreign states can be just as practical and opportunistic in their dealings with China.

But intercultural foreign relations are not at all the same as intracultural relations. Because instead of a common identity there are clashing national sensitivities, any inter-state confrontation on any issue that is more than narrowly technical can arouse the emotions, generating fears, resentment, or mistrust as the case might be, and necessarily affecting relations with the state in question across the board. Yet the December 15–17, 2010, visit of Premier Wen Jiabao to India already cited above was evidently premised on the belief that the Indians would simply set aside the sharp disputes over the status of Kashmir and Arunachal Pradesh (which the Chinese themselves had unilaterally revived) to smartly pursue business opportunities in China. For the purpose, as noted, Wen Jiabao was accompanied by some 400 businessmen. But the Indians are insufficiently pragmatic to behave as Qi, Qin, or Zhao might have done, and the visit unfolded in a chilly atmosphere, with nothing much accomplished, and certainly no goodwill generated by what was officially presented as a goodwill visit.

Exactly the same misapplication of norms has occurred as often as there have been confrontations of late, most notably perhaps the September 7, 2010, incident near the Senkaku Islands (Diaoyutai to the Chinese). This was followed by inflammatory Chinese Foreign Ministry declarations that duly produced anti-Japanese agitations, the arrest of some visiting Japanese executives, a de facto embargo on rare-earth exports to Japan[7]—and very soon thereafter, by Chinese Foreign Ministry statements that recalled the importance of Chinese-Japanese economic relations, called on the public to stop anti-Japanese demonstrations, and invited the Japanese to continue investing in China. It was different for the Japanese, of course: the incident resulted in a long-term reappraisal of Japanese relations with China across the board, and a drastic reversal in the recent trend that seemed to be realigning Tokyo toward Beijing and away from Washington. Only the March 11, 2011, disasters diverted Japanese attention from the "China problem," and then only to intensify efforts to further consolidate relations with the United States. What is tolerated intraculturally, within the family as it were, can easily generate enduring hostility when different cultures clash.

A second and related residue of misapplied *Art of War* intra-cultural norms that distorts China's conduct is potentially much more dangerous. This is the tendency of Chinese officialdom to believe that long-unresolved disputes with foreign countries can be resolved by deliberately provoking crises, to force negotiations that will settle the dispute.

A typical example arose in conjunction with the long-standing and unresolved Arunachal Pradesh/"South Tibet" Zàngnán territorial dispute. In May 2007, one year after the two sides had negotiated an overall negotiating framework,

China abruptly denied a visa application from Ganesh Koyu, an Indian citizen and elite civil servant of the Indian Administrative Service (IAS) born in Arunachal Pradesh, stating that because his birthplace in "South Tibet" is part of China, he would not need a visa to visit his own country.[8]

The applicant was one of 107 young IAS officials who were to tour China as part of their training, one expression of the striving of Indian officials to comply with the spirit of the 2006 Sino-Indian framework agreement for the negotiation of all outstanding issues between the two countries. This was not an incident or accident, and the Chinese consular official who refused to accept the visa application was not acting on his own initiative, but under orders from Beijing. Evidently, the purpose of the visa denial was to provoke a crisis that would then be resolved by negotiations. But the Indian government refused to enter into any such negotiation; instead it withdrew all 107 visa applications, canceled the trip altogether, and edged another inch or two closer to the United States.

Having gained nothing, six months later in December 2007 China's consular officials reversed themselves to grant a visa to a Professor Marpe Sora, also born in Arunachal Pradesh.[9] By then, however, Indian public opinion had been aroused and outraged, generating opposition to cooperative relations with China in general.

It is unfortunate that on this score the Chinese leaders are not better advised by their most faithful friend. Henry Kissinger's *On China* begins with Mao Zedong's October 1962 decision to break the diplomatic stalemate over the border dispute with India:

> Mao had decided to break the stalemate. He reached far back into the classical Chinese tradition. . . . China and India, Mao told his commanders, had previously fought "one and a half" wars. Beijing could draw operational lessons from each. The first war had occurred over 1,300 years earlier. . . . After China's intervention, the two countries had enjoyed centuries of flourishing religious and economic exchange. The lesson learned from the ancient campaign, as Mao described it, was that China and India were not doomed to perpetual enmity. They could enjoy a long period of peace again, but to do so, China had to use force to "knock" India back "to the negotiating table."

Kissinger's admiration is evident:

> In no other country is it conceivable that a modern leader would initiate a major national undertaking by invoking strategic principles from a millennium-old event—nor that he could confidently expect his colleagues to understand the significance of his allusions.[10]

What Kissinger should have noted, of course, was that Mao's surprise attack utterly failed to achieve its objective—far from "knocking" India back to the negotiating table, China's quick victory, which was a humiliating defeat for India, had the opposite effect, making it politically impossible to negotiate a border settlement till this day. To be sure, Kissinger is quite right in seeing the influence of ancient principles in Mao's conduct—but he fails to recognize that the episode is a clamorous example of strategic error induced by the flawed principles of ancient unwisdom.[11]

At present the most dangerous application of the same flawed method is the attempt to use maritime incidents to advance the Chinese claim to the vast oceanic expanses and minuscule dry surfaces of what is officially described as the "Hainan Province Paracels, Spratlys, and Zhongsha Islands Authority." That is the county-level agency that is supposed to exercise sovereignty over the entirety of three disputed archipelagoes in the South China Sea, two of which are not merely claimed by other countries but in part actually occupied— or more truthfully, outposted—by Malaysia, the Philippines, Vietnam, and Taiwan, as well as China.

Moreover, the Chinese have frequently engaged in intimidation tactics at sea, against fishing boats, patrol vessels, and drilling rigs. With firepower ruled out, the Chinese operational method has been to deploy much bigger vessels on the scene than those of the other side, to overawe at least and sometimes to physically induce retreat by threatening collisions. Again, the purpose of these provocations is not to escalate toward war, but rather to create crisis conditions meant to force the other side to focus on the issue, to finally resolve it by serious negotiations. That is all very well, but in the process of provoking a crisis, the

Chinese cannot avoid alerting, alarming, and mobilizing elite and even mass opinion in the target country—and once aroused, public opinion rarely favors concessions.

It is worrisome though not unexpected that Chinese officials seem to have great difficulty in understanding the straightforward nexus that utterly invalidates their method: by attracting attention to whatever is in dispute, crises actually increase its perceived value, making concessions to reach a settlement that much less likely. In other words, to deliberately provoke crises is not at all a good way of solving inter-state disputes. What worked between the Warring States, which shared the same culture, would only cause endless war among today's diverse states.

A third residue of the *Art of War* mentality that distorts and degrades China's conduct, and that militates against the adoption of a correctly nonprovocative grand strategy, is an exaggerated faith in the value of deception as such, as well as of the stratagems and surprise moves that deception allows.

Stratagems and surprise strikes played a large role in the Warring States period, as they did in Renaissance Italy, and for exactly the same reasons: geographic proximity, familiarity, indeed consanguinity, cultural homogeneity—all of them facilitate methods that require in-depth knowledge of the adversary, and easy access.

The obvious merit of these methods is their low cost and capacity to generate high payoffs—they amount to extreme cases of maneuver warfare as opposed to attrition. They are also expressions of asymmetrical warfare in a maneuver mode, of which the most extreme case is to fight an enemy state by "de-capitating its command and control"—that is, by killing its ruler. In 222 BCE, Qin conquered Zhao and threatened Yan. Instead of an army, the Yan sent the celebrated scholar and assassin Jing Ke to kill the ruler of Qin with a poisoned dagger concealed in a presentation map roll (Jing Ke is the protagonist of a government-funded and unwatchable film extravaganza, *Hero*, in Western distribution).[12] He might have succeeded but for the intervention of the court doctor, armed with a heavy medicine box; the infuriated Qin rulers sent an army that conquered Yan.

This example illustrates the obvious defect of such methods: all forms of maneuver warfare, asymmetrical or not, are not only high-payoff but also high-risk, and proportionately so. The fewer the resources committed, the less the redundancy, the smaller the element of brute force, the greater is the efficiency of action, but reliance on very favorable circumstances and very precise execution must also be greater. Only with both good fortune and high skill can one stiletto or poisoned dagger do the work of many swords—when everything works exactly as planned.

Because very fortunate circumstances are unusual by definition and precise execution is a rarity amid the urgencies of conflict, assassination along with all other forms of covert action has always been relegated to a very minor role in Western strategic thought and, indeed, practice. Not so in Chinese strategic literature, in which many prescriptions of

*The Art of War* are predicated on deception. Indeed, the way *(Tao)* of war is equated with the way of deception.[13] And even assassination as such is accorded some prominence: in China's first systematic historiographical work, the monumental *Shiji*, or *The Records of the Grand Historian* (or Grand Scribe) of Sima Qian (Ssu-ma Ch'ien), an entire volume (the eighty-sixth) is dedicated to *The Biographies of the Assassins*, including Jing Ke.[14]

The most dangerous possible confluence of misapplied intracultural norms and misplaced faith in *Art of War* methods would be a Chinese attempt to knock the United States into a negotiating mood by some sort of surprise attack. It must be hoped that Internet speculations about the merits of attacking a U.S. warship, even an aircraft carrier, to strengthen China's hand in claiming jurisdiction over the Western Pacific are merely adolescent fantasies. But it is not especially reassuring that some can be attributed to serving officers of more than junior rank, nor is it reassuring that until quite recently, at any rate, Chinese warships saluted on the high seas by U.S. Navy vessels did not reciprocate and instead switched on their fire-control radars. Most recently, there have been semi-official calls for the use of force to assert China's maritime claims, not against the United States itself but against the Philippines, a treaty ally, as well as Vietnam, its newest informal ally. A recent unsigned editorial in *Global Times*, a voice of the Chinese government of course, is a notable example of such bellicose posturing:

China has been increasingly confronted with sea disputes . . . promoting hawkish responses within China, asking the government to take action. China has emphasized its reluctance in solving disputes at sea via military means on many occasions. . . . But some . . . countries have been exploiting China's mild diplomatic stance . . . the Philippines and Vietnam believe China has been under various pressure. They think it is a good time for them to take advantage of this and force China to give away its interests. Currently, China's mainstream understanding is that it should first go through the general channels of negotiating with other countries to solve sea disputes. But if a situation turns ugly, some military action is necessary. This public sentiment will influence China's future foreign policy. Countries currently in sea disputes with China may have failed to spot this tendency. . . . Thus, the South China Sea, as well as other sensitive sea areas, will have a higher risk of serious clashes. If these countries don't want to change their ways with China, they will need to prepare for the sounds of cannons. We need to be ready for that, as it may be the only way for the disputes in the sea to be resolved.[15]

Especially now that the United States is in the midst of a serious economic crisis, which will undoubtedly result in some reduction of its vast military expenditures, the essential bellicosity of Americans might be overlooked. Like the British, the

Americans are pragmatic and commercial to a fault, but when attacked they behave most unpragmatically and uncommercially, with a decided preference for maximum force even when there are more restrained and cheaper options. Hence, Chinese faith in clever Warring States statecraft, to gain much with just a little violence, an almost symbolic bold stroke perhaps, might collide catastrophically with an altogether more violent American response. The Pearl Harbor precedent should stand as an awful warning of this danger, but then if humans had ever been capable of learning anything from such precedents, their history would not be a record of endlessly repeated follies of war.

When it comes to broad strategic deception, especially when aimed at Americans and the United States, the confidence of Chinese rulers and officials in its feasibility and usefulness is much enhanced by the contrast between their own self-images and their images of Americans and the United States.

In another leftover from the tributary past, the Han usually attribute superior cunning to themselves as compared to the non-Han of the world, as well as more elevated virtues, of course. Americans, on the other hand, they see as especially naive, also as strong and perhaps violent, but easily manipulated. "It is not easy to really know China because China is an ancient civilization . . . [whereas] the American people, they're [*danchun*] very simple [or naive, or innocent—单纯 in the original]." Thus spoke Vice-Premier Wang Qishan on May 11, 2011, extemporaneously in a television discussion, while in

Washington as head of the economic side of the annual China-U.S. strategic and economic dialogue.[16]

For a Chinese official, that was not an unusually arrogant statement. Even miserable and barely literate menials routinely claim that China and the Chinese are too sophisticated to be understood by non-Chinese.

Given this estimate of American discernment, it could well be thought in Beijing that the simplest form of deception—mere concealment, as in the familiar injunction Tāo guāng yǎng huì, "Hide one's capacities and bide one's time"—could be quite sufficient.

Regrettably, it would appear that this assessment has so far proved to be largely correct. Over the years it was triumphantly confirmed as the Chinese watched with increasing incredulity the absence of any American attempt to impede the rise of China, and to the contrary, the many and varied U.S. contributions to China's rapid economic growth, starting with the unilateral opening of the U.S. market to Chinese exports, and then the energetic promotion of China's membership in the World Trade Organization, and all without demanding anything resembling full reciprocity.

Indeed, Chinese unfriendly to the United States have never ceased to spin theories to explain the apparent benevolence of the United States as actually malevolent, in a projection of their own propensity for strategic deception. In one version, the United States vigorously promotes the globalization of the Chinese economy to make it utterly dependent on imported hydrocarbons and raw materials, so that when the time is ripe the Chinese and their government can be subjugated by the mere threat of interrupting the flow of seaborne imports. In another version, the U.S. ruling class relies on cheap Chinese imports long enough to subjugate its own working class before turning on China—and that explains why the deceptively benevolent phase has lasted so long.

Even Chinese who bear no hostility to Americans may still give credence to one of the malevolent explanations, simply because nothing else makes sense to them—why else would the U.S. government go out of its way to accelerate China's rise? Themselves newly emancipated from dogmatic ideology, not many Chinese appreciate even now how rigidly ideological is the framework of U.S. economic policy, especially when it comes to "free trade"—this is an ideology within which protectionism is viewed as a mortal sin rather than as a policy option among others, and in which any consideration of long-term structural consequences (such as deindustrialization) is deemed irrelevant, given the principled refusal to intervene in any case.

....................................

# CHAPTER TEN

# Strategic Competence
## The Historical Record

*Many foreigners*[1] and not only they themselves are inclined to attribute great strategic competence to the Han Chinese, but the historical record does not sustain this belief. That should not be surprising. Great-state autism, the misapplication of intracultural tactics, tricks, and techniques to intercultural conflicts, the ritualistic conduct of warfare, and the fixed Tianxia 天下 presumption of superiority were all obstacles to the situational awareness of Chinese rulers, their ability to formulate realistic grand strategies and to implement them effectively by diplomatic or military means. Hence, though the Han have long viewed themselves as great strategists, they were regularly defeated by enemies neither numerous nor advanced, some of whom were not content with subjecting frontier areas to their rule, instead proceeding to conquer all the remaining lands settled by the Han. Indeed, Han rulers have ruled China for little more than a third of the last millennium.

The last dynasty, the Qīng, whose conventional dates are 1644 to 1912, was established by Tungusic-speaking Jurchen nomad-warriors of forest and tundra led by their Aisin Gioro clan, which invented *Manchu* ("strong, great") as a new ethnic name in 1635, before choosing the auspicious title Qing (*Qīng*, "clear") for their dynasty in 1644.[2] Till the very end, the Manchu rulers preserved their separate ethnic identity complete with their own language and their own script, derived from the Aramaic alphabet via Sogdian, Uyghur, and Mongol; it can still be seen around Beijing in the Qing signboards affixed on historical buildings. (The nationalist claim that the Manchu were quickly and completely assimilated, so that their victories and power were in reality Han victories and Han power, no longer has scholarly standing.)

It was the Manchu who established the borders of contemporary China by gradually conquering the diverse territories that now form the enormous Xinjiang Uyghur Autonomous Region, by encompassing the Mongol tribes whose descendants are now a minority in Inner Mongolia, and by asserting at least a nominal suzerainty over Tibet.

China under the Manchu was thus nothing more than a conquered land alongside the others, yet in contemporary Chinese consciousness the borders of China are those of the Manchu Empire at its peak, achieved with the completion of the conquest of the vast territory of Dzungaria in 1761, under the Qianlong emperor.

It is an interesting case of transposition, but with Manchu garrisons distributed in every Chinese province as occupation troops in effect, its Han contemporaries knew full well that they were not the protagonists of empire, but rather its conquered subjects. Yet today the Han routinely manifest proprie-

tary feelings over non-Han lands conquered by the Manchu—
by the same token Indians could claim Sri Lanka because both
were ruled by the British.

The Ming dynasty that preceded the Manchu, ruling from
1368 to 1644 by conventional dating, was impeccably and entirely Han but it had succeeded the decidedly alien Mongol
occupation. Under Kublai Kan (Qubilai Qan), grandson of
Genghis Khan, the Mongols assumed the symbols and style of
Chinese imperial rule as the Yuan dynasty, whose conventional
dates are 1271 to 1368. Again, the sophisticated Han had been
unable to keep out the rude Mongols, and had to live under
their dominion, destructively predatory at first, and severely
extractive even at its best (not least to pay for the famous network of road-forts cum postal relay and remount stations).

Moreover, in China north of the Yangtze River it was not
Han rule that preceded the Mongols, but rather another Jurchen
dynasty, the Jin established by the Wányán clan that originated in the forest-lands of Manchuria, and whose conventional dates are 1115–1234. The Han dynasty of the Song persisted in the south, but the Han of the historic core of China
centered on the Yellow River lived as subjects of foreign conquerors, whom they had been unable to defeat and keep out of
their lands.

In the north above the Yellow River, including "the sixteen
prefectures," Yānyún Shíliù Zhōu, around and beyond Beijing,
the predecessors of the Jin were also non-Han, but rather Khitans or Qidans, originally Mongolic nomads and mounted

archers from the northern steppes. Under the leadership of their Yelü clan, they established the Liao dynasty, conventionally dated 907–1125, but it is to their original ethnic name that we owe China's now stylish antique appellation Cathay, which is Marco Polo's *Catai* Englished but was not Marco Polo's personal conceit, because *Kitai, Qitay, Khitad,* or *Hitai* is how China is still known going westward all the way to Bulgaria. Not today a well remembered ethnic name, the Khitans or Qidans evidently made a great impression in their time.

Even the Tang dynasty, which preceded the Song (618–907) and which is often viewed as quintessentially "Chinese," included a very strong Turkic-Mongol element, splendidly revealed in the ubiquity of horses, horsemen, and dashing polo-playing horsewomen in its arts. Prominent field commanders drawn from Central Asia's ultimate fighting elite, the wolf-reared Ashinas clan (heroes till now to Turkey's ultranationalists) were an important presence amid the sublime elegance of the Tang imperial court.[3] Han field commanders would have been more familiar with the *Art of War* and kindred military texts, some Han commanders were highly effective, and one was the greatly celebrated Li Jing, 571–649. Yet Tang emperors often preferred to rely on the proven skills of their Ashina-clan field commanders.

What emerges very clearly even from this extremely fragmentary review of China's political history—much of which is indeed not Han history but rather Jurchen, Mongolic, or Turkic—is that the continuing superiority of the Han in all forms of civilian achievement was not matched by their strategic abilities. The Han could produce more and better food with earth and water than any other nation on earth, they could build the most sophisticated cultural and technological superstructure on that material base, but more often than not (twice more often, at least) they could not assess the external environment realistically to identify threats and opportunities, nor could they develop effective grand strategies to muster their relatively abundant resources, to ensure the safety of their lands, populations, and themselves.

Strategic competence was evidently not included in the long list of Han accomplishments, with the result that while Han generals in charge of large armies were busy quoting Sunzi to each other, relatively small numbers of mounted warriors schooled in the rudely effective strategy and tactics of the steppe outmaneuvered and defeated their forces. Moreover, Han intrigues and subterfuges proved vastly inferior to the long-range and large-scale diplomacy that came naturally to the steppe rulers, who regularly coalesced with or against even very distant empires. In the past, the evil consequences of these shortcomings could only be amplified by persisting delusions over the merits of Han strategic culture. Unfortunately, judging by the frequency of Warring States quotations in the discourse of Chinese officials, it seems that the delusions persist.

What also emerges from the historical evidence is the recurrent cycle that weakened dynasties and prepared the way for their destruction. A strong dynasty resulted in internal peace, law, and order. Peace in turn resulted in economic growth, and therefore greater income and wealth differentiation, the rise of the local rich. Wealth differentiation in turn resulted in the transfer of land-ownership from small-holders to richer landlords. Having become sharecroppers and landless field laborers, the ex-peasants became bandits when harvests failed. Bandits in turn became local rebels, and local rebellions merged into large revolts when charismatic leaders emerged. None was more so than Zhu Yuanzhang, who started off as a landless laborer, became a rebel against the Yuan dynasty of the Mongols, rose in rebel leadership ranks, and finally founded the Ming dynasty in 1368 as the Hongwu emperor.

Along the way, there is an inner cycle of decay that starts with wealth differentiation, which leads to the rise of local oligarchs who increasingly control local government, which allows them to accumulate yet more wealth. And within that, there is the innermost cycle of officialdom itself, which starts with scholar-officials who take Confucianism and its obligations seriously, thereby ensuring law and order, which leads to wealth differentiation, which allows the rich to support their children through the examination system until they become officials in turn, who then use their power to further enrich their families, until the system breaks down. Current social realities are probably not coincidental.

CHAPTER ELEVEN

..........................................

# The Inevitability of Mounting Resistance

*The first conclusion*, further confirmed by the contents of two recent, full-scale programmatic documents that officially present China's military and foreign policies,[1] is that China's leaders fully intend to persist in pursuing incompatible objectives: very rapid economic growth, *and* very rapid military growth, *and* a commensurate increase in global influence.

It is the logic of strategy itself that dictates the impossibility of concurrent advances in all three spheres: inevitably, China's military aggrandizement is already evoking countering responses—all the more so because it is so rapid, of course. Those responses in turn are already impeding, and will increasingly impede, China's concurrent advancement in all three spheres, economic, military, and diplomatic, albeit no doubt in varying degrees.

That much is axiomatic so long as independent states persist among China's neighbors and global peers.

As of now, and these are early days, of course, China's rapid military aggrandizement is already evoking hostility and resistance instead of gaining more influence.

95

What remains to be determined are the forms, extent, contents, timing, and intensity of the countering responses of individual countries, and whether and how their separate efforts are coordinated or even combined by pairs of countries, or by ad hoc groups of countries, or even by an organized multilateral alliance under U.S. leadership—though that is a prospect not merely very unlikely but also very undesirable, for it could and most likely would drive the Russian Federation into the Chinese camp, and that could be decisive in itself.

The logic of strategy is not self-executing, but it does force leaders to act, hence some countering responses to China's rise are already under way, in spite of the absence of declared national policies on that score, and the lack of all but very embryonic attempts at international coordination. Just in the last twelve months, these organic responses to perceptions of an increasingly strong and potentially menacing China have included

- the initiation of a strategic dialogue between India and Japan—which has already resulted in practical measures, such as provisions for increased reciprocal attendance at military schools, and closer intelligence cooperation focused on China;
- Japanese aid to Vietnam, also aimed at strengthening its ability to resist Chinese maritime encroachments;
- the 2011 visit to Japan of an Australian prime minister, who arrived with a decidedly strategic agenda explicitly aimed at China;

- a strengthening of Philippines maritime activity to protect claims over Spratly Islands;
- the continued, if glacially slow, reorientation of overall U.S. military efforts from futile tea drinking in Afghanistan to the containment of China; by the end of 2011, spontaneous, uncoordinated, almost instinctive reactions to China's military growth were supplemented by the emergence of a new joint-service planning concept implicitly focused on the Pacific and China, "The Air Sea Battle," which sounds operational but is presented as strategic, and which is equipped with its own advocacy office headed by a three-star officer.

The possible roles of individual countries in a China/anti-China world, as well as organizational arrangements between them, if any, are addressed in later chapters. But the major question must be the *nature* of the countering action. Responses confined to the military sphere, by way of precautionary force-building, counterdeployments, and such cannot long be adequate on their own. If the Chinese economy continues to grow very much faster than that of its neighbors and global peers, and if the percentage of China's gross domestic product allocated to military expenditures is constant, any countering force-building and counterdeployment efforts would soon be outclassed. In the meantime, China's rivals could even fall behind if they consume more resources for military preparations that lead to nothing yet still consume resources that could have been invested for economic growth.

Large military expenditures aimed at China must therefore be closely questioned, for they would not actually respond to the problem of destabilizing growth, while on the other hand nothing resembling a general China/anti-China war with armies in the field, naval battles, and conventional air bombardments is possible in the nuclear age. China may be making exactly the same colossal error that Imperial Germany did after 1890, but this is not a devolution that ends with another 1914, another war of destruction. The existence of nuclear weapons does not preclude all combat between those who have them, but does severely limit its forms as each participant is compelled to foreclose or at least contain the risks of escalation to the nuclear level. That still allows China to engage in inherently localized combat with India in the form of border skirmishing, and perhaps it could allow somewhat more extensive military action against a non-nuclear state, albeit with the lively possibility that it would be assisted by the United States or the Russian Federation if that state were Mongolia, or one of the Central Asian republics, not to speak of U.S. allies and quasi-allies.

Preparations to deter, and if needs be defend, against the possible military actions that the nuclear inhibition would still allow for China—not an attack on Japan, for example, or anything more than a localized border war with India—are necessary, of course, to dissuade these attacks or at least deny escalation dominance to the Chinese.

But such necessary preparations cannot be sufficient—they cannot embody all the resistance that China must arouse if both its rapid economic growth and proportionate military aggrandizement persist in coming years.

The axiom that independent states will by all possible means resist losing their independence will inevitably be expressed in the only way that the impossibility of large-scale war still allows, by "geo-economic" means—the logic of strategy in the grammar of commerce, as explicated above, and detailed below. If China persists in using its economic growth to acquire proportionate power as well, developing harmoniously internally while disrupting power balances and harmony externally, the response must be aimed at impeding its economic growth, if it is to be to be effective at all.

Military expenditures, by contrast, might be not only irrelevant but even counterproductive, if they end up accelerating the relative speed of China's economic growth.

The ineluctable necessity of slowing down China's economic growth will be more easily accepted by other countries more inclined to mercantilist approaches, but for the United States, it will collide with a most sacrosanct ideological dogma, as well as with politically important economic interests. *But strategy is stronger than politics.*

......................................

# CHAPTER TWELVE

# Why Current Policies Will Persist

*China's persistence* on its path toward vast troubles, if not ruin, as it exceeds its culminating level of unresisted achievement, is "overdetermined" by a multiplicity of factors:

- *Great-state autism*, which diminishes situational awareness, a malady shared with the United States and the Russian Federation as well as India, but at least proportionately greater in the Chinese case, and much aggravated by relative inexperience on the international scene. The specific effect is to reduce the ability of the regime as a whole to perceive international realities with clarity, and notably the mounting hostility tracked even by commonly available opinion polls.
- *Historical residues* in China's external conduct, deriving from the tributary system and the presumption of centrality within the concentric circles of the Tianxia. The specific effect is to inspire heavy-handed conduct, and to induce underestimations of the importance of whatever signals of mounting resistance from the outside world that do filter through the autistic barrier.

- *Ressentiment,* both popular and CCP elite hostility directed at outside powers, often well concealed but strongly felt and sometimes abruptly expressed, which derives in the first instance from the century or so of China's pre-1949 weakness, with the resulting intrusions and invasions, but ultimately perhaps from the many centuries of Han subjection to culturally inferior alien conquerors. The specific effect is to induce powerful emotional opposition to the very idea of limiting China's military aggrandizement, even if at some level there is a degree of intellectual recognition of its inevitable consequences.

- *The influence of the PLA* and the military-industrial establishment on Chinese policies and conduct. There is no need to engage with the complexities of the subject to presume that the PLA and related interests would not support the abandonment of China's proportionate military growth, to instead favor the military stagnation that would best serve China and the Chinese peoples as a whole. Given the current level of military capabilities, the PLA's declared policy of continued, rapid growth is quite understandable, and it seems that it is also supported by public opinion. Alas, the logic of strategy often calls for policies that are unpalatable, and sometimes downright unnatural.

- *The multiplicity of other expressions of Chinese power—* organizations able and willing to pursue expansionism perhaps for their own purely internal motives, which include state-owned enterprises, as well as integral parts of the state apparatus. Without listing each organization, consider what just one lowly part of the government structure, the law-enforcement command of the Administration of Fishery and Fishing Harbor Supervision (*zhōng huá rén mín gòng hé guó yú zhèng yú gǎng jiān dū quán lǐ*), officially part of the Ministry of Agriculture, can do all on its own. Even while goodwill missions and charm offensives were all the rage at the end of 2010 after a rough year for Chinese diplomacy, on December 26, Zhao Xingwu, director of the Fishery Administration (here FA), energetically declared his own policy that went in the directly opposite direction:[1]

> China will intensify management of the fishing in-
> dustry in its territory. Normal patrols to safeguard
> fishing around the Diaoyu Islands in the East China
> Sea [= Japan's closely patrolled and now garrisoned
> Senkaku Islands] will be organized in 2011.
> Protection of fisheries through accompanying pa-
> trols will be improved around the Nansha Islands . . .
> to crack down on illegal fishing.

The Nansha so blithely cited are better known as the Spratly Islands, more of which are outposted or even garrisoned by Vietnam, Malaysia, the Philippines, and Taiwan than by China.

The FA already had a formidable fleet with 2,287 ships and boats, including 528 built just in the past five years, including the very modern 2,500-ton *Yuzheng 310* long-range corvette. But evidently the FA is far from satisfied. Zhao Xingwu's speech proceeded to make that clear:

> Current Chinese patrol ships are too small, and cannot guarantee long-distance escort trips. . . . Sea patrols are different . . . because if anything happens [= incidents] it takes much longer for backup forces to reach the scene, and if the vessels themselves aren't sufficiently prepared there's no other resources they can turn to, and that makes it difficult to deliver timely protection.

The FA's *Yuzheng 310* is not small at 2,500 tons and in any case there is also the 4,000-ton *Yuzheng 311*. As for "other resources," there is the 15,000-ton replenishment ship *Yuzheng 88*—these are all substantial naval vessels, repainted in white. Whatever China's top leaders may say at summit meetings about harmonious collaboration, it is evident that Mr. Zhao Xingwu has his own plan: get more ships (and aircraft), be more active in asserting Chinese power over contested seas, achieve escalation dominance when incidents ensue.

There is worse. The most active and more consistently aggressive Chinese maritime service is not the Fishery Administration but rather the China Maritime Surveillance (CMS) organization Zhongguo Haijian of the State Oceanic Administration. Its primary mission is to patrol China's exclusive economic zone—the 200-nautical-mile zone around every speck of land that is itself claimed territory. On that basis, China is now claiming the entirety of the South China Sea, including tracts hundreds of miles from its coasts but almost within sight of the Philippines; the standard formula of the official Xinhua News Agency is that "China has more than 18,000 kilometers of coastline and three million square kilometers of territorial waters." (The South China Sea is estimated at 2.59 million square kilometers.)

The CMS has its own aircraft as well as 3,000-ton *Haijian-83* large cutters among other ships, though the 1,500-ton *Haijian-51* fast cutters have more often featured in confrontations with the Japanese. Nor is the CMS lacking in ambition: its deputy director, Sun Shuxian, has been quoted as saying: "The force will be upgraded to a reserve unit under the navy, a move which will make it better armed during patrols . . . the current defensive strength of CMS is inadequate." Accordingly, the CMS is also in the process of acquiring new cutters, some of which are very substantial 4,000-ton warships of commensurate combat value, and thus "better armed during patrols."

In addition to the dynamically expansive FA and even more active CMS, there is also the Maritime Safety Administration (MSA) of the Ministry of Transport. With 20,000 people classed as operational, it exceeds both the FA and the CMS, while its substantial fleet includes the 3,000-ton *Haixun-11* and *Haixun-31* cutters, not to be confused with the *Haijing 1001*, the most modern vessel of the Maritime Police, which is part of the People's Armed Police, and yet another player in a crowded field.

Thus the Standing Committee of the Politburo of the CCP may order the Foreign Ministry to replace arrogant threats with smiling reassurance—as it certainly did at the end of 2010; but to ensure that they too would participate in the effort, avoiding rather than provoking incidents, Politburo inspectors would have to remain aboard FA, CMS, and MSA vessels, as well as those of the PLA navy—whose warships, as we have seen, have been known to reply to the standard underway greeting with silence, while switching on their fire-control radars.

One more factor is the peculiar phenomenon that might be called China's "acquired strategic deficiency syndrome" (ASDS) whereby both ordinary common sense and even a weary awareness of the paradoxical logic of strategy are displaced by a distinct tendency to rely excessively on deception, stratagems large and small, and "barbarian-handling" techniques that devolve into gamesmanship. China's ASDS, which amounts to the habitual overuse of perfectly sensible methods of making the most of one's resources, derives from the aforementioned strategic unwisdom of the ancients, and it generates unwarranted confidence in the ability of the Chinese government to dissuade resistance by strategic deception, and to cleverly outmaneuver such resistance as is manifest nonetheless.

The specific consequence of China's ASDS at this time in its history, when its ascent is still fragile in some respects, or at any rate not yet fully accomplished or irresistibly consolidated, is to dissuade the one and only correct countermeasure to rising global resistance: the mitigation of its cause, by slowing aggrandizement. Instead, China's ASDS favors ultimately counterproductive tricks and maneuvers that can only add to the barriers of distrust. They in turn obscure the many positive aspects of China's evolution in its immense diversity, including the multiple, indeed divergent policies manifest in its governance. Overreliance on deception increases the tendency of security-minded officials and also many opinion-makers outside China to see only menacing expansion all around, and invasiveness far too often, instead of the broader reality that includes the global benefits of China's rise.

The significance of each of the factors listed above in keeping China on its present course is debatable, of course, and perhaps they are all less important than is here suggested. *But there are so many of them.* As against their powerful multiplicity, there is only a dimmed perception of mounting opposition to China's aggrandizement, and the misapprehension and underestimation of its consequences, which indeed evoke more *ressentiment* and hubristic contempt than prudent restraint.

....................................

# CHAPTER THIRTEEN

# *Australia*

## Weaving a Coalition

*All states invariably assert* formal claims to absolute sovereignty, but not all states are sustained by political cultures equally refractory to any subordination to foreign powers, a category to which even the British mother country was gradually consigned during the twentieth century. Legal barriers to specific foreign activities may be effective within their remit in any case, as with cabotage prohibitions, but an abundance of legal barriers to foreign activities suggests that the political culture is *not* so refractory to foreign influence after all, and the same is true of excessively manifest national sensitivities—they are encountered most often in the very countries most likely to be subservient to greater power.[1]

Australia is not of that ilk, and moreover for all its ever-increasing ethnic diversity, it fully retains the Anglo-Saxon trait of bellicosity. Only that quality can explain how a country so very far removed from all but one of the world's conflict zones has sent its troops to fight in so many wars since 1945: the Korean War, the Malayan Emergency, the Indonesia Confrontation, the Vietnam War, the Somalia futility, the East Timor stabilization, the Solomon Islands intervention, and at much greater cost, the protracted wars in Afghanistan and in Iraq.

It is not surprising, therefore, that Australia has been the first country to clearly express resistance to China's rising power, and to initiate the coalition-building against it that is mandated by the logic of strategy.

Already in 2008, when the self-imposed restraints of "Peaceful Rise" were still in effect—that is, before the hubristic turn in Chinese conduct—the Australian government was redacting *Defending Australia in the Asia-Pacific Century Force 2030 presented in the Defence White Paper 2009* (not an annual event; there is no 2010 edition).[2]

Chinese officials have persistently denounced the *White Paper* as alarmist and inflammatory. That is interesting in itself because to the contrary, the authors were evidently striving hard to present a balanced assessment in the most moderate language, as may be seen by perusing the complete segment on China, under the heading "Strategic Implications of the Rise of China":

4.23 Barring major setbacks, China by 2030 will become a major driver of economic activity both in the region and globally, and will have strategic influence beyond East Asia. By some measures, China has the potential to overtake the United States as the world's largest economy around 2020. However, economic strength is also a function of trade, aid and financial flows, and by those market-exchange based measures, the US economy is likely to remain paramount.

4.24 The crucial relationship in the region, but also globally, will be that between the United States and China. The management of the relationship between Washington and Beijing will be of paramount importance for strategic stability in the Asia-Pacific region. Taiwan will remain a source of potential strategic miscalculation, and all parties will need to work hard to ensure that developments in relation to Taiwan over the years ahead are peaceful ones. The Government reaffirms Australia's longstanding "One China" policy.

4.25 China has a significant opportunity in the decades ahead to take its place as a leading stakeholder in the development and stability of the global economic and political system. In coming years, China will develop an even deeper stake in the global economic system, and other major powers will have deep stakes in China's economic success. *China's political leadership is likely to continue to appreciate the need for it to make a strong contribution to strengthening the regional security environment and the global rules-based order.* [Italics added]

Here the authors are proactively encouraging the Chinese to act moderately, in the guise of predicting that they will so act.

4.26 China will also be the strongest Asian military power, by a considerable margin. Its military modernization will be increasingly characterized by the development of power projection capabilities. A major power of China's stature can be expected to develop a globally significant military capability befitting its size. But the pace, scope and structure of China's military modernization have the potential to give its neighbors cause for concern if not carefully explained, and *if China does not reach out to others to build confidence regarding its military plans.* [Italics added]

Here the authors are arguing that an emollient diplomacy could offset "China's development of a globally significant military capability." They do not consider what must happen next: once neighboring countries are duly mollified because the Chinese government has built confidence in its good intentions, how will they react when they see that China continues to pursue "a globally significant military capability" that dwarfs their own?

4.27 China has begun to do this in recent years, but needs to do more. If it does not, there is likely to be a question in the minds of regional states about the long-term strategic purpose of its force development plans, particularly as the modernization appears potentially to be *beyond the scope of what would be required for a conflict over Taiwan.* [Italics added]

Here the authors set a much lower limit on the magnitude of China's acceptable military strength than the aforementioned "globally significant military capability"—to wit, armed forces that have a regional and not a global reach; that are sized to fight the forces of Taiwan but not those of, say, Japan; and that are functionally limited to what would be needed to conquer Taiwan, rather than to carry out a wider range of military operations.

With this the authors come close to an implicit affirmation, if not endorsement, of the tacit pan-Asian consensus that China is entitled to try to seize Taiwan by force of arms, even if it should not do so; for Australia, evidently, as for others in Asia, but not for Japan or the United States, that is implied by the de jure "One China" position all these countries share.

Since the *White Paper* was published, Australia has been acting accordingly to increase its powers of resistance, both by making significant investments in long-range military capabilities[3] and, more consequentially perhaps, by assiduous coalition-building.

The Chinese government's expressed preference—or insistence, if it can get away with it—is to deal bilaterally with all comers, notably over its maritime claims; that would of course ensure very favorable power-balances for the Chinese side at each remove.

Australia's preference is the diametrical opposite: to institute a working system of collective security in East Asia and the Western Pacific that remains undefined but for its priority goal: to ensure that no participating country has to confront China on its own in a territorial or other security negotiation, or actual confrontation if it comes to that.

It is easy to determine that this would require an up and running consultative mechanism, which may or may not be an offshoot of ASEAN such as the "ASEAN Defense Ministers Meeting Plus"—minus at least one of the "Plus" countries if it is to work). As for maritime confrontations specifically, it may require standing arrangements for fast gatherings of fishery-protection, coast guard, or even naval vessels when needed. But all this, in regard to what is abbreviated below as "joint talk" or "joint action," remains in the future, still being the subject of bilateral consultations rather than any actual planning.

Still, what is already happening is quite sufficient to show that the Australian government is determined to redirect its long-standing bilateral dialogues with the countries of interest to the new strategic aim of coalition-building to resist China's expansionism.

That much emerges very clearly even from the official presentation of Australian-Vietnamese relations in the joint document issued on September 7, 2009, whose very title, "Australia–Viet Nam Comprehensive Partnership," is symptomatic of the drive with which both sides are acting.[4] After prior headings on other matters ("Expanding Political Ties and Public Policy Exchanges"; "Promoting Economic Growth and Trade Development"; "Ongoing Development Assistance and Technical Cooperation"), there comes the explicit heading of interest: "Building Defense and Security Ties":

Australia and Viet Nam recognize that the security and prosperity of both countries is linked to a secure future for the Asia-Pacific region. Reaffirming their respect for national independence and sovereignty, Australia and Viet Nam will work together in regional forums to develop credible security architecture [= collective security mechanisms] and promote regional confidence-building measures to minimise the risk of conflict in the region.

That is mostly the joint-talk component; next comes the joint-action component:

Australia and Viet Nam will foster greater openness and cooperation in the defence relationship by continued personnel exchanges and human resources training, ships visits and by strengthening the exchange of views on regional and security issues of mutual concern through an annual dialogue between officials from the foreign and defence ministries.

Given that the two sides are cooperating on all sorts of other things, including people trafficking (there are resident Australian police attachés in Vietnam), it is interesting to note that on successive occasions they go out of their way to assign a higher priority to the inherently China-directed security relationship. That is made explicit in a Vietnamese government communiqué, "Viet Nam Marks Army Day in Australia," issued on September 12, 2009.[5] After listing the Australian officials attending the ceremonial gathering, it added: "They all agreed that since the two countries first established diplomatic ties in 1973, they have both seen major progress in various fields, *especially in security and national defence*" (emphasis added). By 2012 the two countries had progressed to the point of engaging in a full-scale strategic dialogue, to coordinate practical action.[6] The action, China's rise, evokes reaction, in this case coalescence. Naturally Vietnam, as very much a frontline state, is more advanced on this path than others—but the others are following.

The complex case of Indonesia is discussed in Chapter 18, while Australian-Malaysian security relations are the most linear, because bilateral defense cooperation is explicitly identified as such under the formal arrangement of the "Malaysia-Australia Joint Defence Program," which replaced earlier arrangements in 1992. It covers Australian training for Malaysian military personnel, officer cross-attachments, and annual military exercises.

That would already go a long way to preparing the ground for "joint action" to build a system of collective security, in the event that "joint talk" does not dissuade confrontations. But in addition, the 1971 "Five Power Defence Arrangement" (FPDA),[7] although born as a last-gasp expression of Britain's "East of

Suez" role, remains in force, and more to the point it is still in operation.

Formally, it commits Australia, New Zealand, and the United Kingdom "to consult on a response to any armed attack or threat against Malaysia or Singapore," uncompromisingly and unabashedly placing the latter in the role of neocolonial wards. Since 1971 the United Kingdom has abandoned the last of its Far Eastern pretensions, and New Zealand has retreated from international military activism (it is present in Afghanistan, but only with a "reconstruction team" that includes soldiers rather than a combat unit). But Australia still forges ahead, having taken over the FPDA as its framework of choice for combined training exercises because it includes Singapore as well. Needless to say, maritime security has been identified as the top priority.

Singapore is not a contender in the Spratly Islands dispute, but its government is activist by nature and fully intends to participate in any emerging system of collective security designed to contain China. Moreover, Singapore pursues a very ambitious military policy, whereby it maintains disproportionately large military forces for a city-state with 3.1 million citizens: these include 77,000 personnel on active duty and 350,000 ready-reservists. Much more unusually, these forces are kept at a high state of overall effectiveness and combat readiness with serious training and first-rate equipment, including the most advanced U.S. combat aircraft and Israeli air-launched missiles.

Not surprisingly, there is an important military as well as more broadly "security" element in Australian-Singaporean relations, which became the subject of a specific agreement on August 12, 2008 ("Memorandum of Understanding on Defence Cooperation" signed by Prime Minister Lee Hsien Loong and Prime Minister Kevin Rudd). Among its practical expressions, the Singaporean armed forces conduct training and full-scale exercises that their home territory could not possibly accommodate in the spaciousness of the Shoalwater Bay Training Area and Oakey Airfield in Queensland, as well as at RAAF Base Pearce in western Australia.

Under the heading of joint talk, on the other hand, while the two countries pursue all other forms of cooperation under their standing biennial "Singapore-Australia Joint Ministerial Committee," the 2009 edition ended with fairly explicit language for a communiqué, when it came to strategic cooperation.[8] First, under the heading of bilateral security cooperation, the statement read:

> 4. The Ministers noted that the bilateral defence relationship had grown deeper and broader in scope, based on a history of close cooperation and shared *strategic* perspectives . . . [Italics added]
>
> 5. The Ministers underlined the importance of cooperation between our armed forces to confront common threats to our security. . . .

Then, under the anodyne title "Further Areas of Bilateral Cooperation," the text continued:

> 17. The Ministers exchanged views on a wide range of global and regional issues. They noted that the United States, China, Japan and India all had important roles to play in maintaining security and stability in the region. The Ministers undertook to continue to work closely together to promote regional cooperation, stability and prosperity.

Nothing dramatic, yet the statement reveals the logic of strategy at work—the rise of China induces the coalescence of the threatened.

Each of these Australian initiatives derives from a prior and broader decision to take the initiative in building a structure of collective security piece by piece, and not just leave it all to the Americans. That is an attitude ultimately rooted in the revisionist consensus on Australian history in the two World Wars, in which the Australians—as the revisionists argued— paid a greater price for a smaller benefit because they supplied troops for others to command (actually it was more like entire divisions under their own generals for British Corps and Army chiefs to command). The greater price was the supposedly disproportionate number of casualties. The smaller benefit was the feeble weight of Australia in peacemaking; the Australians would have put Emperor Hirohito on trial, for instance.

This ancient history was given a reprise after the Americans took over the tutelage role of the British, in the wake of the Australian engagement in the Vietnam War, in which Australian casualties were trivial by Gallipoli standards (500 killed, 3,129 wounded) but which was assessed in retrospect as the wrong war, and clumsily fought. The derived lesson was that if Australia passively follows the Americans, Australia might be led in the wrong direction, and incompetently to boot at the tactical level. The same was true of the Iraq war. Casualties were much fewer, but the outcome is not viewed as a success, given the end-state of the country, which happens to be a major source of illegal migrants for Australia.

Once again, as the documents reviewed above show very clearly, Australians view themselves as facing a strategic threat—this time from a China that is growing in every way and very fast, and that shows every sign of wanting to expand territorially as well. But this time the Australians evidently do not want to wait until summoned to serve under American leadership, in whose competence their faith is less than perfect: they fear that the United States will act too soon or too late, too vigorously or not strongly enough should there be a crisis—or simply an increased level of Chinese pressure that calls for a response. Even hard-line Australians, moreover, want to deter China and contain it as necessary while preserving the best possible relations with the widest possible spectrum of Chinese, anticipating much more cooperation than hostility in the long run.

At the same time, Australians do not doubt the good intentions of the United States, nor its ultimate capacity to rise to every occasion, and its firm reliability in defending Australia if it comes to that—a confidence reaffirmed in November 2011 when the two governments announced that U.S. troops would be based in Australia for the first time since World War II; the chosen location, Darwin, in the Northern Territories, is less than 400 nautical miles from Indonesian territory.[9] Australians in turn always do the necessary in peace and war to retain their status as the second-best ally of the United States, claiming precedence over other contenders—and not only because of their privileged role in signals intelligence (only Australia, Canada, and New Zealand fully participate in U.S.-British communications intelligence efforts).

These two potentially opposed attitudes toward the United States, one weary and the other trustful, are conjugated by the certainty that independent Australian initiatives designed to construct elements of an overall system of collective security will always add something to, and never detract from, the overall capacity of the U.S.-Australian alliance to contain China. For example, the Australians have an excellent connection with the Malaysian armed forces, with which the United States does little, and they can still play a similar bridging role with Indonesia as well. As for Vietnam, on which see Chapter 15, the Australians can still add to that country's security relationship with the United States, vigorous though it is, if only because of their less activist stance on human rights issues.

The synergy of Australia's bilateralism with its U.S. alliance commitment reaches its apogee when it comes to Japan. From the Australian point of view, it was disturbing that the ongoing political fluidity in Japan could suddenly elevate a figure such as Ozawa Ichiro to national leadership in 2009, notwithstanding his dubious background[10] and notably complaisant attitude toward China. The Australian reaction was to refocus on Japan and boldly strive to influence its foreign policy, undeterred by the great difference in scale and wealth.

The clearest manifestation of so much boldness was the visit of Prime Minister Julia Gillard to Japan in April 2011, in the immediate aftermath of the March tsunami and the ensuing disasters (naturally, she made a point of visiting the northeast, defying radiation fears). In addition to what might have been expected for the occasion, in a very carefully prepared April 22 speech at the National Press Club of Japan, Prime Minister Gillard clearly emphasized the priority of collective security, not least by making it the first substantive subject after mentioning the disaster and the help sent by Australia:

Japan is Australia's closest partner in Asia. . . . So we had Australian aircraft, working with the Japan Self Defence Force, ferrying Japanese supplies, while using US bases in Japan and with the support of the United States.

We talk a lot about trilateral Australia-Japan-US cooperation. But this was the talk put into action . . . as Prime Minister, I am committed to this most important security relationship. Japan and Australia are close strategic partners.

We face a number of shared security challenges. . . . Australia's relationship with Japan on security and defence issues has grown to become one of the closest and most important that either of us has . . . our Foreign Affairs and Defence ministers meet regularly for "2 + 2" meetings.

This is the only "2 + 2" meeting that Japan has with any country other than the United States, and one of only two "2 + 2" meetings that Australia has in Asia. . . . We have stepped up our participation in joint military exercises with one another. . . . Australia is keen to see new opportunities for co-operation.[11]

She went on to specify the concrete result: the implementation of the Australia-Japan Acquisition and Cross Servicing Agreement, ratified by both Japan's Diet and the Australian Parliament, which allows military forces on each side to provide logistic support for the other. Given the vast distances that condition Australia's strategic engagement with the world, this was a critical passage, which has already opened a new phase of more frequent and more ambitious security cooperation with Japan and its armed forces. As it is, transport, supplies, and maintenance support are being actively exchanged. With this, Japan is no longer confined to security cooperation with the United States alone, and that too is important in itself.

In addition, Prime Minister Gillard revealed that advanced negotiations were under way on an Information Security Agreement as well, to provide a legal framework for the exchange of classified information by way of studies and analyses and—far more important in a crisis—for the instantaneous exchange of operational intelligence between the command posts and even platforms of both sides.

Further, Prime Minister Gillard unveiled an agreement in principle to jointly develop a "new vision for defence cooperation" between Australia and Japan, whose purpose as she described it left no room for doubts: to "improve our mechanisms for bilateral cooperation in the event of another crisis or emergency, either in Japan or Australia or in the region more broadly." The meaning of "crisis" in this context is made perfectly evident by its pairing with "emergency," one being human and the other natural.

The very detailed enumeration of all the different practical steps being taken to increase not only policy coordination but also joint military action had the evident purpose of giving as much substance as possible to the security relationship—a frankly military substance, that is, if only because diplomatic cooperation is taken for granted. The Japanese were duly impressed, not least because they are well aware of the great part that exports to China have in Australia's unprecedented prosperity. Having put military cooperation at the very top, Prime Minister Gillard addressed the foreign-policy coordination only at the end, but in categorical terms:

> Regional prosperity cannot be assured through a strong economic framework alone. It also requires a robust security environment.

She then defined that desired situation by affirming the unity of Japan and Australia in favoring "a continued forward presence" of the United States in the Western Pacific; that plainly referred to both American military forces, including the aircraft carriers that the Chinese view as intrusive, and American diplomacy: "Stability and security depend vitally on the integral role of the United States." But that was not enough, according to Prime Minister Gillard, who went on to stress the need to develop "the right regional architecture to encourage cooperation on security challenges and the peaceful settlement of disputes." In this context the word "architecture" refers to a set of highly specific agreements on how to deal with a highly specific problem: Chinese maritime claims whose scope keeps expanding— by December 2011, Chinese media were defining China's *territorial* waters, and not just its exclusive economic zone, as encompassing almost the entirety of the South China Sea. But the prime minister did not, of course mention China as an actual or possible threat, though in reality nothing else could justify all the bilateral efforts she mentioned, and the high costs of operating Australian forces thousands of miles from their home bases. The threat was not mentioned because there is only one candidate for that role, given that the Australians have no plans to fight in Korea.

Australia's diplomatic activism had the additional merit of allowing the more diffident leaders of Malaysia, the Philippines, Singapore, and Vietnam to respond to China's hubristic post-2008 conduct by just standing by and nodding, until they were ready to speak out. It was much the same in Japan in April 2011.

Again, what happened in East Asia to change its politics is nothing more than the logic of strategy in action, with very real consequences for China, whose conduct initiated the action-reaction sequence: instead of facing only bilateral relationships with its neighbors, inevitably governed by China's greatly superior magnitude, China's relations with its neighbors have been "multilateralized," not least because of Australian initiatives that preceded American efforts in that same direction. That is the "architecture" which is to be "robust"—the functional equivalent of a multilateral security treaty.

..........................................

# CHAPTER FOURTEEN

# *Japan*

## Disengaging from Disengagement

*For a country* both praised and blamed for its slow-moving conservatism, Japan's China policy and its reciprocal U.S. policy have been extraordinarily changeable in recent years.

In small part because of the wear and tear caused by the U.S. military presence in a crowded country, and especially by Marine Corps Air Station Futenma, virtually in a city center, in much larger part because of a post-2008 assessment that the United States was declining while China was offering rapidly expanding opportunities, without necessarily being less benevolent in the long run, the Japanese elite consensus was beginning to drift toward a closer connection with Beijing, even at the price of a more distant connection with Washington. That shift was only incipient and was still resisted quite strongly by most Foreign Ministry professionals, among other elite Japanese, but it did have some serious if variegated political support.

First, there was an older-generation attitude, exemplified by former prime minister Nakasone Yasuhiro (in office 1982–1987), a Tokyo-based navy officer in the Second World War, which combined guilt feelings for Japanese misdeeds in China with a lively awareness of growing opportunities for Japanese business, and a benign interpretation of Japan's past and possible future within the Chinese Tianxia.[1] According to this view of its history, Japan had evolved successfully in its early centuries in a state of subjective independence within what Chinese rulers nevertheless perceived as their hegemonic sphere. The implication for the future was that Japan could continue to prosper even if it were inside rather than outside China's security perimeter, because of the expansion of China's strategic reach. The United States has no special role in this vision of the future other than to fade away quietly. This view is of course also congruent with a pessimistic view of Japan's future, according to which nothing will interrupt its decline into a middle power with a diminishing and aging population.

Alongside this philosophical position that has its merits, there was in 2009 the much cruder stance of Ozawa Ichiro—America down, China up, let's go with China and that way we will not need Marines in Okinawa anymore. In more nuanced fashion, there was also the consideration that China could control North Korea whereas the United States could only retaliate against it in the event of a nuclear attack on Japan, and other such calculations.

More simply perhaps, Ozawa happens to dislike Americans, and besides, as secretary-general of the Democratic Party of Japan, long in opposition, he needed a differentiated foreign-policy stance to oppose the eternal recurrence of the Liberal Democratic Party (LDP).

On December 10, 2009, Ozawa was able to enact his policy intentions on the grandest scale by leading no fewer than 143 Democratic Party of Japan (DPJ) Diet members and 470 staff and political supporters on a visit to Beijing, under the framework of the ongoing "Great Wall" exchange program between his party and the CCP.

Clearly form prevailed over substance—it was a processional tribute-bearing visitation without the tribute—but there was a thirty-minute meeting between Ozawa and Hu Jintao; unsurprisingly, they agreed to "strengthen Japan-China relations and accelerate the pace of DPJ-CCP exchange." The East China Sea, adulterated *gyoza* (as in Chinese exports of), and China's lack of transparency in its defense budgeting were mentioned but obviously could not have been discussed in a serious fashion.

Nevertheless, after the meeting, or more accurately, the audience,[2] Ozawa declared that the encounter had contributed to the development of friendly relations, which is fair enough. But he also said that he had introduced himself to Hu as the "director of field operations for Japan's Liberation Army"— liberation from the long-ruling LDP? from bureaucrats? from the United States? All three, no doubt.

On the second day of the visit, December 11, Ozawa met with Defense Minister and PLA General Liang Guanglie to "express his concern over China's continuing military buildup." Ozawa said that he had told Liang: "There is sentiment in Japan that sees China's modernization as a threat. If Japan were to strengthen armaments, it would not bring good results for the future of Japan and China."[3] Liang's reply was of course that the PLA "serves to protect a large territory and border and definitely does not seek hegemony."

In other words, nothing was negotiated and nothing was conceded in Beijing, yet December 2009 marked a low point in U.S.-Japan relations at the political level. Nevertheless the dominant bureaucratic view in the Foreign Ministry and the unanimous view in the Defense Ministry remained unchanged,[4] namely, that China had unambiguously become the "main threat" to Japan's security, that its relative capabilities were increasing rapidly, and that Japan therefore needed to

a. increase its own military strength;
b. safeguard the U.S. alliance by overcoming all problems along the way, starting with the Okinawa/Futenma controversy; and
c. broaden the basis of its own security by participating in the effort to build a collective security framework for East Asia as a whole.

Naturally there was considerable tension between the two ministries and the Ozawa-dominated Democratic Party of Japan. They came under attack as part of a broader Ozawa campaign against the upper echelon of the state bureaucracy as a whole, which he labeled undemocratic and ineffective. He also accused the Ministry of Foreign Affairs of being too tough with China, too soft with the United States.

Because the bureaucrats in general could be blamed for Japan's protracted stagnation, the anti-bureaucracy campaign was quite successful, even as the DPJ was losing ground and Ozawa in particular fell into legal difficulties for the usual reasons, murky campaign finances merging into simpler forms of corruption. That only intensified DPJ attacks on the Foreign Ministry and the party's insistence that policy must be made by (DPJ) politicians and not by bureaucrats. Even a broad redirection of Japan's foreign policy away from the United States and toward China did not seem impossible at the time.

A high point of the China-Japan rapprochement of 2009 was the joint press communiqué issued in Beijing on March 20, 2009, by Defense Minister Hamada Yasukazu (who declared, when coming into office: "My mission is to make Japan a more comfortable country for people to live in") and China's defense minister, General Liang Guanglie.[5] The significance of this text is that it announced joint initiatives that went much beyond confidence-building measures between adversaries, to provide the rudiments of a collective security arrangement, or even an embryonic alliance:

During the talks, the two sides [agreed to]:

1. Continue high-level exchange of visits. To return Minister Hamada's visit to China, Minister Liang Guanglie will pay a visit to Japan in 2009.

2. Hold defense and security consultation between the two defense ministries in Tokyo in 2009.

3. Build on the China-Japan defense and security consultation to strengthen communication between policy departments, exchange views on issues of mutual interest such as international peace keeping, combating natural disasters and anti-piracy, and step up cooperation in information sharing, particularly in anti-piracy operations in the Gulf of Aden and Somali waters.

4. To return the visits to Japan by Chinese Air Force Commander, Navy Commander and Deputy Chief of the General Staff since 2008, Japanese Chief of Ground Staff, Chief of Maritime Staff and Chief of Air Staff will visit China. . . .

5. Continue consultation to establish at an early date the maritime contact mechanism between the defense ministries of China and Japan. . . .

6. Continue mutual visits of navy ships on the basis of the first mutual visits conducted respectively in 2007 and 2008. Chinese naval vessels will visit Japan in 2009.

7. Step up consultation at the working level and promote the implementation of the annual defense exchange plan. The two sides will discuss the possibility of inter-service staff officer dialogue involving all services including the Joint Staff of Japan.

8. Explore exchanges between Military Area Commands of the Chinese People's Liberation Army (PLA) and armies of the Japanese Ground Self-Defense Force.

9. Continue to conduct exchanges between field-grade and company-grade officers under different frameworks.

10. Push forward exchanges between the National Defense University of China and Chinese Academy of Military Science and the National Institute for Defense Studies of Japan, and between Chinese universities like the PLA University of Science and Technology and Dalian Naval Academy of the PLA and the National Defense Academy of Japan. . . .

[In conclusion] Minister Hamada expressed thanks to Minister Liang Guanglie.

In the absence of a concurrent sworn statement from Hamada Yasukazu that it was all done with the utmost insincerity to deceive the innocent Chinese, this list of joint initiatives was startling, and certainly alarming.

But everything changed very suddenly with the Senkaku fishing intrusion incident of September 7, 2010, mostly because of the reckless Chinese reactions, which included riotous attacks on Japanese-affiliated shops, the arrest of visiting Japanese business executives, the interruption of rare-earth shipments to Japan, and a maximally provocative (if legally necessary) demand from the China Ministry of Foreign Affairs for compensation and an apology.

The overall effect was to crystallize underlying anxieties about China's intentions and even coherence—anxieties obviously intensified by the rapid increase in Chinese power. The impact on Japanese opinion was therefore not merely strong but downright structural. It was perfectly evident in the aftermath (though not perhaps to Chinese decision-makers) that the change in Japanese attitudes to China would be lasting, and could not be undone by goodwill visits and charm offensives.

The immediate result was that Ozawa and like-minded others were silenced, and could no longer oppose the Foreign and Defense Ministries as they proceeded with their triple effort to build a stronger defense and a stronger U.S. alliance, and a broader framework of collective security, more or less along Australian lines. The Futenma polemic did not go away any more than the noisy Marine Air Station that occupies the core of Okinawa's Ginowan city, but the volume of the controversy was drastically reduced.

Even before the Senkaku incident, there was a pattern of increasingly provocative Chinese behavior.[6] Interceptions of military aircraft approaching Japanese airspace provide the readiest quantification: between 2009 and 2010 the number of Air Self-Defense Force interception sorties increased from 274 to 386. Of the aircraft intercepted, 264 were Russian, a 30 percent increase that measures the revival of Russian military activity in the Far East. Only 96 of the offending aircraft were Chinese, but that marked a *250 percent* increase over 2009. The closest intercept (of two Y-8 long-range surveillance aircraft) occurred within 50 kilometers of Japanese airspace. Interestingly, some Japanese observers correlated the increase in Chinese intrusions not with the overall increase in PLA activity but rather with the advent of the DPJ in Japan's government and the subsequent tensions in the Japan-U.S. military relationship. They were supported in this by an unnamed Defense Ministry official who was quoted as saying: "[Foreign countries] might have been testing Japan's defense capability as they regarded Japan-U.S. relations as weakened."[7]

The March 11, 2011, "Great East Japan earthquake" and more catastrophic tsunami naturally had very powerful effects on every aspect of Japanese life, not least the Japan Self-Defense Forces, in whose case, however, the effects were contradictory. On the one hand, a reallocation of public spending is under way that will deny any large increase to the Defense Ministry and the Japan Self-Defense Forces, barring a very sharp rise in the perceived threats to Japan. But on the other hand, Japan's armed forces may gain some more funding and certainly will not lose any—as other ministries will—not only because China is neither forgotten nor forgiven, but also even more perhaps because the armed forces were almost the only effective instruments of the state in coping with the successive disasters unleashed by the earthquake.

Indeed, Japan's armed forces visibly performed much more than adequately, acting compassionately (in conducting dignified burials), heroically (hosing water on reactors emitting dangerous levels of radiation), efficiently (in distributing food), uncomplainingly (in difficult, often dangerous conditions), and on the largest scale with ground, air, and naval elements—100,000 personnel (40 percent of total) were committed immediately.

This was actually the very first opportunity of the Self-Defense Forces since their creation to display to the Japanese public their overall quality, and some of their physical capabilities (Prime Minister Murayama Tomiichi, the first and only Socialist prime minister, refused to order the armed forces he had long opposed into action for the January 1995 Great Hanshin earthquake). Among the immediate images relayed to the public, there was a burly soldier carrying a rescued old lady on his back, a helicopter rescue of eighty-one dockworkers who had been swept out to sea on a hulk, and a rescue of schoolchildren stranded on a school rooftop—and these early dramatic episodes were followed by many more.

The Self-Defense Forces are bound to benefit greatly from the resulting attitudinal shift in Japanese public opinion—it is the final emancipation of Japan's military from the ignominy of 1945.

Therefore, even at a time of severe budgetary stringency, the defense budget may well increase sooner rather than later, if only because its current spending is so small as a percentage of the gross domestic product (below 1 percent) and of total government spending (3 percent in the 2009 fiscal year).

Hence, Japan is the one country that could accommodate a sharp increase, even a doubling, of its military spending without changing its overall fiscal balance.

It is even possible that the emphatic taboo against the acquisition of aircraft carriers might end, if only because of the public's heightened appreciation of their utility for disaster relief as well as for sea-control operations at a time when China, in the person of Defense Minister General Liang Guanglie, has officially acknowledged its intention of acquiring aircraft carriers. In response to a question from Japan Defense Minister Hamada Yasukazu in Beijing on March 20, 2009, Liang Guanglie reportedly said: "China needs to develop an aircraft carrier as it is the only major power in the world operating without one"[8]— thereby implicitly defining carrier-less Japan as not a major power.

The March 2011 disasters and the subsequent relief operations also radically changed public perceptions of the significance of U.S. forces in and around Japan. That the USS *Ronald Reagan*, along with USS *Chancellorsville* and USS *Preble*,[9] arrived on the scene very quickly to serve as an air and resupply base for rescue and relief helicopters directly opposite the most critically affected tract of the Fukushima coast was not half the story: first, all civilian airports within range were inoperative or their capacity was greatly reduced, thus greatly enhancing the carrier's relative value; second, the *Ronald Reagan* also acted as the base for Maritime Self-Defense Force (S-70) helicopters, visually demonstrating an extreme degree of interoperability and trust (alien helicopters, that is, U.S. Army and U.S. Air Force machines, let alone foreign helicopters, are never allowed to land on Navy carriers); thirdly, the sailors aboard the *Ronald Reagan* and its escorts *were knowingly exposed to radiation* at a rate of one month's worth of naturally occurring radiation per hour; finally, all of the above distinctions between a de rigueur and "above and beyond" assistance mission were made amply known to the Japanese public by an exceedingly effective U.S. Navy public relations effort. Itself very sensitive to radiation dangers, the Japanese at large were profoundly moved by television imagery of American sailors being decontaminated (with freezing water) while hard at work on the carrier's deck in support of Japanese rescue helicopters. It is symptomatic that a very popular Japanese multivideo blog on the rescue operations as a whole actually began with several videos of *Ronald Reagan* operations.[10]

The controversy over the Futenma Marine Corps Air Station—indeed a colossal irritant to the surrounding Ginowan city (unsurprisingly, Ginowan has a Japan Communist Party mayor)—has been a good indicator of the overall state of the Japan-U.S. security relationship in recent years.

In 2009 it seemed possible that, rather than confront the difficulties of relocating the noisy Marine Corps Air Station elsewhere in Okinawa or elsewhere in Japan, the Japanese government would demand the removal of U.S. forces from Okinawa altogether—and indeed a 2014 deadline was set. Now, by contrast, in the aftermath of the attitudinal shifts in regard to both China and the American military presence, the two governments have simply abandoned any intention of relocating the base.[11]

It was in this radically altered context that the April 2011 visit of the high-spirited Australian prime minister, Julia Gillard, took place, providing an excellent opportunity for the much-chastened DPJ leadership to finally repudiate its original strategic stance, and instead reaffirm the centrality of the Japan-U.S. alliance, even while embracing the proffered vision of a complementary East Asian (minus China)—Australian alliance as well.

With this, two of the three Foreign Ministry/Defense Ministry countermeasures against Chinese military aggrandizement are in place, and now the expansion and diversification of Japanese military capabilities is impeded only by extreme fiscal stringency—instead of by the very stiff domestic political opposition that had always been the insurmountable barrier.

One may doubt that it was the aim of Chinese policy to strengthen Japan's alliance with the United States, or to emancipate to some degree Japan's potential for military strength. But both were the inevitable result of China's accelerated military aggrandizement.

The Nakasone vision of a Japan prospering within China's Tianxia, indeed within its strategic perimeter, was never a feasible alternative because it required not only an improbably tactful, indeed unfailingly courteous, Chinese government, but also a powerful yet quite unthreatening China—an impossible contradiction.

As for the notion that Japanese business interests would favor, or even seek to impose, pliant policies for business reasons—China is certainly a large and growing market, and rumors to that effect did circulate during the September 2010 Senkaku confrontation—it would be far more plausible if true profit-maximizing at all costs businessmen in the Chinese style were in charge of Japanese corporations, rather than their managers with their Samurai-style concept of loyal service.

As compared to other Japanese, the managers of the larger, politically more significant corporations are far more focused on international politics, much more knowledgeable about the outside world, and correspondingly more conscious of the central importance of the very things that are lacking in China, beginning with democracy and the rule of law—not worshipped as in the Anglo-Saxon world, but still highly appreciated as the best available *gaijin* substitute for Japanese self-control. Moreover, of all Japanese, those most active in doing business in China are the least likely to support Japan's national subordination to the CCP.

There is a contrary view, to be sure, but so far it is heard from journalists rather than businessmen—most recently to the effect that whereas pre-tsunami it was enough for Japanese companies to have assembly plants in China to serve the Chinese market, now with the post-tsunami power cuts they must also move the production of subsystems and components to China to supply non-Chinese markets as well. Symptomatically, this functional argument is preceded by a lamentation on the nullity of the Japanese government and the country's demoralization.[12]

Yet it is only the willing acceptance of subordination to China that could interrupt the countermeasures against its rising power that the logic of strategy ineluctably requires from Japan—and strategy is always stronger than politics and all its inhibitions.

That is just as well, because strategy will require a far greater sacrifice from the Japanese political system than the cessation of Antarctic whaling to show respect for the valiant Australian ally: the setting aside, if not formal abandonment, of the greatly cherished claim to the Hoppō Ryōdo, the so-called Northern Territories known as the southernmost Kuril Islands to the Russians, who have occupied them since 1945.

The Kuril Islands are not insignificant outcrops: Etorofu, Kunashiri, and Shikotan Islands have a combined land area of 4,854 square kilometers—1,874 square miles—not counting the fourth component of the Hoppō Ryōdo, the Habomai Rocks.

The Japanese, moreover, have a strong legal case, as do the other countries that were diminished by Soviet annexations at the end of the Second World War: Poland, Czechoslovakia, and Romania, although the latter was the only one of the three that attacked the Soviet Union in alliance with Germany, while Japan did not, and was itself attacked, as was Poland.

But in the emerging international context, Japan's strong legal case for restitution is irrelevant. If China continues to grow very rapidly both in economic capacity and in its military strength, not merely in the years but in the decades ahead, Japan's continued independence will increasingly depend on the overall strength of the anti-China coalition. Japan's own resolve and American support would be of critical importance, of course, but the alignment of the Russian Federation would also be exceedingly important and could indeed be decisive, both because of itself and because of the neighboring states—Mongolia, Kazakhstan, Uzbekistan, Kyrgyzstan, Tajikistan, and Turkmenistan—which the Russians continue to influence in important ways. As their only credible security guarantor against an overbearing China, and as protector presumptive against assorted fanaticals from the Islamic lands to the south, the Russian Federation is unlikely to lose its hegemonic role in Central Asia. That obviously magnifies its strategic importance, especially in geo-economic terms.

If in response to some major Chinese aggression or bloody repression, the United States and like-minded countries were to interrupt commerce with China—a perfectly possible alternative to a military escalation inhibited by nuclear fears—China could still purchase all the fuel and raw materials it would need from the Russian Federation and its allies—if they were themselves not already part of the coalition.

However outlandish an interruption of commerce may now seem, it could quickly become the policy option of choice if there were an attack on Taiwan, or a large-enough massacre of Tibetans, Uyghurs, or Mongols (or rebellious students). That is so quite independently of any geo-economic reactions. Both American and European Union military trade with China was interrupted by the bloody repression of the 1989 Tiananmen student demonstrations, and it has yet to resume.

If its raw-material needs could be supplied by Russia and its lieges, China would not be so vulnerable to an interruption of seaborne trade, thus weakening the strongest instrument of power against an aggressive China that could actually be employed without the imminent danger of precipitating a general war that might even become nuclear.

By contrast, if the Russian Federation and its allies were to participate in the interruption of commerce, joining the United States, Japan, Australia, and all other participants, China would truly be encircled by a coalition too strong to be defied—a coalition that would need no soldiers but only customs officials to apply immediate and powerful pressure on the Chinese government.

Anticipation of such an outcome is likely to deter misconduct at least as well as, if not better than, the much less credible threat of force. Failing that, if misconduct is not dissuaded, it might be interrupted and revoked insofar as possible, once the interruption of commerce by the coalition becomes reality—if it does include the Russian Federation with its very well-resourced allies and dependents.

It follows that if a China/anti-China world does emerge—a most undesirable outcome but better than a China-dominated Asia—Moscow would be its strategic pivot, conferring much leverage to its rulers, who would certainly use it to the full.

That would no doubt cause vast difficulties for the United States and its allies, especially if the Russian government were to remain as authoritarian as it now is. That would greatly complicate all forms of cooperation, because authoritarian Russian leaders would simultaneously strive to perpetuate popular suspicions of the outside world, including Russia's new strategic allies. (Stalin's regime did that unabashedly throughout the Second World War, with no great difficulty or ill consequence for its own hold on power.)[13]

On the other hand, cooperation with Russia and Mongolia should not be so complicated for Japan, because it would be exclusively economic in content, and limited to commercially profitable activities, with nothing more needed from the two governments than a favorable attitude. (Given that Japan's most vehement anti-Russian rightists are also vehemently anti-Chinese, it should not be impossible for the Japanese government to overcome right-wing opposition in a time when Chinese power is rising, while Russian power is at best stagnant.) That would be enough to open the way for Japanese investments and management activities in the Russian Federation, and more specifically in its Dalnevostochny Federalny Okrug (Дальневосто́чный Федера́льный о́круг), the "Far Eastern Federal District." It stretches across the vastness of eastern Siberia all the way to the Pacific and Arctic shores, but its entire population of six million or so is smaller than that of the nearest Chinese city, Harbin (Hā'ĕrbīn); Mongolia's entire population of under three million is likewise no larger than that of the city of Baotou, in China's Inner Mongolia Autonomous Region (Nèi Měnggu). Understandably, both the Russian and the Mongolian governments are concerned not only by the possible long-term implications of the population imbalance, but also by the ever-increasing level of local Chinese economic activity.

Hence, from the point of view of both governments, it would be much better if instead of Chinese investors, managers, and technicians, there were other foreigners from less threatening countries further away—anything to dilute the Chinese presence and contain its growth.

While the Japanese are much respected by the Mongolians but not especially well-liked by the Russians, they certainly qualify as desirable foreign investors and developers, and they have all the required organization, technology, market-absorption capacity, and capital.

Capital comes last and not first, because what both Mongolia and the Russian Far East need is much more the activity than just the capital. For Mongolia, Japanese activity would increase the skill base, whereas for the Russian Far East, it would serve by helping to retain the population in place. If one person is employed locally by a Japanese company, that is one person less that might emigrate to more comfortable parts of western Russia—for in addition to low fertility rates, depopulation has also been caused by substantial internal migration, to the Moscow region in particular.

Japan could do much to enlist the Russian Federation for the anti-China coalition—indeed, it could do more than any other country. It may be true that Japanese and Russians are not especially sympathetic to each other, and it is certainly true that Japanese business corporations that have done business with the Russian Federation, and with the Soviet Union before it, have periodically had unsettling experiences—including the arbitrary and patently dishonest revocation of contracts. But if the Japanese government accepts the strategic imperative, it will set aside the "Northern Territories" question, refrain from futile complaints,[14] and stop discouraging Japanese business activity in the Russian Far East. That in itself would preclude symmetrical Chinese activity in the region, while serving as a powerful incentive to Russian participation in the anti-China coalition.

# CHAPTER FIFTEEN

# *Defiant Vietnam*

## The Newest American Ally?

*A willing acceptance* of subordination to China is not a Vietnamese trait, to say the least, in spite of immediate proximity and an extreme imbalance in overall power. Moreover, the close similarity between the ideology and inner-party practices of the local Communist Party (Đảng Cộng sản Việt Nam, VCP) and those of the Chinese Communist Party (CCP) and their joint inheritance of Leninist methods, Stalinist techniques, and secret police tricks, only sharpens the resolve of VCP leaders to resist CCP intentions for Vietnam.

The unambiguous 1975 victory of Communist Vietnam against the United States and its local allies, auxiliaries, and expeditionary allies also reinforces its government's determination to resist Chinese power wholly and firmly—in effect to negate the bilateral imbalance of power.

To simply deny the balance of power because of ignorance, pride, or a transcendental creed, to refuse the accommodations and concessions that the realities of power require, is an unfailing prescription for yet greater losses and worse humiliations, if not utter destruction.[1]

But that is not an error the VCP leadership is likely to commit, because another legacy of the long struggle that finally resulted in victory in 1975 is a diplomatic, military, and comprehensively strategic culture characterized by bitter realism, and quite free of military adventurism or wishful thinking about the workings of regional and world politics.

Accordingly, the government of Vietnam has only refused to bend to China's much greater power when it could actually negate its superiority, whether with its own military strength or by finding allies willing to deter China on its behalf.

That is how Vietnam survived the February 1979 Chinese invasion—or rather counterinvasion, for in January some 150,000 Vietnamese troops had invaded, defeated, and occupied China's ally, the Cambodia or Kampuchea of the autogenocidal Khmer Rouge.

With other motives as well but most immediately to force the Vietnamese to withdraw from Cambodia, on February 17, 1979, the PLA attacked in twenty-six sectors of the 480-mile border with at least 200,000 troops and perhaps as many as 250,000.[2] The operational-level aim was apparently to wear down Vietnam's army by forcing it to defend the provincial capitals near the border: Laocai, Caobang, Dong Dang, and Long Son. Neither the strategic nor the operational aims were achieved: the Vietnamese did not retreat from Cambodia nor did they send their field army formations to defend against the PLA's invasion thrusts. They instead contained them with border troops alone (some 100,000 men), who mounted a harassing, dogging, and pouncing elastic defense, complemented by many cross-border raids to attack PLA supply lines, ammunition stores, and fuel dumps.

Hence, while the Chinese did advance in several directions, reaching depths of 30 to 40 kilometers, thereby overrunning several provincial capitals, their advance was slow—it required some seventeen days of fighting—and casualties were high, with the round number of 20,000 killed, wounded, or captured often cited.[3] Having started the war on February 17, the PLA withdrew on March 16, having failed to "teach Vietnam a lesson" or force the abandonment of the occupation of Cambodia.

Military strength employed skillfully—and the retention of a large operational reserve, indeed the totality of the field forces (even those in Cambodia were redeployable) to cope with further offensive waves—was the necessary but not sufficient condition to preserve Vietnam from a fifth era of Chinese domination.[4]

Absent the counterpoise of a Great Power ally that could dissuade renewed war on a much larger scale, Vietnam could have been faced with successive PLA offensives on a yet larger scale, which were ultimately bound to be overwhelming.

But Vietnam did have the requisite alliance: the November 1978 Treaty of Friendship and Cooperation with the USSR, which, ironically, was apparently imposed as a precondition for Soviet military assistance (and certainly increased Chinese hostility[5]) and granted access to the Da Nang and Cam Ranh Bay facilities and anchorages to the Soviet navy and long-range air force.

Soviet military aid (estimated at US$800 million in 1978) paid for Vietnamese operations in Cambodia, and after the Chinese attack it increased to an estimated US$1.4 billion, including the replacement of equipment lost in combat.

More important, the treaty and the aid went a long way to committing the Soviet Union to defend Vietnam if it needed succor—if necessary by attacking China in the north, because of the very great logistic difficulty of sending Soviet ground forces all the way round to Vietnam. In 1979 the two sides were certainly mobilized on the largest scale on the Sino-Soviet border, with some thirty Soviet armored divisions aimed squarely at Beijing.

In addition, it is possible that the PLA did not try to bomb Vietnam from the air or employ tactical aircraft in support of its ground forces, not only because of Vietnam's war-experienced and abundant air defenses, but also because superior Soviet fighters could have been sent into action in response—and not necessarily by an expeditionary deployment to Vietnam.

Everything conspired to divide China and Vietnam in the aftermath of the 1979 fighting: ethnic antipathy, brutally manifest in the recurrent persecution of Vietnamese of Han extraction; historic resentment because of the many centuries of Chinese domination; new bitterness caused by the war just fought; competition for regional influence in Indochina, starting with Cambodia; land borders disputed at many points; and incompatible maritime claims.

But there was one thing that united China and Vietnam especially after 1989: both the CCP and the VCP were greatly threatened by the delegitimization of Leninist Communism as such, made explicit by the collapse of European Communism and the prompt dismantlement of its entire edifice of seemingly rooted institutions and seemingly established modes of existence. In China's case, the repercussions had already made it necessary to protect the regime with firearms in the heart of Beijing.

At a time when China had not yet started on its present path of accelerated military aggrandizement, and when the Cambodia rivalry was attenuated, the common ideological and political threat to the CCP and the VCP was seemingly the motivating factor for the "normalization" of relations negotiated secretly at first, and then publicly announced by Secretary-General of the CCP and Chairman of the Central Military Commission Jiang Zemin and Secretary-General of the VCP, Do Muoi.[6]

That in turn led to the start of border negotiations, first on the principles and precedents to be followed (the 1887 and 1895 Franco-Chinese agreements[7]), which were agreed by 1993. With that, border delimitation could begin.

But six more years passed before the two sides signed a border treaty in 1999, because of many obstacles, some of which retain their significance till this day.

One was that the Chinese side wanted to focus on delimiting the land borders and the Tonkin Gulf, in order to allow cross-border trade and sea ventures as soon as possible (cross-border trade was then the preferred remedy for the poverty of remote peripheries everywhere in China). The Vietnamese side, by contrast, wanted to negotiate on the other two disputes as well, over the Paracel Islands (some forcibly seized by China in 1974 after a battle with South Vietnamese naval forces) and the Spratly Islands.

The Chinese won this argument, but the result is that maritime disputes are unresolved till this day. Another obstacle was the reluctance of officials on both sides to negotiate as they were directed to do by their respective governments. There was no goodwill, let alone bonhomie, and none developed. The PLA, moreover, reportedly refused to participate in the border delimitation work.[8]

Finally, in July 1997, Jiang Zemin and Do Muoi met again (after six years) and agreed to order their respective negotiators to reach agreement by December 31, 1999. Agreement was duly reached—albeit not before December 30—essentially on a 50/50 basis. That was not the end of it, however, but only the beginning of epic wrangling over the placement of the 1,533 boundary markers. It took three years to place just six.

Finally, on February 23, 2009, ten years after the signature of the delimitation agreement, the very last boundary marker, number 1117, was placed—not coincidentally in Pingxiang, in the Guangxi Zhuang Autonomous Region, opposite Vietnam's

Lang Son, where the 1979 fighting had been especially intense and destructive.[9] The Foreign Ministry spokesman's statement on the ceremony held by State Councilor Dai Bingguo and Vietnam's Deputy Prime Minister Pham Gia Khiem was brief: "The two sides resolved complicated issues in a frank and friendly manner." The maritime disputes remained unsolved and unmentioned.

As noted above, the China problem for neighboring countries is not just a matter of arrogant words or intrusive deeds that they themselves may have experienced; nor it is limited to the scope of unresolved territorial disputes, but rather arises from China's very rapid military aggrandizement as such, whose vast potential is destabilizing power balances everywhere. Future power is not discounted, as is future money, but to the contrary, it is anticipated, as has been noted. That is the threat to the independence of China's neighbors inherent in its military growth.

That applies to Vietnam as well—indeed more so, because both popular and institutionalized interpretations of Vietnam's periods of subordination to China have none of the benign dimensions evoked by some in Japan and by many more Koreans. On the contrary, the national identity of the Vietnamese was formed by resistance to invasions from China, and that is why, when the ostensibly internationalist VCP won control of South Vietnam in 1975, it immediately acted to expel as many Hoa (ethnic Han Vietnamese) as possible, with many physically driven over the border or sent off in precarious boats. What is certain is that prevailing Vietnamese attitudes to the Han and their country are incompatible with a contented, or even a resigned, participation in a China-centered Tianxia. In any case, cultural complexities aside, the Paracel and Spratly Islands are not insignificant excuses for a quarrel, as in the case of the Dokdo/Takeshima islets, among other such cases. They comprise hundreds of islands, rocks, and reefs, which between them claim Exclusive Economic Zones that add up to some 648,000 square miles.

One instrument of resistance is still the military strength of the Vietnamese armed forces, which suffer from severe technological limitations but reportedly not from any lack of fighting spirit and basic competence. But just as in 1979, Vietnam also needs a Great Power ally to be able to confront China if it comes to that, and it has seemingly found one in the United States, and prospectively India and Japan as well.

Perfectly willing to take the initiative—coalescence is a natural reaction to China's aggrandizement but does need enactment—the Vietnamese used their 2010 chairmanship of ASEAN to "internationalize" the maritime disputes by forming a multicountry negotiation forum. Their aim, obviously, was to force China to negotiate in a multilateral setting.

The original U.S. position had been one of passive neutrality on the Spratly Islands claims of all the parties—Brunei, China, Indonesia, Malaysia, the Philippines, and Taiwan, as well as Vietnam. Even at the start of 2010 that remained the U.S. position, so that the Vietnamese were reduced to asking for no more than a U.S. reaffirmation of its own principles of transparency (no more overnight installations on reefs and rocks), of the rule of law, and of the freedom of the seas and navigation.

But Vietnam's diplomacy, aided by its American friends, starting with ex-POW Senator John S. McCain III, as well as by Australia, succeeded in changing U.S. policy—unless that change too was an unintended consequence of China's military aggrandizement. At the July 2010 ASEAN Regional Forum Foreign Ministers Meeting in Hanoi, U.S. Secretary of State Hillary R. Clinton reiterated that freedom of navigation is a U.S. "national interest," that the United States opposes the use or threat of force by any claimant—neither of which were new positions—but then also declared that "legitimate claims to maritime space in the South China Sea should be derived solely from legitimate claims to land features," a new position that undermines China's claims to the entire ocean area while supporting Vietnam's.

There was an immediate and (reportedly) angry response from Foreign Minister Yang Jiechi, who attacked all those who had raised the issue at the meeting, claiming that the entire area was nothing but sovereign Chinese territory, just another part of Hainan Province. It was a ringing, impeccably nationalistic ("leftist") affirmation by a foreign minister whom country-bred nationalists may view as far too much of an internationalist—he certainly lived in London and Washington for many years—"It is all ours, there is nothing to discuss."

Yet less than five months later, at the December 2010 ASEAN meeting in Indonesia, the Chinese delegation agreed to negotiate in just the multilateral setting that Vietnam and the United States had called for, at least for the purpose of defining a *multilateral* Code of Conduct.

Several different reasons could each explain the Chinese reversal.

One possible reason was that the retreat was a particular application of the more general retreat from the post-2008 hubristic excesses ordered by the CCP's highest echelon, as explained and justified in Dai Bingguo's long article "Adhere to the Path of Peaceful Development" (Jianchi zou heping fazhan zhi lu), released on December 6, 2010, just before the ASEAN meeting,

Another possible reason is that the Chinese claim cannot gain global acceptance simply because the Spratly Islands are plainly a very long way from China and much closer to the coasts of the other claimants—except Taiwan, symptomatically. The map is hostile to the Chinese claim, while invocations of ancient overnight visits by nameless fishermen can only evoke ridicule.

A third possible explanation is that the original uncompromising Chinese stance made the dispute a very effective anti-China coalition-building device: indeed, it roped in both the erratic Philippines and the habitually recalcitrant Malaysian government.

A fourth possible explanation is that Secretary of State H. R. Clinton is very persuasive or that Secretary of Defense Robert Michael Gates is very persuasive, because he spoke on the same lines at the ASEAN Defence Ministers Meeting Plus held on October 2010 in Hanoi—that entity, "ADMM+8", had been decreed into existence by the acceptance of a Vietnamese and Singaporean initiative at the May 10–11 Hanoi meeting of the original ADMM+6 of members and partners (China, India, Japan, Australia, New Zealand, and South Korea), with the additional two being the Russian Federation and the United States.

The declared purpose of bringing in the two powers was to "enhance the legitimacy of ASEAN as a regional cooperative bloc, and the engagement of the US and Russia in East Asia." But the actual result was of course to weaken China's strength in that forum, where it had been the sole Great Power—yet one more result of the inevitable reaction to its military aggrandizement. (It is also possible that the Vietnamese welcomed a forum that could instantly become a collective security council by deducting 1 from the plus-8 of the ADMM, i.e., China.)

But the most likely explanation is simply that Vietnam is by far the most active of the Spratly Islands contenders, and that China's uncompromising stance on the dispute had brought about a U.S.-Vietnamese rapprochement that started off as a diplomatic partnership but was becoming a tacit military alliance as well, and one that could be all too effective.

This was not an inevitable outgrowth of the 1995 establishment of diplomatic relations between the United States and Vietnam. It has been Chinese initiatives, conceivably not even coordinated in Beijing, that have driven Vietnam into closer relations with the United States. Consider this incomplete summary of recent maritime incidents:[10]

On February 2, 2010, a Chinese patrol boat stopped and boarded a Vietnamese fishing craft and seized its catch, navigational aids, spare parts, and tools.

On March 22, 2010, Chinese patrol boats detained a Vietnamese fishing boat and its twelve-member crew who were sheltering near Woody Islands in the Paracels. Chinese authorities demanded payment of a US$10,000 fine. This prompted a protest by Vietnam on March 30.

On April 13, 2010, a Chinese naval patrol seized a second Vietnamese fishing boat and its crew of nine near Da Loi Island (near the Paracels) and demanded payment of a US$10,000 fine.

On May 4, 2010, Chinese Fishery Administration officials seized a Vietnamese fishing boat in the Paracel archipelago and demanded a fine of US$8,000.

In June, China seized three Vietnamese fishing boats and arrested the crew in waters east of the Gulf of Tonkin and near the Paracel Islands.

On September 11, 2010, China seized a Vietnamese fishing trawler and arrested its crew of nine in waters near the

Paracels. Four days later, China officially notified Vietnam that the boat had been seized and the crew detained for violating China's territorial waters.

Vietnamese fishermen are not like their much-televised Alaskan counterparts: US$10,000 is an immense, indeed impossible, sum for them. Nor did matters improve in 2011. On May 13, the Vietnamese Foreign Ministry protested the unilateral Chinese proclamation of a fishing prohibition in the Hoang Sa (Paracel) archipelago from noon May 16 to noon August 1. The announcement was made just before, on May 11, by a posting on the Hainan Province Haikou Municipal Government website. That forced the VFM spokeswoman Nguyen Phuong Nga to issue a categorical declaration:[11]

> Vietnam has indisputable sovereignty over the Hoang Sa (Paracel) and Truong Sa (Spratly) archipelagos and sovereignty and jurisdiction over its exclusive economic zone and continental shelf. . . . China's unilateral execution [sic] of a fishing ban in the East Sea is a violation of Vietnam's sovereignty over the Hoang Sa archipelago.

Politically, Vietnam and the United States should have been firmly separated by the persistence of the VCP dictatorship with the consequent and chronic violations of human rights and the institutionalized denial of democratic political rights.

By contrast, the VCP government of Vietnam has excellent reasons to strive for good relations with the CCP government of China, and vice versa. Unless all reality is overlooked to consider the family-owned Latino dictatorship and the family-owned Korean shamanistic cult as communist parties, ideological solidarity between *governing* Communist parties has become a very rare commodity, indeed it is limited to the CCP and VCP. Moreover, the Vietnam government has excellent economic reasons to cooperate with China as much as possible.

Indeed, a careful study of Sino-Vietnamese relations by a specialist summarizes just such strivings:[12]

> There is an apparent paradox in Sino-Vietnamese relations. On the one hand, these two countries are experiencing arguably the greatest friction over territorial disputes in the South China Sea in recent years. There is palpable Vietnamese nationalist anti-Chinese sentiment among large sections of the political elite.
>
> Vietnam's military establishment has stepped up its self-help efforts with major big-ticket arms procurements including more Sukhoi-30 multirole jet fighters and diesel powered Kilo-class conventional submarines. On the other hand, high-level party, state and military leaders continue to exchange visits and speak of bilateral relations in effusive terms. [The author goes on to describe the web of interparty as well as intergovernment relations.]

But always and everywhere, strategy is stronger than politics (and stronger than trade), and the result in this case also is one more politically unnatural alliance decreed by the logic of strategy. What a U.S.-Vietnam alliance might mean was anticipated in low-key fashion by the "Lower Mekong Initiative," comprised of the United States, Vietnam, Cambodia, Laos, and Thailand (the "lower" helpfully excludes China and its then quasi client Myanmar).[13] It is all about water and fish and such, but interestingly the protagonists are the respective foreign ministers (hence a meeting was held in conjunction with H. R. Clinton's October 2010 Hanoi visit). The LMI's agenda includes everything— climate change, fighting infectious disease, education policy, river management information-sharing (the Mekong River Commission and the Mississippi River Commission agreed to pursue a "sister river" partnership to share expertise and best practices). Then there is the minor agenda item that provides the fuel for it all: the LMI is to monitor and coordinate responses to the construction of dams—particularly but *not exclusively* those being built in China. Encirclement light (the *not exclusively* is a fine touch) still encircles.

What a U.S.-Vietnam alliance might mean was also anticipated in much more dramatic fashion by the August 2010 visitation of the USS *George Washington* (CVN 73) carrier strike group, including USS *Curtis Wilbur* (DDG 54), USS *Chung-Hoon* (DDG 93), and USS *McCampbell* (DDG 85), as well as the deliciously well-named guided-missile destroyer USS *John S. McCain* (DDG 56).

This event is best described by two different texts, one produced by the U.S. Navy's public relations staff, and the other by one of the CCP's more skilled propagandists.[14] The U.S.

Navy's version was severely factual, if somewhat tongue in cheek:

> [The] weeklong series of naval engagement activities with the Vietnam People's Navy . . . [were] . . . centered around non-combatant training, such as damage control, search and rescue, and skills exchanges like cooking and maintenance events. Friendship-building events such as medical and dental civic action projects, . . . and U.S.–Vietnamese Navy sporting events.

Surely nobody could possibly feel threatened by Americans and Vietnamese busy with dental, cooking, and sporting events.

Naturally, Vietnam's notables were not overlooked:

> A group of government and military leaders flew from the city of Ad Nang to the aircraft carrier USS *George Washington* (CVN 73) to meet with Navy leadership and observe the strike group as it operates in the South China Sea.

Those operations presumably were not dental or culinary. Nobody had to fly to visit the USS *John S. McCain*, which docked in Ad Nang from August 10. Unnecessarily, the release explained that "the ship is named for the father of Sen. John McCain, a respected figure in Vietnam who was a prisoner in Hanoi during the Vietnam War." After one more mention of "medical, dental, and engineering civic action . . . [and even] community service events," the release quoted Rear Admiral

Ron Horton, commander, Task Force 73, about the purpose of it all: "Exchanges like this are vital for our navies to gain a greater understanding of one another, and build important relationships for the future" (presumably not only a dental and culinary future).

Next, the release recapitulated recent port visits to Vietnam: two in 2008; the first "fly out" in 2009 to the USS *John C. Stennis* (CVN 74); also in 2009, U.S. 7th Fleet flagship USS *Blue Ridge* (LACK 19), and the guided-missile destroyer USS *Lassen* (DDG 82), not coincidentally commanded by a Vietnamese American officer, Commander H. B. Le—who duly attracted much media attention—and earlier in 2010, the hospital ship USNS *Mercy* (T-AH-19).

Far more significantly, given the difficult logistics of U.S. Navy operations so very far from its home ports, the release also notes that Vietnam is offering the most critical element of a home port:

> The rescue and salvage ship USNS *Safeguard* (T-ARS 50), and the dry cargo-ammunition ship USNS *Richard E. Byrd* (T-AKE 4) [were repaired] by Cam Ranh Shipyard, Hong Koi Port, Van Phong Bay.

The second text is an August 13, 2010, article, "The United States and Vietnam Must Not Behave Unscrupulously in the South China Sea," by the well-known commentator Kao Weimin in the Chinese-language Hong Kong newspaper *Ta Kung Pao*.[15] Founded in 1902 to promote democracy in imperial

China, it has promoted other aims since it came under CCP control in 1949, as Kao Wei-min's article demonstrates:

> Following Hillary's [*sic*] claim in Vietnam in July that "the United States has national interests in the South China Sea," the US carrier *George Washington* and the destroyer *John S. McCain* . . . will stage an "unprecedented" joint sea exercise in the South China Sea. . . . The question of "how to deal with a more self-confident China" is triggering argument in American media and academic circles. Some [say] . . . that the United States urgently needs "a new China strategy," [starting in] . . . the South China Sea.

In the pre-aggrandizement era, China could count on the automatic support of what are still called, anachronistically, "nonaligned countries." Malaysia, all too Western but for its obsessively Muslim rulers, is invoked, along with others prudently left unnamed:

> However, Malaysia and others have warned the United States: "You cannot interfere in high spirits in the South China Sea, you will only bring trouble there" . . .
>
> On 10 August, the US destroyer *John S. McCain* docked at Tien Sa in Da Nang port in central Vietnam . . . news from the US Seventh Fleet greatly boosted the whiff of gunpowder in the visit: "The destroyer *John S. McCain* and the carrier *George Washington* will stage an

'unprecedented' joint military exercise with the Vietnamese Navy." . . .

It is not difficult to see . . . that Vietnam is deliberately using this kind of exercise to bump [*sic*] into the present complex South China Sea situation, otherwise it should send a powerful message of friendship to China to balance the effect of the exercise.

A nice thought: even if threatened and seeking American protection against it, Vietnam's government should still affirm an absent friendship for China because it is China and thus deserving of courteous deference in all circumstances.

Yet the writer went on to offer an entirely realistic explanation of the new U.S.-Vietnam amity, which he prudently attributed to anonymous others rather than himself:

> *Public opinion* has pointed out that the reason why the United States and Vietnam, enemies during the Cold War, can embark on a honeymoon today is entirely due to Vietnam's antagonism towards China over the island dispute, and the United States is trying to contain China's power expansion in the South China Sea; the concerns of the two countries have coincided again. . . . *China's territorial ambitions are already causing unease in Vietnam.* [Italics added]

Kao Wei-min then switched back again to blame the United States, under the subtitle "Frequent US Confused Roaring at China." Having just explained by way of interposed public opinion that it was China that started the process by threatening Vietnam, he blithely contradicted himself to find the protagonist in the United States, whose attitude he writes "is becoming more and more hard-line . . . articles blaming China are tending to gather together in American media."

What comes next reflects a peculiar aspect of the prevailing Chinese outlook on international politics, which contains its own distortions and makes it that much harder for highly intelligent Chinese analysts and decision-makers to reason intelligently. Never naive, and never inclined to take the virtuous affirmations of foreign governments seriously, these days most Chinese observers seem to fall into the opposed error of viewing materialistic motives as not merely important, as they certainly are, but all-important to the exclusion of all else. That is how Kao Wei-min next reasons, to confidently predict that it is the United States and not China that will be isolated, because the Americans have only warships whereas China has the money. ASEAN countries might be inclined to seek U.S. favor over the South China Sea issue, but they also realize that the United States "cannot help them except in the military and security aspects," while "economically [they] depend more and more on China."

Such exaggerated faith in (nondialectical) materialism is just as naive as its opposite would be—if governments habitually subordinated security and power concerns to moneymaking, human history would have evolved very differently, in an altogether better fashion, with fewer follies perhaps, and certainly with fewer crimes. Alas, it is only in Homer's version of the Trojan War that heroic warriors sensibly enough fight for pretty captives, silver, and well-wrought armor, instead of the much uglier ideologies and political compulsions or even personal dictatorial ambitions that actually cause modern wars.

Kao Wei-min next evokes unspecified "Malaysian media" as the voice of reason, claiming that they "published an appeal to all sides to keep calm," and attributing to them the injunction that "Washington cannot intervene in regional affairs in high spirits [sic]; to do so will only cause trouble." That sets the stage for the author's own admonition, which comes off as plaintive, belying his own previous confidence in the workings of materialism:

> Faced with the play between the powers, and with excessive US interference in the South China Sea, ASEAN countries *should vigilantly explain* that the United States should . . . not behave unscrupulously in the South China Sea. [Italics added]

But even though China's conduct in the South China Sea "has been restrained" according to the author, who claims that China can safeguard both its "rights and interests" and also "overall stability" because it is not "in confrontation with the countries on its periphery" (news to them, presumably), Vietnam is isolated as the supposed exception. In its case there *is* confrontation, which the author blames wholly on Vietnam, because it is "very selfish and only thinking about itself without thought for the periphery." Vietnam, he writes, has often displayed a "hard-line" attitude on the South China Sea territorial issue, *"and also displayed resolve that it does not shrink from fighting over the islands there"* (italics added). For Kao Wei-min, evidently, Vietnam is a strange beast because it is willing to fight for the territory it holds or claims. It should be sensible and yield to superior force, evidently (victims who idealistically resist superior force instead of prudently yielding are very irritating for aggressors). Moreover, its officials "are so bold"—not a compliment, given the deference they should show—that they actually name China as the antagonist, and worse still, they "are bringing others into the fray." This time the author cites "international opinion" as the voice of reason:

> Certain [Vietnamese] officials have publicly named China. International opinion now holds the view that Vietnam is making efforts to internationalize and multilateralize [*sic*] Sino-Vietnamese disputes over South China Sea territory, and wants to enlist the help of the United States, *currently* the world's strongest power, to counter China in the South China Sea. [Italics added]

What follows is a veiled warning: "Vietnam [is] aggravating Sino-US confrontation. . . . Chinese society's dissatisfaction with Vietnam is rapidly accumulating; this is bound to have a complex effect on China's future Vietnam policy." The restrained language of indirection ("complex") normally serves to mitigate the harshness of confrontation, but in this case the veiled warning was immediately followed by a direct military threat. That indeed was seemingly the aim of the entire disquisition: to intimidate Vietnam by arguing that U.S. naval power could not protect it if China decided to attack, overland presumably:

> Should China and Vietnam truly come into confrontation, no aircraft carrier of any country can make Vietnam secure. . . .
>
> Vietnam must not play a dangerous game between China and the United States; that is playing with fire.

What makes this article so revealing is that Kao Wei-min first cites "public opinion" to frankly admit that China's territorial expansionism is the cause of it all ("the United States is trying to contain China's power expansion"; "China's territorial ambitions are already causing unease in Vietnam"), but then goes on to argue in effect that because China is China, Vietnam should shut up ("officials have publicly named China") and concede what it wants, because "no aircraft carrier of any country" can protect it from China's unleashed strength.

Of this warning, all one can say is that it would be far more credible if directed at some other nation. For the Vietnamese, by contrast, it is not dissuasive at all but rather positively an encouragement to persist in resisting China. For the core of their national identity is the giant-killer complex so manifest in Vietnam's war against the United States, which originated in the formative experience of resisting an even greater power than any Chinese empire: the world-conquering Mongols, who attacked in 1257–1258, and then in 1284–1285 (after the formation of the Yuan dynasty), and again in 1287–1288. The Mongols were defeated each time. Only after the Mongols retreated did the Vietnamese pay tribute. Undoubtedly they would willingly do so again—after defeating the PLA once more.

That the Chinese rulers, for whom Kao Wei-min is a skillful spokesman, should know nothing of their historic neighbors would be inexplicable, except for the dense barrier of great-nation autism. That is a very natural trait in the greatest nation, and it could have been harmless, if China were not intent at present on pursuing aggrandizement as well. As it is, a classic escalatory trigger has been contrived by the incendiary combination of obstreperous Chinese autism, Vietnamese defiance, and the Palmerstonian activism of the United States. It could be activated the next time the Chinese try to seize a reef, rock, or shoal.

# CHAPTER SIXTEEN

# South Korea

## A Model Tianxia Subordinate?

*As already noted*, all independent states invariably assert their absolute sovereignty, but not all states are animated by political cultures equally resistant to subordination to foreign powers—some are just more pliant than others. The usual motivation is fear, but in the case of South Korean attitudes toward China, fear is only a secondary and indirect factor that derives from China's presumed ability to leash or unleash North Korea. The greater motivation, rather, is a combination of deep cultural respect for China and the Chinese—highlighted by elite (not popular[1]) resentment against the United States and Americans—and above all, a lively awareness of the ever-increasing relative importance of China's market for South Korea. Again, while all strive to pursue economic advantage, not all do so with equal intensity—and compared to Koreans even the Japanese are unfocused, while the Chinese are downright self-indulgent.

Respect for China and the Chinese survives current Korean perceptions of their business practices—which in any case are significantly less unfavorable than those of Japanese, Europeans, or Americans. This tendency dates back at least to Ming times, and was the subject of impartial study before the

CCP's rise to power in Beijing, with folklore as the empirical basis.[2] That study therefore records popular respect for China and the Chinese, but it was elite Koreans, and more precisely the bureaucratic meritocracy, the Yangban class, that was the protagonist of a unique imitation cult: following the thirteenth-century introduction of neo-Confucianism, Korean devotees identified themselves as "lesser Chinese," though the ruling Joseon (or Chosŏn) dynasty became a Qing tributary only in 1636.

Subsequently, Korea's fate was such that it is the Japanese rather than the Chinese impositions that are still bitterly resented; Chinese cultural influence is only reviled, paradoxically in North Korea, to the point that it only allows the use of the Hangul Korean alphabet, with Chinese characters (Hanja) actually prohibited (there is of course much more Hanja than Hangul in the corpus of Korean literature).

As for the anti-Americanism of educated younger South Koreans—they find it easy to explode in anger at any mere accident, and readily accuse their political leaders of servility to the United States—this scarcely requires explanation, for it is rooted in the most common of human sentiments: unreciprocated bounties easily become humiliations. (When Nubar Pasha was told that a junior clerk was spreading vile rumors about him, he replied: "And yet I do not recall that I ever conferred any benefit upon him"—"Et pourtant je ne me rappelle pas lui avoir conféré aucun bienfait.")[3] In the Korean academy, the notion that the Korean War was an American or even a

Sino-American plot enjoys surprising credence, while much less explicitly there is ample racial and racist resentment for decades of GI couplings with Korean women. Such is the unmentioned subtext of agitations and exaggerations.[4]

No doubt more significant is the finding that South Koreans are more inclined than Japanese or Europeans to believe that China will become the country's most important trade partner, ahead of the United States, whose importance is anticipated to decrease. According to the above-mentioned detailed poll released in 2011, the average scored importance of economic relations with China is expected to increase over the next ten years, as compared to 2005, from 7.62 to 8.02 in South Korea, as opposed to 7.51 to 7.93 in Australia, for all its vast raw material exports to China, and 7.15 to 7.45 in the Philippines. Concurrently, the economic importance of the United States is expected to decline: average score down from 8.00 to 7.82. To be sure, for South Koreans the economic importance of China is not merely a matter of corporate or national significance but can be of personal significance as well: more than any other nationality, individual South Koreans have found good self-employment in the largest Chinese cities as experts in all fields, from dernier cri hairdressing to industrial quality control.

South Koreans also have distinctly more favorable views than other respondents of the impact of the Chinese economy on their interests. Between 2005 and 2010 the number that viewed China's economic rise positively remained stable at 49 percent—remarkable considering that China is a direct export competitor for the Koreans; in Australia, by contrast, favorable views declined from 54 to 52 percent between 2005 and 2010, even though China does not compete with Australia and became a much larger market for it over those years; in Japan, those who had positive views of China's economy declined from 35 to 23 percent. This is the psychological and political background of the current strategic relationship between the Republic of Korea and China. That relationship is also of course a derivative of the more immediately significant strategic relationship between the Republic of Korea and North Korea. The latter has different aspects, of course, but only one is really significant in the Sino–South Korean context: the very peculiar reluctance—indeed refusal—of the South Koreans to deter North Korean armed provocations in the normal manner of countries in conflict, that is, by prompt, convincing, and proportionate retaliation.

It is understood by all that it is the United States that is supposed to deter any large-scale North Korean aggression of strategic significance, with its global military capabilities; but it is the South Koreans with their very large and well-equipped armed forces in place that are supposed to deal with localized, onetime, attacks—armed provocations that have no operational continuity. This understanding was formalized and greatly broadened in its application with the 2007 U.S.–South Korean agreement to transfer (by April 2012) operational control of Republic of Korea (ROK) forces even in wartime from the current UN (that is, U.S.) command to ROK command.

What has happened in practice, however, is that the South Koreans have not responded to North Korean provocations, remarkably even in the case of really damaging attacks, notably the March 26, 2010, sinking of the 1,200-tonne corvette *Cheonan* with the loss of 46 of the 104-man crew. Within two months it was definitely determined that the *Cheonan* was split in two by a torpedo, but the South Koreans still did not retaliate, even though the North Korean navy offers many comparable targets.

Next, on November 23, 2010, a sudden North Korean artillery barrage on Yeongyeong Island some 75 miles from Seoul killed four, wounded many more, and left a substantial built-up area in ruins. This time also there was no prompt, convincing, and proportionate retaliation—instead, some rounds of artillery belatedly fired in response were deliberately aimed at empty wasteland.

The exact reasons for South Korea's refusal to follow the customary practices of deterrence are irrelevant when it comes to the strategic consequences (even stock market concerns have been mentioned!), for in any armed conflict excuses are pointless. The reason certainly cannot be the fear of a yet more damaging North Korean response—the excuse sometimes cited—for that would mean that the South Korean armed forces cannot deter anything at all, given that it is the United States that is responsible for deterring any full-scale attack or outright aggression.

Nor could the particular composition of the South Korean government in 2010 explain its passivity—indeed, its president was elected on a supposedly "hard-line" platform.[5] What counts is the impact on Chinese–South Korean relations. The disingenuous Chinese response to every inter-Korean incident (all initiated by North Korea, so far) is to piously ask both sides to "show restraint," and to call on all concerned to resume the China-hosted "Six-Power talks." In the meantime, China maintains cordial relations with North Korea at the government level, fraternal interparty relations, and collegial intermilitary relations, founded on selectively glorious shared memories of the Korean War. China also continues to provide North Korea with economic help that is most probably essential for the survival of the regime—which can always do without basic necessities for the starving population at large, but which does need decent food and the usual consumer goods to preserve elite cohesion (local customers predominate in the always well-stocked Pyongyang Number One Boat Restaurant moored off Kim Il Sung Square). There is a substantial unrequited trade imbalance (US$1.25 billion in 2008), and that may well measure the magnitude of the Chinese subsidy.

That seems to be money very well spent, because it gives the Chinese leaders a reliable leash on North Korea—a leash that is, of course, useful only insofar as North Korea continues to be aggressive periodically; no leverage can derive from a leash on a dog that never bites.

Whatever South Korean governments may state or believe, their refusal to retaliate promptly, convincingly, and proportionately for North Korean attacks, makes them, in effect, dependent lieges, both to the United States, for the deterrence of all-out war, and to China, for the deterrence of onetime attacks. For all their protestations, the South Koreans evidently prefer it this way. But this is not a satisfactory situation for the United States, which thus faces alone the costs and risks of safeguarding the Republic of Korea from North Korea, while having to divide its influence over it with China, which can always discipline the ROK government by threatening to unleash the North. There is little call for that now, because the South Koreans are deferential to Beijing and pathetically eager to attribute great merit to the Chinese leadership for keeping North Korea on a tight leash. A May 9, 2011, report from Beijing in the English-language version of the *Choson Ilbo* is a case in point:[6]

> North Korean leader Kim Jong-il requested [from] the Chinese . . . the latest in military weapons . . . last May, according to a source in Beijing. . . . China turned down the request, he said. "Kim Jong-il returned to North Korea from China last May in a bad mood," the source said. ". . . Among the weapons that Kim asked for from China were 30 Jianjiji Hongzhaji fighter-bombers[7] loaded with C-801 and C-802 anti-ship missiles. . . ." The source said Kim was convinced that North Korea should be prepared for a counter-strike from the United States and South Korea after the sinking of the *Cheonan* last March. [He] also apparently tried to convince China that any attacks

from the South and U.S. could spread to China. . . . Kim repeatedly told the Chinese leadership that North Korea had not sunk the [ship], even though Beijing sternly asked him about the incident three times.

After the Chinese refusal, the *Choson Ilbo* report noted that Kim Jong-il left Beijing abruptly, missing a scheduled theatrical performance.

The Beijing source that attributed such prudent restraint to Chinese leaders in refusing the aircraft to the impetuous North, would have been more credible had his report not echoed another, published in the same *Choson Ilbo* eleven months earlier:[8]

North Korea asked China to provide it with the latest J-10 fighter jets and other hardware but was rejected, it emerged Wednesday. . . . Kim Jong-il made the request to Chinese President Hu Jintao when he visited China in early May. But Hu apparently told Kim that China will protect and support him if attacked. Observers guess this is the reason why Kim left a day earlier than scheduled.

In both versions, the Chinese restrain North Korea by denying it strike aircraft in 2010; in both versions Kim Jong-il impolitely leaves one day earlier than planned, but in the 2010 report he is denied the *J-10* lightweight single-seater, whereas in the 2011 version of the same episode he is denied the two-seat *JH-7*: evidently China's moderating influence is increasing.

A particularly unseemly form of deference to China is the persistent refusal to grant a visitor's visa to the Dalai Lama, a figure widely respected in Korea, and not only among Korean Buddhists. Even when a wholly apolitical Nobel Peace laureates' conference was convened in South Korea in 2006, the Dalai Lama was refused a visa, with the unembarrassed explanation that China is Korea's number one trading partner and, in addition, that China's help was needed to persuade North Korea to give up its nuclear ambitions.[9]

After that, however, South Korea acquired a supposedly "hard-line" president, Lee Myung-bak, and on June 27, 2010, the Dalai Lama was able to commune with more than 500 Korean Buddhist monks—but only at the Intercontinental Grand Hotel of Yokohama, Japan,[10] having again been refused a visa. Whatever the U.S.-Korean alliance might comprise, values are not included.

So long as the Republic of Korea continues to respond to deadly North Korean attacks with plaintive words alone—praiseworthy no doubt for those who love peace above all else—it could only subtract from, and not add to, any coalition meant to dissuade Chinese aggrandizement. If South Korea with its present policies is, most unwisely, admitted to its councils, it could only weaken the collective resolve of a coalition to resist China, especially if any concrete action is called for—for example, joint maritime patrols of contested waters. Nor is South Korea likely to participate with its own forces if such decisions were nonetheless implemented, for fear that China would retaliate by relaxing its leash on North Korea or even applying the goad.

By contrast, the Republic of Korea under its present policies could combine membership in China's Tianxia as a sort of "lesser Chinese" subordinate, with the persistence of the U.S.–South Korean alliance. After all, the United States is quite used to its one-sided commitment and exacts no price for free-riding, whereas the South Koreans are obviously more inclined to be lieges than to accept the costs and risks of providing for their own security.

There is oblique evidence of this refusal to assume responsibility in South Korea's eagerness to pursue quarrels with Japan that are entirely devoid of strategic significance, and of course entail no risk whatever of forcible punishment. Even in 2010, in between deadly North Korean attacks that were neither deterred nor punished, thirty-seven members of the ROK Congress formed a forum to promote Korea's territorial claim to Japan's Tsushima Island, which the Koreans call Daema-do. Others rejoice in Korea's possession of the Liancourt Rocks, known as Takeshima to the Japanese who claim them, but which the Koreans call Dokdo. The *Korean Times* runs a permanent essay competition on the ownership of the islets, with no prizes for finding merit in Japanese claims. How this alleviates South Korea's acute and pathetic vulnerability is left unclear.

In December 2011, in a brutal episode, a member of South Korea's Coast Guard was killed and another was wounded by Chinese fishermen arrested with their boat for illegally fishing in Korean waters.[11] It was reported at the time that since 2006 some 2,600 Chinese boats had been arrested in similar circumstances—catastrophic pollution spreading out from the Chinese coasts, compounded by overfishing, is now driving desperate Chinese fishermen ever outward. But neither the extensive depredation of their coastal waters nor even the killing diverted resentment from the preferred, and of course utterly inoffensive, target: on December 14, 2011, a statue of a demure Korean girl representing a "comfort woman" was unveiled directly in front of the Japanese Embassy, to commemorate the 1,000th weekly demonstration demanding compensation, and of course to cause maximum irritation to a country that is no threat at all to South Korea.[12] Strategic escapism is not that uncommon a phenomenon in world politics, but it does make its practitioners unfit as active allies, and all the more easily intimidated by those who really threaten them.

# CHAPTER SEVENTEEN

# *Mongolia*

## Northern Outpost of the Coalition?

*Mongolia is Vietnam's twin* and South Korea's polar opposite when it comes to relations with China, for it could not survive as an independent state within the Chinese orbit, even though China did legally, formally, and finally renounce its claim to all of Mongolia with the 1962 border treaty and 1964 boundary protocol (which added another 10,000 square kilometers to Mongolia's 1.5 million). Prior to that, by the usual appropriation of ownership that still persists in the case of Tibet, Chinese governments had rejected Mongol declarations of independence (from 1911), claiming that Mongolia was part of "China" because the Manchu Qing dynasty had ruled both Mongol and Han-Chinese lands, as well as those of many other nationalities, of course. By that criterion, as noted, Sri Lanka could claim India.

Today there are no annexationist threats from Beijing, but as a landlocked country with only two neighbors, Mongolia must rely on the other to safeguard its independence—and that too somewhat precariously, because Russians remember too well the unfailing obedience of the pre-1990 Mongolian People's Republic to the Soviet Union.

Another vulnerability is demographic—though it could become a strength one day perhaps. There are only some 2.5 million Mongols in the vastness of Mongolia, but there are about 4 million in China's Inner Mongolia Autonomous Region (where almost 80 percent of its population is Han), with 1.5 million more Mongols in Xinjiang and elsewhere in China, as well as some 400,000 Buryat Mongols in the Republic of Buryatia of the Russian Federation.

In theory, because of its independence and because it contains the ancestral sites of the nation, Mongolia should be the cultural center for China's more numerous Mongols as well, exerting corresponding influence in Inner Mongolia. One obstacle, however, is that there is not much cultural capital in the Mongolian language, given the almost universal use of Russian (and now some English) in higher education instead of Mongol. Another obstacle is that in 1946, by Stalinist dictate, the Cyrillic alphabet was imposed for Mongol as well, while by contrast the Mongols of China retain the historic Mongol script derived from cursive Aramaic and Hebrew, via the Syriac, Sogdian, and Old Uyghur alphabets.[1]

As a landlocked country with only two neighbors, both of which have imperial dimensions and at least latent imperial pretensions over it, Mongolian governments have made great and not unskillful efforts to interest other countries in their own. They did duly evoke the distant benevolence of the United States, which is both appreciated and of small net value in enhancing Mongolia's independence because it evokes an almost symmetrical Russian displeasure—which matters more. Japan is the obvious third party that should have been able to offer a significant counterweight to the suffocating embraces of China and the Russian Federation. The establishment of diplomatic relations in 1972 generated little activity, but after the 1990 liberalization there was a sustained effort of both sides to communicate and cooperate, with many expressions of reciprocal interest and no historic antipathies standing in the way.

Many official visits ensued, and there is even a standing committee for economic cooperation, but in spite of much goodwill, in the end the narrow base of the Mongolian economy and Japan's high-end orientation defeated optimistic expectations. As of 2009 (last available data), Japan absorbed less than 1 percent of Mongolia's exports as opposed to China's 74.1 percent, Canada's 9.4 percent, and 3.4 percent for the United States. It supplied 6 percent of its imports, as opposed to Russia's 34.6 percent and China's 31.7 percent. Japanese investments came to 3.4 percent, as compared to China's 51.1 percent, Canada's 10.6 percent, and South Korea's 6.7 percent. Japan has been the largest aid giver to Mongolia, at US$40 million per year, but that too will be eclipsed somewhat by the US$300 million over five years of the U.S. Millennium Challenge Account.

With typically Japanese self-criticism, the Japan Ministry of Foreign Affairs blames only one side: "It is extremely important that Japan engage substantially in the development of Mongolia's . . . resources, conduct large-scale investment, and create a mutually beneficial relationship."[2] That injunction came after a rueful assessment that took note of the lack of Japanese business investment in Mongolia, whereas "the presence of neighboring China and Russia is overwhelming. In addition, the Republic of Korea's influence increased dramatically, with the expansion of small- and medium-sized investments (restaurants, esthetic clinics, [other] services . . . [and 30,000 labor permits for Mongolian workers]."

South Korean activity in Mongolia undoubtedly profits both sides, but it does not help to relieve Mongolia's strategic impasse, because the Republic of Korea's government will certainly not serve as a counterweight to China, or to Russia for that matter. Also, in a manner perhaps not paradoxical, the South Korean presence in Mongolia generates goodwill for the Chinese and Japanese, because of a peculiar ethnic incompatibility, and the much more ordinary resentment generated among the deprived by Korean shopkeepers who are both irreplaceable and visibly alien. Matters were not helped by a scandal that featured a Mongolian teenager, a South Korean ambassador, a pregnancy, and a refusal to pay child support.[3]

Perhaps the Japanese government will act on the earnest plea of its Foreign Ministry, and perhaps it will be successful in energizing Japanese activity in Mongolia, building a major presence that would then acquire its own political significance, so that Japan could emerge as something of a strategic counterweight to China. Subject to that happy evolution, however, Mongolia's ability to resist China's potentially overwhelming influence will continue to depend almost exclusively on the countervailing influence of the Russian Federation.

In a China/anti-China world, if Russia were to come out on the same side as China, Mongolia would at best have the exiguous autonomy of a mutually convenient buffer state, and at worst it could be reduced to a condominium with figurehead government. On the other hand, if the Russian Federation does reject an authoritarian convergence, to instead join the anti-China coalition to preserve its control of eastern Siberia in the long run, and its influence in Central Asia more immediately, Mongolia would once again become the indispensable and well-protected outpost it was during the decades of Soviet-Chinese confrontation. But this time it would concurrently obtain the benefits of good relations with the United States, Japan, and the rest of the coalition.

In the meantime, the force fields of commerce, geopolitics, and geo-economics intersected in the disposition of "Five Hills," Tavan Tolgoi, in the Tsogttsetsii district of Ömnögovi Province in southern Mongolia—indeed, in the southernmost part of the country, hence adjacent to China and far from Russian territory. This bit of geography is highly relevant because there is an open-pit mine in Tavan Tolgoi that since 1967 has been extracting valuable low-sulfur coal. Its output has been very unimpressive by world standards, but that is only so because the extraction has been confined to the merest fraction of Taval Tolgoi's vast coal deposits, one of the very largest in the world; according to a conservative estimate limited to the most cheaply recoverable upper layer, it holds 1.5 billion metric tons of coking coal and 3.6 billion tons of thermal coal, and could produce 30 million tons a year for at least thirty years. Along with almost every other global mining company, the China Shenhua Energy Company pursued mining rights, and plans were made for the rapid construction of a rail link from Tavan Tolgoi to the Inner Mongolian railway hub of Bayan Obo (Báiyún Èbó Kuàngqū in Chinese) a mere hundred kilometers from the border. The Chinese steel industry and its coking coal suppliers have been importing coal from much further away, and were of course very keen to start importing from the abundance of Tavan Tolgoi.

Many things happened thereafter, including the revocation of concessions already granted after a change of government in 2011, but the final outcome was that no Chinese company has been allowed to participate in the extraction, and the dedicated rail link from Tavan Tolgoi will run to the Russian border much further away, rather than to Bayan Obo. In 2010 Russia's transportation minister, Igor Levitin, announced a $1.7 billion plan, a very large investment that could only be recovered by carrying Tavan Tolgoi's coal to Russian ports for export to Japan, South Korea, and China too—but only via Russia.[4]

The Mongols had reacted to China's ever rising geopolitical pressure with a geo-economic denial, evidently to contain Chinese influence—and they made their motivation quite explicit.[5]

·······································

# CHAPTER EIGHTEEN

# *Indonesia*

## From Ostracism to Coalition

*Indonesia's successive governments* have not always been especially stable, broadly representative, or particularly effective, but they have always claimed a distinct regional primacy because of the sheer magnitude of the country's population and vast geographic extent, which is entirely disproportionate to its land area, very large though it is. In population, at more than 237 million in 2011, Indonesia far exceeds the next ASEAN members, the Philippines with some 94 million and Vietnam with 87 million. In total land area, Indonesia's 1.9 million square kilometers greatly exceed Vietnam's 331,000 square kilometers, and only the Malaysian Federation is of similar size. As for the archipelago of 6,000 or so inhabited islands, it is of continental dimensions with maxima of 5,000 kilometers from east to west and 1,700 kilometers from north to south. Counting surrounding seas, Indonesia's universally recognized territory amounts to some 5 million square kilometers, with an exclusive economic zone that adds 5 million more.

For all their expansive territory, until 1993 successive Indonesian governments operated under the assumption that sheer distance would guarantee their immunity from China's maritime claims, which by then had already troubled Brunei, the Philippines, Malaysia, and Vietnam, as well as Japan, and of course Taiwan in a different way, as a rival co-claimant. Indeed, as late as 1991, Indonesia's foreign minister Ali Alatas warned of the danger of conflict implicitly among other parties, over the Spratly Islands, seemingly edging toward proposing mediation under Indonesian auspices.[1]

That was just as well, because almost uninterruptedly from the establishment of Communist rule in 1949, China was in any case viewed as the "main threat" by the dominant faction of the Indonesian armed forces, even without a known territorial dispute. Nor was this merely a nominal threat meant mostly for planning purposes. In spite of China's then extremely limited strategic reach—and even now it is severely constrained—there was acute concern over a danger that was deemed ominous even personally, and at times imminent. China was not very near, but regional wars of communist insurgency certainly were, and they were then vigorously supported by China both in Malaya and later in Indochina. There was, above all, the internal threat of an uprising by the Partai Komunis Indonesia (PKI), the world's third largest Communist Party—until the failed PKI coup and subsequent anti-PKI countercoup and massacres of 1965.

The Chinese government was accused of being complicit with the PKI, both by virtue of interparty connections and support (manifest in CCP publications), and because of the perceived role of Indonesia's Chinese population within the PKI. That was a role greatly exaggerated by racial and religious prejudice, and twice over, because only a rather small proportion of Indonesians of Chinese extraction identified with Communist China, and even fewer had any links with its authorities; and also because the role of ethnic Chinese within the PKI was not dominant outside the largest cities, and there were virtually no Chinese in the PKI stronghold of Bali.

Nevertheless, official legislation and administrative policies after 1965 reflected both exaggerations: public Chinese religious rituals were banned, Chinese-language schools were shut down, the public display of Chinese characters was prohibited, and Chinese were encouraged to adopt Indonesian-sounding (that is, mostly Muslim) names.[2] Most of this legislation (not quite all) has been revoked, but in the meantime the rise of political Islam within Indonesia, and intensifying religious compulsion, have intensified social pressures against the mostly non-Muslim Chinese, many of whom are hardly Chinese in anything but their non-Muslim religion. The Islamists stimulate a constant, if mostly latent, hostility, with occasional outbursts of murderous violence.[3]

In theory all this is either in the past or unrelated to Sino-Indonesia state relations. In practice it is the subtext that colors reciprocal perceptions—Chinese officials despise Indonesians as self-indulgent, yet periodically violent with their Chinese compatriots, defined expansively (though only some have access to Chinese citizenship). As for Indonesian officials, they are congenitally suspicious of Chinese intentions, and not only over the long term.

Chinese policy has not served to dispel suspicion over its most immediate object: the Natuna Islands, 150 miles from Borneo, 1,000 miles from the nearest Chinese coast on Hainan Island, and about half that distance to the nearest Chinese outpost in the Spratly Islands, Cuarteron Reef,[4] itself established only in 1998 after a March 14 skirmish with the Vietnamese at Johnson South Reef.

Suspicion is aroused, not because the Chinese are claiming the Natuna Islands or have ever done so, but rather the contrary: the Chinese have issued periodic denials that there is any dispute between the two countries over the islands. Thus in June 1995 the Ministry of Foreign Affairs spokesman Chen Jian stated categorically, "There is no dispute between China and Indonesia on possession of the Natuna Islands." That should have been entirely reassuring, but then Chen Jian added: "We're willing to hold talks with the Indonesian side to settle demarcation of this area," without elaborating further.[5]

There was no need: two years earlier in the 1993 Indonesian-sponsored Surabaya workshop on the Spratly dispute, the Chinese side had greatly surprised the Indonesians—who thought they were helping others to resolve their own disputes while having none of their own—by claiming the waters east and northeast of the Natuna Islands on the basis of their now famous "dotted line" or "nine-dash" map,[6] whereby Chinese territory loops a long way south from China and very near Indonesia, Malaysia, the Philippines, and Vietnam so as to encompass virtually all of the South China Sea.

When the ownership of small islands of scant worth is disputed, it is almost invariably said nowadays that there is oil in the waters round about or at least gas, and in large amounts of course. It is no doubt comforting to believe in the prevalence of economic rationality in matters of war and peace and territory, in spite of millennia of evidence to the contrary (and so it was that the Falklands/Malvinas were endowed with entirely undiscovered vast oil reserves when men died in fighting over them). The seas around the Natuna Islands, by contrast, definitely do contain vast gas deposits, and oil as well, with production already under way and much more to come, so the dispute mattered as such even if nothing ensued from it, because it would inhibit investment and stop or slow the exploitation of the reserves (as it happened, however, an Indonesian-Exxon quarrel did that efficiently enough).

There was no possibility that Indonesia would renounce its claim, but neither did the Indonesian government vigorously dispute Chen Jian's unreassuring reassurance—that is not the Indonesian way, they are not Vietnamese, they prefer avoidance to defiance. Foreign Minister Ali Alatas accordingly replied to Chen Jian: "We appreciate the spirit in which the spokesman [Chen Jian] made the statement. But Indonesia does not see it has a sea border problem with China, or the necessity to have sea border delimitation. China is far away to the north.... On Natuna, there is no claim from China and there has never been a problem between China and Indonesia. So there is no question to be discussed."[7]

The Chinese proceeded to do nothing to advance or abridge the Natuna offshore end of their vast claims, while the Indonesian default position as the party in possession was of course to do nothing. In the meantime, the Chinese had good reasons to be well satisfied with the policy of Indonesia's leaders toward the U.S. military presence in their region—they were against it, under a ghostly survival of classic nonalignment in 1950s style that inherently disfavored the United States, which in turn had reasons to sanction Indonesia over human rights and the repression in East Timor.

But that was before the sequence of accidents and incidents that transformed Indonesia's strategic outlook, notably including the 1998 and 1999 Chinese appropriations in the Spratly Islands, with lethal violence against Vietnam, and with real mischief in dealing with the Philippines, if the pun be allowed, because Mischief Reef is squarely within the Philippine exclusive economic zone, measured from the nearest coastline.

The greater transformation, however, occurred in U.S.–Indonesian relations.

The January 2005 Bandar Aceh tsunami rescue and relief operations introduced the most Muslim and thus the most anti-Western, hence anti-American, of all Indonesian populations to the virtues of the U.S. Navy. By the end of that same year Indonesia's solid progress in democratization and the safeguarding of human rights allowed the resumption of the U.S.–Indonesian military relationship, in the first instance through the International Military Education and Training program. Also, under a "National Security Waiver," congressional restrictions on Foreign Military Financing (FMF) for lethal defense articles were relaxed. It took much longer to resume full military cooperation—the prohibition of assistance to Kopassus, Indonesia's version of the U.S. Special Operations Command, and as such implicated in repressive operations, was not voided until July 2010.[8]

As for the U.S. Navy, having first arrived in humanitarian style it could return in proper naval fashion, for its sea-control abilities suited the Indonesians very well by then—another achievement of China's unskillfully overbearing foreign policy.

Then Australia stepped in once again to provide what the United States could not, a stable, treaty-like security alliance, in the form of the 2006 "Agreement between the Republic of Indonesia and Australia on the Framework for Security Cooperation."[9] One of its preambles marked a distinction between the two parties on one side, and China on the other: "Recognising that both Parties are democratic, dynamic and outward-looking members of the region and the international community." The declared purposes of the agreement included: "to provide a framework for deepening and expanding bilateral cooperation . . . on matters affecting their common security as well as their respective national security."

Under "Defence Cooperation," the agreement contains highly substantive positions—typical expressions of Anglo-Saxon concreteness that Indonesian officials would have resisted but for China's alarming behavior, including:

> The closest professional cooperation between their Defence Forces; . . . Regular consultation on defence and security issues of common concern; and on their respective defence policies;
>
> Promotion of . . . capacity building of defence institutions and armed forces of both Parties including through . . . training, exercises, . . . and [the] application of scientific methods to support capacity building . . . activities; Cooperation in the field of mutually beneficial defence technologies and capabilities, including joint design, development, production, marketing and transfer of technology as well as developing mutually agreed joint projects.

Then under "Intelligence Cooperation," the agreement calls for "the exchange of information and intelligence on security issues between relevant institutions and agencies."

"Maritime Security" had its own specific provisions that are no doubt of interest to China, including "enhancing existing Defence and other cooperation activities and capacity building in the area of aerial and naval maritime security."

The Chinese government might have mitigated, if not reversed, the very unfavorable shift in Indonesia's overall strategic alignment by a tactful retrocession from their maritime pretensions. But when the Chinese were given the opportunity, they instead reasserted their maximal claim, and in very abrasive fashion: in June 2009 the Indonesian navy detained 75 Chinese nationals and their eight fishing boats off the Natuna Islands. In response, Qin Gang, Foreign Ministry spokesman in Beijing, described the area as *Nansha*, the summary Chinese term for the Spratly Islands as a whole—adding in typically bullying tones: "China is strongly dissatisfied with Indonesia for having detained Chinese fishing boats, and it demands that the Indonesian government immediately release the fishermen and boats."[10] But having adopted one tone, Qin Gang immediately switched to another, tripping over the intercultural boundary with the typically intracultural presumption that one can scold one minute and warmly embrace in the next: "China and Indonesia [are] 'strategic partners,' . . . The two countries should settle the problem as soon as possible in the spirit of friendly consultation and maintaining the overall situation of bilateral relations." Then came the territorial claim, in a reference to "the waters around China's Nansha Islands," to which Qin Gang added: "China is gravely concerned about this incident."

Under the rubric of strategy, the Indonesians may have other shortcomings, but they are not lacking in subtlety. Just as they long tried to ignore the Natuna claim to give the Chinese an opportunity to quietly forget it, now they will not renounce any partnership with Beijing, strategic or not. But they are striving to ensure that they can contain Chinese pressures with means of their own—or of friendly others, as the case might be. On May 26, 2010, for example, Rear Admiral Among Margono, commander of the Eastern Fleet Command of the Indonesian navy, supported by a band, ceremoniously welcomed in Surabaya the arrival of USS *Tortuga* (LSD 46), USS *Vandegrift* (FFG 48), USNS *Salvor* (T-ARS 52), and the U.S. Coast Guard cutter *Mellon* (WHEC 717) for a joint exercise, "part of the . . . Cooperation Afloat Readiness and Training (CARAT)" program of six original partner nations, Brunei, Malaysia, Philippines, Singapore, and Thailand as well as Indonesia.[11] Such a flotilla could not win another battle of Midway, but its presence alone would inhibit the bigger-ship bullying tactics repeatedly witnessed in the Spratly archipelago in recent times.

Given its structured security connection with Australia, which itself has the closest possible alliance with the United States, Indonesia needs no formal arrangement to signify its membership in the emerging anti-China coalition. Although its own military strength is and will remain unimpressive, Indonesia could exert pressure on China if it comes to that by limiting its commodity shipments to China now that Indian demand keeps rising—the precedent set by China when rare-earth shipments to Japan were withheld is valid for all. If a crisis were to escalate further, Indonesia's archipelago astride China's shortest westward sea routes might also offer opportunities to apply pressure.

There is no audible "who lost Indonesia" debate in Beijing, but there should be. Indonesia is not another Vietnam, whose national myth cannot be in good working order without an ongoing confrontation with China. True, Indonesia is not South Korea either, and definitely not a candidate for profitable obedience in a gilded Tianxia cage. But as late as 1993 and indeed later, it was still set to consolidate relations with China while remaining distant from the United States and its ally Australia. Now, by contrast, it has emerged as an important member of the anti-China coalition.

As for the benefit to China of having pursued the policy that antagonized Indonesia, its advocates would no doubt argue in internal Politburo discussions that China's vast maritime claim—most of the South China Sea—has only a fragile basis in debatable historiography, dubious cartography, and the occupation of only a few places, so that it must therefore be asserted with maximum vigor. That in turn is best done by insisting on claiming the most distant zone off the Natuna Islands, against the largest country among the rival claimants.

This would all make sense within its own gamesmanship terms, that is, within the artificially circumscribed context of an imaginary China that has no other international relationships but with its maritime rivals, and no other international priority but to maximize its maritime possessions, or at least its claims. As it is, it is yet another manifestation of China's acquired strategic deficiency syndrome.

............................................

# CHAPTER NINETEEN

# The Philippines

## How to Make Enemies

*From a Chinese and strategic point of view*, the Republic of the Philippines was little more than an extension of the United States until September 16, 1991, when the Philippine Senate amid great displays of emotion voted 12 votes to 11 to reject a treaty that would have leased the Subic Bay Naval Station to the United States for another ten years.[1] Instead, the last U.S. sailor departed on November 24, 1992, and by then the United States had already evacuated Clark Air Force Base, which had been heavily damaged by a 1991 volcanic explosion.

Under the 1947 Military Bases Agreement, concluded at a time when the Philippine government could not have disputed any American request, the United States also operated a number of smaller installations, but "Clark" and "Subic" were very much more than just another air base and another port among the many others then in use by the United States in Europe and East Asia. In addition to ample housing, airfields, hangars, depots, and docks, the two vast complexes also included a full range of maintenance facilities and repair workshops of industrial dimensions, including a full-scale shipyard and a 600-foot dry dock at Subic.

From the U.S. point of view, Clark and Subic supported the entire American military posture in the Western Pacific. From the Philippine point of view, they provided employment for many thousands, including highly skilled, well-paid craftsmen and administrators. In addition, however, U.S. personnel purchased intimate personal services from local females on a vast scale, and did so under unusual modalities exceptionally humiliating for Philippines at large, including, no doubt, the twelve senators who voted to end it all. For everyone understood the scenes outside Clark and Subic as metaphors for the entire U.S.-Philippine relationship of structural inequality and demeaning subordination.

Although the 1991 vote did not repeal the 1952 U.S.-Philippines Mutual Defense Treaty, it did remove all American forces and thus changed fundamentally the strategic disposition of the country, potentially opening it up to Chinese influence as never before. There were impediments, to be sure, including a historic Chinese ethnic presence in the Philippines that had its negative as well as positive aspects and strong links with Taiwan—though the Philippines preceded the United States by four years in switching diplomatic recognition to the PRC on June 9, 1975. Overall, however, the Chinese were very well positioned to supplant the United States as the benevolent greater state on the scene that could gradually evolve into a potentially protective power.

Since then, however, Sino-Philippine relations have unfolded in the different ways that have become normal under the deadly workings of what was earlier defined as China's acquired strategic deficiency syndrome:

- economic relations have grown and have become more diversified, with a merchandise trade balance weighted in favor of the Philippines because of its large commodity exports;
- a sequence of bilateral agreements on economic and related matters have been successfully negotiated, without prejudicing Philippine-Taiwan relations in any substantive way; and
- China's overbearing, even threatening, conduct has driven the Philippines back into a protective relationship with the United States.

There are multiple overlapping contending claims over large parts of the South China Sea, as we have seen, but two very recent documents suffice to define the Sino-Philippine contention.[2] One is a *Note Verbale* sent by the Philippine Mission to the secretary-general of the United Nations on April 5, 2011, to reply very belatedly to two Notes Verbales sent by the PRC on the same day May 7, 2009. Although neither was addressed to the Philippines, one being a reply to Vietnam and the other to Malaysia, because both Notes Verbales referred to "extended continental shelves" in the South China Sea and other "relevant waters as well as the seabed and subsoil thereof" as indicated on the usual nine-dash Chinese map,[3] the Philippine Mission was "constrained to respectfully express its views":

First, the Kalayan Island Group (KIG) [the Spratly Islands, claimed and in part occupied by the Philippines] constitutes an integral part of the Philippines. . . .

Second, the Philippines, under the Roman notion of *dominium maris* and the international law principle of *"la terre domine la mer"* . . . necessarily exercises sovereignty and jurisdiction over the waters around or adjacent to each relevant geological feature in the KIG. . . .

Third, since the adjacent waters of the relevant geological features are definite and subject to legal and technical measurement, the [Chinese] claim . . . reflected in the so-called 9-dash line map . . . would have no basis under international law. . . . Sovereignty [belongs] to the . . . Philippines.[4]

The Chinese replied in turn on April 14, 2011—within nine days of having received the Philippine note, amazing swiftness amid the languor of the UN—and did so in the strongest possible terms:

China has indisputable sovereignty over the islands in the South China Sea and adjoining waters . . . [its] . . . related rights and jurisdiction are supported by abundant historical and legal evidence. . . . The contents of the [Philippines'] Note Verbale . . . are totally unacceptable to the Chinese Government.

The so-called Kalayaan Island Group (KIG) claimed by the Republic of Philippines is in fact part of China's

Nansha islands. . . . Since 1970s, the Republic of Philippines started to invade and occupy some islands and reefs of China's Nansha islands. . . . [These] acts constitute infringement upon China's territorial sovereignty. Under the legal doctrine of *"ex injuria jus non oritur"* the Republic of the Philippines can in no way invoke such illegal occupation to support its territorial claims.[5]

Both letters ended in classic fashion as each Mission availed itself of the "opportunity to renew to the Secretary-General of the United Nations the assurance of its highest consideration." That was duly polite, and each side did spell its Latin aphorisms correctly, but nothing can alter the pre-1914 flavor of the exchange, from a time when Notes Verbales asserting incompatible territorial claims and denouncing intrusions, let alone invasions ("started to invade and occupy some islands and reefs of China's Nansha islands") were the usual preliminary to war.

No Sino-Philippine war is imminent, but there already is warlike conduct by way of sudden occupations and overnight constructions, and by maritime harassment. There are also immediate consequences. By May 10, 2011, President Benigno Aquino III at an ASEAN meeting in Jakarta called on the other claimants to the Spratly Islands—Brunei, Vietnam, and Malaysia—"to take a united stand against the recent aggressive actions from China."[6] In this case, words followed action: President Aquino had earlier ordered the Coast Guard to provide security to oil exploration vessels, in the wake of a March 2, 2011, incident at Reed Bank near Palawan, in which two white-painted Chinese gunboats (No. 71 and No. 75) tried to drive away by harassing maneuvers the Philippine Department of Energy vessel M/V *Venture*.[7]

More action followed. On May 15, 2011, President Aquino with his cabinet flew aboard the USS *Carl Vinson* CVN 70 (by then redubbed the "Bin Laden shark-feeding vessel" in the vernacular press) as it headed for Manila for a port call with USS *Shiloh*, USS *Bunker Hill*, and USS *Gridley*. The Philippines Armed Forces spokesman Commodore Jose Miguel Rodriquez referred to the arrival of the nuclear-powered aircraft carrier as exemplary of "the strong defense relations of the two countries" (referring to the U.S.-Philippine Visiting Forces Agreement approved by the Philippine Senate in May 1999).

Two days before this effective bit of aircraft-carrier diplomacy, there was more definitive action than a ship visit: on May 13, 2011, the Philippine Navy received a Hamilton-class "Weather High Endurance Cutter" from the U.S. Coast Guard under a Foreign Military Sales credit; it will undoubtedly be deployed mostly off the disputed Spratly Islands—locally, the Kalayan Islands. The designation "cutter" hardly describes accurately a substantial warship of 3,250 tons that will be by far the largest patrol ship in the Philippine Navy (as the BRP *Gregorio del Pilar* PF-15), with a crew of 167, exceptional endurance (14,000 miles unrefueled, but in this case significant for long periods on station), modern armament (including the 20-mm *Phalanx*), and a helicopter hangar and deck. Certainly the

*Gregorio del Pilar* will be well suited for the bigger-ship games-manship that the Chinese have favored—it dwarfs the 1,500-ton Chinese patrol vessels that have operated in the Spratly archipelago. The transfer was described as "an expression of America's commitment to help the Philippines protect its maritime domain."[8]

It can definitely be said that Sino-Philippine relations have evolved very dynamically—there is nothing like a territorial claim pressed aggressively, if the aim is to ruin amity. A mere seven months before President Aquino's strong statement on the need to confront China, and his highly meaningful descent on the USS *Carl Vinson*, the Chinese government had been very pleased indeed by the Philippine stance on the South China Sea dispute, in contrast to sinister American scheming,[9] as depicted in a more than semi-official publication:

> The disturbed waters around China reflect how changes in the political landscape between China and the United States are laying the foundation for a future Asian power struggle. . . .
>
> "Strategically speaking, China has very limited influence on neighboring countries and keeps a low profile in diplomacy," said Shi Yinhong, a senior scholar of American studies at Beijing-based Renmin University. "But the US possesses long-term military advantages and sticks to its hegemonic ideals," Shi said.

In a regional security forum held in Vietnam last month, US Secretary of State Hillary Clinton claimed a US "national interest" in this region. . . .

"But the US' desperate demonstration of its military strength [re the visit of the USS *George Washington* task force to Vietnam] gives away its fear of weakness deep inside," Rear Admiral Yang Yi wrote in a commentary published in Tuesday's *Nanfang Daily*.

Yang said the US is now provoking ASEAN nations in order to disrupt their relations with China. . . .

Clinton, urging a multilateral solution, claimed in Vietnam last month that the US was concerned that conflicting claims to the Nansha and Xisha Islands [Spratly and Paracels] were interfering with maritime commerce, hampering access to international waters.

It is at this point that the praiseworthy Philippine intervention occurred:

But the situation was further complicated last week when the Philippines, a close ally of the US, said Southeast Asian nations did not need US help in solving territorial disputes with China over the South China Sea.

"It's ASEAN and China. Can I make myself clear? It's ASEAN and China. Is that clear enough?" said the Philippines Foreign Secretary Alberto Romulo, who was ASEAN chairman in 2007.

Shi said the Philippines doesn't want US intervention to further complicate the South China Sea issue.

The Chinese were so well pleased by Romulo's outburst that it was also cited in Kao Wei-min's August 13, 2010, programmatic article in the *Ta Kung Pao* (see Chapter 15).[10] Referring to the same Clinton speech in Hanoi, it noted:

> On the same day, Philippine media revealed the attitude expressed the previous day by Foreign Minister Romulo that "the South China Sea negotiations do not need American intervention."
>
> *These [ASEAN] countries are also clear that the United States cannot help them except in the military and security aspects, while . . . economically [they] depend more and more on China. . . .* The attitude expressed by the Philippine foreign minister is based on this consideration, and is also aimed at making clear to the international community that the Philippines is not a US pawn. [Italics added]

The Philippine Republic is still not a U.S. pawn, but its government no longer pleases the Chinese so well. Nor can the Chinese complain overmuch of American incitement, because declared U.S. policy has been impeccably conciliatory. Only two months before the May 2011 U.S. naval visitation, the U.S. ambassador to the Philippines, Harry Thomas Jr., was quoted quoting Secretary of State Hillary Clinton enjoining moderation on her Philippine counterpart:

> "When Secretary Clinton spoke to DFA Secretary Del Rosario on Sunday, they spoke about the need for all claimants to resolve these issues at the negotiating table peacefully. We take no sides in this. We think all claimant states should sit down together, iron out their claims, and then work with China via ASEAN for a Code of Conduct for the South China Sea in the Spratly Islands. . . .
>
> "The most important thing for all countries is to realize that over $5 trillion in international commerce goes through the South China Sea. And that's why we support freedom of navigation. But all this should be done peacefully, at the negotiating table. And that is so, so important," he said. Thomas said he has also discussed these matters with the Chinese Ambassador to the Philippines, Liu Jianchao, saying "we talk about these things."[11]

To be sure, the United States was primarily advising the Philippine government to settle the intra-ASEAN disputes, then reiterating the need for a united ASEAN front, and only then encouraging the latter to "work with China" for a Code of Conduct, everyone's default position for now. As noted, by the end of 2010 the Chinese Foreign Ministry agreed, after long resistance, to negotiate with an ASEAN-wide delegation, and to do so on a U.S.-suggested "Code of Conduct" to boot.

But a second Chinese player was ready to rekindle the dispute with the Philippines by harassing the oil exploration ship in March 2011, and a few weeks later a third Chinese player seemingly intervened as well. It was reported on May 20, 2011, that two Philippine Air Force OV-10 Broncos (top speed 288 mph) on a reconnaissance patrol over the Reed Bank basin of the Kalayaan [Spratly] Islands were approached and "buzzed" by two Chinese MiG-29 Fulcrums (top speed 1,490 mph).[12] General Eduardo Oban Jr., chief of staff of the Philippine Armed Forces (AFP), declared that "the incident would not deter the AFP from enforcing its mandate to . . . protect the nation's territorial integrity as well as its maritime resources." As it happens, the arrival in Manila Bay of the USS *Carl Vinson* and its Strike Carrier Group I was imminent at the time of the incident. Colonel Arnulfo Marcelo Burgos Jr., of the AFP Public Information Office, helpfully explained, "The mutual support and assistance both countries provide to each other contributes largely to strengthening our capabilities as military institutions."

In a manner utterly incoherent, damagingly contradictory, yet by now almost customary, the visitation of the Chinese MiG-29s preceded by three days the arrival of a Chinese delegation at the highest government level below the presidency, headed by the minister of national defense, General Liang Guanglie, and State Councilor Dai Bingguo, for an extended (May 21–25), full-dress "goodwill" visit. The Chinese Embassy announcement explained that "[the visit] is expected to further advance China-Philippines friendly relations, specifically military exchanges and pragmatic cooperation, thus enriching and enhancing the strategic cooperation between our two countries."

The U.S. stance over the South China Sea disputes is not unsubtle, but it seems that no competition in subtlety is under way. On June 23, 2011, Albert del Rosario, foreign secretary of the Philippines, asked U.S. Secretary of State Hillary Clinton to clarify U.S. policy on the China-Philippine confrontation in the South China Sea under the 1951 Mutual Defense Treaty. He also asked for surplus U.S. warships to upgrade the capacity of the Philippine navy to "defend maritime borders." Secretary Clinton reassured del Rosario on both points.[13] Once again, Chinese conduct has driven a possible partner into the arms of the United States. By 2012 the return of the U.S. Navy to its old base at Subic Bay was the subject of hopeful speculation in the Philippines.

........................................

# CHAPTER TWENTY

# *Norway*

Norway? Norway!

*Although Norway notoriously* has vast maritime possessions, exclusive economic zones amounting to 2,385,178 undisputed square kilometers as opposed to China's 877,019, it faces no Chinese claims as yet. On the other hand, its Nobel Committee did give the 2010 Peace Prize to Liu Xiaobo, a Chinese citizen convicted and imprisoned by due process of Chinese law for advocating human rights—a criminal, that is. The Chinese could have retaliated symmetrically by awarding the newly instituted Confucius Prize to a convicted Norwegian criminal, but instead it was reportedly left to Chinese food-safety inspectors to respond by holding up Norwegian salmon imports long enough to spoil the fish.

The extra "quality controls" on Norwegian fresh salmon were introduced a few days after the December 10, 2010, prize ceremony, once Chinese health inspectors reported that "traces of drugs" and/or bacteria had been found in thirteen shipments of salmon.[1] "We cannot get fish in there at all," was the reported comment of Henning Beltestad, CEO of Norway's Leroey Seafood Group (an overstatement: salmon exports to China in 2011 were running at 30 percent of the 2010 level), while a stalwart

Viking, Lars Berge Andersen, "a lawyer who assists Norwegian companies in China," added: "I am very worried about the long-term effect for Norwegian businesses in China." The interim beneficiary is Scotland, now allowed to export fresh salmon to China for the first time. Jamie Smith, spokesman for the Scottish Salmon Producers' Organization, said that Chinese health inspectors had not interfered with his fish.

Long before the Nobel announcement, after curtly dismissing Norwegian claims that the prize committee is independent, the Chinese Foreign Ministry did warn that there would be retaliation if the prize were given to the convicted criminal. Yet six months later the Norwegians were very surprised by its severity: it comprised the interruption of political contacts, the freezing of "very promising" trade negotiations, and the lethal unfreezing of Norwegian salmon held up in Chinese customs sheds—while Chinese companies, by contrast, were "increasingly active" in Norway, without impediments to be sure. In December 2010, as the Liu Xiaobo scandal was erupting, China Oilfield Services announced a contract with Norway's Statoil for drilling in the North Sea. In January 2011, China National Blue Star purchased the Norwegian Elkem mining company for US$2 billion, and the Norwegian company Orkla joined Aluminum Corp. of China Ltd. to serve Chinese high-speed railway projects. (But the signature was affixed by Orkla's Swedish subsidiary, Sapa, in the presence of the Swedish ambassador. "There is no need to be provocative," explained Orkla spokesman Johan Christian Hovland.)[2]

In Oslo a Chinese Embassy spokesman helpfully explained that Sino-Norwegian relations are "in difficulty" because the Peace Prize was given to "a Chinese criminal." He made it clear that it was Norway's duty to repair relations with China, though he failed to add how that might be done, although one Norwegian executive, Henrik Madsen, did suggest a remedy for the future: broadening the Nobel committee to include non-Norwegians to weaken its link to Norway—something best ensured by including CCP members, no doubt. Other businessmen suggested that Norway simply stop awarding prizes to foreigners far away.[3] For all of Norway's riches, one can always want more, so that the businessmen's complaints against the four women and three men who select the winner were not simply dismissed—there was an impact, and prospective Chinese candidates may be overlooked in the future.[4]

This entirely trivial episode holds a serious lesson: no doubt for nontrivial political reasons, the Chinese government cannot at present successfully manage its international problems, not even very minor ones such as the award of an unofficial prize to a Chinese dissident. In the case at hand, in addition to antagonizing a few Norwegians and a somewhat greater number of disinterested souls around the world, and in addition to enhancing enormously the resonance of Liu Xiaobo's name globally and within China as well, the Chinese government incurred further diplomatic costs when it set out to try to persuade countries with resident representation in Oslo to withhold their ambassadors from the award ceremony. It succeeded with the usual suspects, authoritarian or venal, or both: Russia, Kazakhstan, Tunisia, Saudi Arabia, Pakistan, Iraq, Iran, Vietnam, Afghanistan, Venezuela, Egypt, Sudan, Cuba, and Morocco. (Perhaps the U.S. government should have exerted counterpressure on the aid recipients among them.) On the other hand, strenuous and exceptionally insistent attempts that evoked not a little ridicule and contempt in Oslo's small diplomatic community failed with forty-six other countries.

Aside from its particular, almost comical, aspects, this episode is not atypical of China's recent international conduct in being both highly energetic and definitely counterproductive.

# CHAPTER TWENTY-ONE

# The Three China Policies of the United States

*It is customary to criticize* the administration in office for "not having a (grand) strategy" and for not having a policy for this or that country. But this accusation certainly cannot be advanced in regard to China policy, because there is not merely one of them, but three—two of which are moving in diametrically opposed directions.

Yet, as we shall see, the remedy cannot be to reduce three to just one, but rather it must be to add a fourth policy, a geoeconomic policy. It alone can offer the possibility of preserving a long-term power equilibrium with China.

*The First U.S. China Policy: Vigorous Promotion of China's Economic Growth.* The most familiar U.S. China policy is that of the U.S. Treasury, both for itself as the keeper of American public finance and as the institutional advocate in the councils of the U.S. government for private finance, or at least for the major "Wall Street" firms that operate internationally.

This policy, which has been faithfully executed and indeed strongly reaffirmed by the current secretary of the Treasury, Timothy Franz Geithner, focuses entirely on the benefits to

U.S. public finance of cheap capital from China's huge foreign-currency reserve, and to U.S. consumers and businesses alike of having unconstrained access to the cheapest possible imports of manufactured goods as well as raw materials, because in effect they increase the U.S. standard of living without (inflationary) income increases, and reduce input costs to businesses.

From that point of view, the chronic, very large Chinese merchandise trade surpluses with the United States—overwhelmingly because of manufactured goods—are not a problem but merely register the magnitude of the benefits received.

The U.S. Treasury is naturally highly cognizant of the benefits to U.S. public finance, and to private financial entities also, of having access to cheap Chinese capital—capital originally generated by China's chronic and very large trade surpluses, a function of the very high (50 percent, plus or minus) average Chinese savings rate, and which is used by the Chinese authorities to acquire U.S. Treasury bonds, bills, and notes as well as other dollar instruments, specifically in order to increase the relative value of the U.S. dollar against the yuan and thus help perpetuate Chinese trade surpluses. Chinese industrial policy is thereby the very mechanism that makes cheap capital available to U.S. public and private finance. For this reason, instead of being criticized on this score, China is the beneficiary of the U.S. Treasury's especial solicitude. One more factor that may affect U.S. Treasury attitudes toward China is sociological, so to speak: because its highest echelon is staffed almost entirely by former or future employees of the leading financial firms, there is a natural sensitivity to the importance of Chinese officialdom and state enterprises as future clients.

By contrast, the U.S. Treasury has no expertise in, no organizational responsibility for, nor indeed any intellectual interest in the condition of the U.S. manufacturing sector. Far from having an industrial policy to promote manufacturing in general or specific sectors thereof, in its everyday bureaucratic operations the U.S. Treasury is indifferent to the condition of U.S. industry, and specifically to the sharp decline, or outright disappearance, of entire industrial subsectors because of the unconstrained inflow of cheaper imports, notably including imports from China. (The normal Treasury stance in that regard is that the lost jobs were evidently uncompetitive, poorly paid, and not worth having anyway).

Only the U.S. International Trade Commission, an organization that is small and weak both politically and institutionally, has any sort of jurisdiction in that regard, and it too is strictly limited to "dumping" cases—in which, moreover, it applies stringent standards to determine if *serious* damage was caused to American industry, with no mandate to prevent it beforehand. Nor is the commission empowered to protect American industry from the chronic undervaluation of the Chinese yuan. Although it is contrived by the systematic purchase of U.S. dollar instruments, it is not defined as "dumping" even though it affects all product categories instead of just one.

On the other hand, the U.S. Treasury, which does have jurisdiction over the currency, and thus currency manipulation as well, reacts if at all, and then only verbally, only under lively pressure from the U.S. Congress at the behest of industrial or trade union interests.[1]

Secretary Geithner has followed his predecessors in periodically asking his Chinese counterparts to let their currency rise when the volume of complaints mounts—but he does so with evident reluctance, and with no suggestion that any sanctions would follow if the undervaluation persists. When he insists, he sounds plaintive, not menacing, for indeed there is no intention whatever to act if defied. Accordingly, the Chinese feel free to ignore these occasional requests, though in the past they have sometimes allowed at least temporary and small increases in the relative value of the yuan in response to particularly intense U.S. congressional complaints, and/or to contain domestic inflation.

On such occasions, the U.S. Treasury makes much of the very small rise in the value of the yuan, abundantly praises the Chinese for their flexibility, and cites it as evidence of the forthcoming end of systematic undervaluation. Characteristically, on May 10, 2011, after the annual U.S.-China Strategic and Economic Dialogue meetings, Secretary Geithner told reporters: "We are seeing very promising shifts in China's economic policy."[2] He then said that the United States still hopes that China will move more quickly to allow its currency to rise in value against the dollar and will also allow it to appreciate against the currencies of its other major trading partners. The same report quoted the Chinese as also promising "to end discrimination against foreign firms looking to secure lucrative government contracts and to open the mutual fund and car insurance sectors to U.S. firms."[3] This was not a new promise; it had been made before in 2010, 2009, 2008 . . .

At the same time, the U.S. International Trade Commission published the results of its investigation entitled "China: Effects of Intellectual Property Infringement and Indigenous Innovation Policies on the U.S. Economy."[4] Its overall estimate was that the losses to U.S. firms amounted to approximately $48 billion in the year 2009 alone, not counting legal and other expenditures of $4.8 billion to contain losses of intellectual property in China. It was also estimated that approximately 923,000 U.S. jobs were lost. Secretary Geithner did not address this report or the subject thereof during the China-U.S. dialogue or afterward. Nor did any other component of the U.S. government propose to undertake any retaliatory action, or even ask for compensation. Instead, promises to do better in the future were solicited from the Chinese—and duly obtained, of course.

Given the narrowly financial focus of the U.S. Treasury, the very limited jurisdiction of the International Trade Commission and its lack of retaliatory powers, the nullity of the U.S. Department of Commerce, and the absence of any department of industry in the U.S. government (a reflection of free-trade ideology), there is no possibility of any serious government intervention to stop or at least contain the extensive deindustrialization caused by large and chronic trade deficits in manufactured goods.

Nor is any part of the U.S. government charged with safeguarding U.S. technology from diffusion to China or anywhere else—unless it is specifically military or at least "dual-use" technology. That is so even though it is universally recognized that the overall competitiveness of the U.S. economy derives in large degree from its technological edge, and even though much of the technology now productively employed in the private sector was originally developed by the U.S. government, or with its funding. Remarkably, this failure to control technological diffusion even extends to the U.S. aerospace sector, in spite of its obvious importance both militarily and economically. This failure has a number of peculiar characteristics:

First, in many of its subsectors, distinctions between civil and military, and barriers to the transfer of know-how from one to the other, are weak or nonexistent.

Second, the aerospace industry accounts for a good part of all remaining U.S. manufacturing exports.

And third, aerospace is the one sector in which desistance from technology transfers to China could easily be negotiated with all others, because in each specialty there is usually only one European and/or Japanese supplier, and both European and Japanese firms are

inherently more reluctant to share their technology
with the Chinese than are their U.S. counterparts.

Nevertheless, as if it were no different from, say, the soft-drink
industry, there is no U.S. policy to control the diffusion of nonmilitary aerospace technology, or even to monitor the process.
In the absence of any U.S. government action, critical U.S.
aerospace technologies are now being transferred to China via
joint ventures with the state-owned COMAC (Commercial
Aircraft Corporation of China Ltd.), or other subsidiaries or
affiliates or associated companies of China's civil/military AVIC
(Aviation Industry Corporation of China), which manufactures
jet fighters, bombers, missiles, and other military equipment as
well as civilian aircraft.

These joint ventures—evidently the preferred mechanism
for the Chinese side, for less than evident reasons as well[5]—
serve broader purposes, indeed the general advancement of
China's industries as a whole, but more immediately they are
absolutely essential for two current entirely civilian aircraft development programs: the 70- to 100-seat ARJ21 "regional" pas-
senger jet, an unpromising entry in a crowded market, and the
much higher priority 150- to 200-seat C919 airliner, intended to
compete directly with the omnipresent Boeing 737 and Airbus
320 series. A partial list of current joint ventures includes:[6]

Flight controls, Parker-Hannifin + AVIC, in Xian,
Shaanxi Province

Jet engines and blades, Pratt & Whitney + AVIC, in Xian, Shaanxi Province

S-92 helicopter tail/stabilizer, Sikorsky + Changhe Aircraft Industries Corporation (helicopter producer for the People's Liberation Army), in Jingdezhen, Jiangxi Province

Communications, navigation equipment, Rockwell-Collins + China Electronics Technology Avionics, in Chengdu, Sichuan Province

Jet engine components, Pratt & Whitney + Chengdu Engine Group, in Chengdu, Sichuan Province

Hydraulic and fuel systems for the C919, Parker-Hannifin + AVIC, in Nanjing, Jiangsu Province

Environmental control systems, Honeywell + China Research Institute of Aero Accessories, in Nanjing, Jiangsu Province

Turboprop components, Pratt & Whitney (Canada) + China National South Aero-Engine, in Zhuzhou, Hunan Province

Avionics for C919, GE Avionics + AVIC, in Shanghai

Fuel, hydraulics for C919, Eaton + Shanghai Manufacturing, in Shanghai

Weather radar for C919, Rockwell Collins with AVIC, in Wuxi, Jiangsu Province

Auxiliary power units, Honeywell + AVIC, in Nanjing, Jiangsu Province

Electrical systems for the C919, Hamilton Sundstrand +
   AVIC, in Nanjing, Jiangsu Province

Fly-by-wire controls, Honeywell + AVIC, in Xian,
   Shaanxi Province

Landing gear and nacelles, Goodrich + Xian Aircraft, in
   Xian, Shaanxi Province

Engine nacelles, Nexcelle + AVIC, under negotiation

Aluminum structures, Alcoa + COMAC, under
   negotiation

Composite structures, Boeing + AVIC, in Tianjin

There is not much U.S. aerospace technology—civil or
military—that is not in the possession of the companies that
have entered or are entering into joint ventures with AVIC or
its affiliates—whose declared intent is to compete with Boeing
as well as Airbus for market share, and which also designs,
develops, or copies tactical aircraft and bombers for the PLA
air force and navy.

The Chinese, moreover, can certainly expect to obtain access to more technology—much more perhaps—than is contractually to be provided by the joint ventures. One reason is
that joint ventures inherently offer many opportunities for
cyber penetrations, or more physical forms of technological
theft.[7] That the loss of technology may occur in much less
sinister ways, starting with ordinary conversations among fellow professionals, does not reduce its consequences. And it is

also a documented fact that joint ventures facilitate the re-cruitment of agents in place, with U.S. citizens of Chinese origin almost routinely targeted.[8]

To be sure, technological leakage from aerospace joint ventures is merely a subset of the broader diffusion of U.S. technology to China, most of it not misappropriated, of course, but rather contractually transferred by the leading U.S. corporations. It is not their managers' proclivity, and still less their responsibility, to calculate the long-term effects on the overall condition of the U.S. economy of all technological transfers to China. Next-quarter impacts on their own firms is as far as they try to calculate, and there matters rest, given the absence of any broad U.S. industrial policy in that regard.

The great flow of technology transfers to China is in turn merely a subset of the unbalanced U.S.-China economic relationship as a whole, which is beneficial for Americans as consumers, borrowers, and financiers above all, while being harmful to Americans as workers and producers, but which is evidently so entirely beneficial to the Chinese that it shapes the entire "American policy" of the CCP, with the overriding aim of perpetuating that unbalanced economic relationship[9] for as long as possible, or rather until China emerges as the richer and more advanced country.

For that high purpose, to sit through tiresome "strategic and economic dialogues," and even to listen almost politely to futile lectures on human rights or democracy, for that matter, is a small price to pay; and for that high purpose all else must await a more propitious moment, whether it is the forcible annexation of Taiwan or the seizure of the vast ocean areas that China is now claiming in all directions. Tāo guāng yǎng huì ("Hide one's capacities and bide one's time") is a much simpler formulation than Peaceful Rise or Peaceful Development, but serves just as well.

Of that the best evidence is the China policy of the U.S. Treasury, which seeks to perpetuate exactly the same unbalanced economic relationship, in spite of the deindustrialization caused by the chronic trade deficit in manufactured goods. Objectively if not subjectively, the U.S. Treasury, under its current leadership as before, actively favors China's economic growth and technological advancement—having no departmental responsibility, or perceptible concern, for the inevitable relationship between China's overall economic and technological capacity and its resulting military aggrandizement. That is simply not part of the Treasury brief, and there has been no presidential intervention to make it so.

*The Second U.S. China Policy: The State Department Confronts China.* This second China policy is nowadays very vigorously promoted by Secretary of State Hillary Rodham Clinton, with varying degrees of support from her top officials. It certainly values cooperation with China whenever it is forthcoming, but recognizes that it is more often an opponent of the United States, both multilaterally at the UN Security Council and other venues, and bilaterally in its dealings with the United

States itself, its allies, and third parties of U.S. interest, including rogue regimes, both in regard to concrete American interests and also values.

In that regard specifically, matters deteriorated somewhat after 2008, both because of an unexpected recrudescence of repression within China itself, and also because of increased Chinese activism in promoting antidemocratic practices abroad. One very recent example is the Chinese co-sponsorship, with the Pakistan government, of a "media university." Pakistan's minister for information and broadcasting, Dr. Firdous Ashiq Awan, defined its purpose as

> national-interest oriented media training, to change people's perception about Pakistan, and to prepare press attaches sent to other countries to respond to western media propaganda. State interest should be protected at every cost but sometimes, media organizations go beyond limits and cause irreparable loss to the state interest.[10]

Another example, which also illustrates the willingness of the Chinese government to cooperate with rogue regimes, is even more egregious, because it would specifically serve to increase the repressive capacity of a violently repressive regime: the Chinese financing of a "Robert Mugabe School of Intelligence" in Zimbabwe—the one form of educational investment unneeded in that once-flourishing country now despoiled by the very same Robert Mugabe and his minions. The mission of the new school is officially described as "addressing the current global challenges"; unsurprisingly, only "invited candidates" will be enrolled. The curriculum provides for the following disciplines: Cryptology, Linguists, Signals Intelligence Analysts, Human Intelligence Collectors, Military Intelligence (MI) Systems Maintainers and Integrators, Counterintelligence Agents, Imagery Analysts, Common Ground Station (CGS) Analysts, Intelligence Analysts, Signals Collector, and so on, all to be trained by Chinese instructors.[11]

Unlike the U.S. Treasury, whose policies are premised on a product-improved China, which should never be penalized because it is perpetually on the verge of allowing the yuan to rise in value, and to finally enforce its own intellectual property laws, the State Department accepts the continuing reality that makes China different from other non-allies, such as India, for example, and similar to the Russian Federation and Venezuela, for example—to wit: China cooperates with the United States only when its interests demand such cooperation, whereas it habitually opposes the United States whenever its interests allow such opposition. Opposition is the default mode, cooperation is the advertised mode. By contrast, India, for example, often opposes the United States, but it does so each time for some positive reason of its own, good or bad, not merely because it can do so. This, in turn, in the current State Department view, warrants energetic opposition to China whenever it engages in expansionist conduct, although the need to resist the expansion of China's power as such is not yet recognized even as a policy concept, let alone accepted as a policy goal.

Accordingly, the U.S. State Department has reacted very energetically to China's expansionist pressures against Vietnam over the Paracel and Spratly Islands, against Laos, Thailand, and Cambodia by way of dam construction on the upper Mekong River, against Brunei, Malaysia, and the Philippines also over the Spratly Islands, and against Japan through the Chinese claim for the Senkaku Islands and surrounding seas.

Likewise, while Secretary Geithner of the U.S. Treasury, once a student in China and a former China specialist at the profitable firm of Kissinger Associates Inc., has been earnestly convivial at his frequent meetings with Chinese officials,[12] U.S. Secretary of State Hillary Clinton has openly and repeatedly clashed at ASEAN meetings with China's minister of foreign affairs, Yang Jiechi (though he is scarcely her counterpart inasmuch as the Ministry only implements and does not formulate policy).

Among other things, just in the last two years or so, Secretary Clinton has:

- publicly insisted that the Spratly Islands dispute must be managed multilaterally between China and all the affected ASEAN members, and not bilaterally between big China and each "little country"—in Yang Jiechi's words. After flatly refusing the U.S. demand at two ASEAN meetings, after failing to intimidate Vietnam or to persuade the others, the Chinese, as noted above,

finally agreed to multilateral talks on a "Code of
Conduct" in December 2010.

- declared that the Senkaku Islands are fully included in
the 1960 U.S.-Japan Treaty of Mutual Cooperation
and Security, thus rejecting the Chinese claim in
actuality, even though in general principle it is not
U.S. policy to affirm or deny the territorial claims of
other countries.

- initiated in 2009 the U.S.-funded "Lower Mekong
Initiative" with Vietnam, Cambodia, Laos, and Thailand; the qualifier "lower" neatly excluded China and
its quasi ally, Myanmar's then rogue regime.[13] It is all
about water and fish, but interestingly the protagonists
are the respective foreign ministers, not the ministers
of agriculture and fishery. And while the agenda includes everything under the sun—climate change,
infectious disease, education, river management, and
more—there is also a supposedly minor aim that in
reality matters the most: to coordinate responses to the
construction of dams, particularly, but not exclusively
(a nice touch), those being built in China.

- vigorously pursued every possible opportunity to
expand cooperation with India that has any degree of
strategic significance, striving hard to overcome all
manner of bureaucratic, institutional, and cultural
obstacles on both sides, and trying to make the most of

the new opportunities made possible by the U.S.-India
"123 Agreement"[14] for Civil Nuclear Cooperation.

That 123 Agreement was merely a necessary preliminary for
the U.S.-India nuclear activities, but it amounted to a colossal
undertaking in itself, politically, bureaucratically, and diplomatically. It was not indeed one achievement but many:

- Against very intense internal opposition (antiprolifera-
  tors on the U.S. side, autarchy advocates on the Indian
  side), after strenuous negotiations, on July 18, 2005,
  India's prime minister Manmohan Singh and U.S.
  President George W. Bush agreed on a "framework"
  whereby India undertook to physically separate its civil
  and military nuclear facilities and place the former
  under International Atomic Energy Agency (IAEA)
  safeguards.
- The Bush administration for its part had to induce the
  U.S. Congress to amend the Atomic Energy Act of 1954.
- India next had to negotiate an inspection agreement
  with the IAEA, a delicate matter given the concurrence
  of noninspected military activities.
- The United States then had to secure a unique exemp-
  tion for India with the multinational Nuclear Suppliers
  Group (NSG) export-control cartel—not at all easy,
  given that the NSG had been formed in the first place
  at U.S. initiative as a response to India's first nuclear
  test in 1974.

Yet a mere three years and three months from the original Bush-Singh agreement, on October 1, 2008, the U.S. Congress voted its approval of the U.S.-India nuclear cooperation agreement, and on February 2, 2009, the India-IAEA agreement was also finally completed, allowing the newly installed Obama administration to start its own efforts to realize the broader strategic potential that had been opened up, in addition to nuclear cooperation as such.

The removal of restrictions on U.S. arms transactions with India, legally mandated in retaliation by the original 1974 nuclear test, was of course very important but did not remove what still remains the greatest obstacle to U.S. arms sales: the profound incompatibility between the methods, procedures, customs, and ambitions of the Indian state-owned aerospace and defense industry, itself controlled with an extreme degree of centralization by long-serving authoritarian managers and brahminic chief scientists of stupendous arrogance, and ponderous U.S. aerospace and defense corporations, with their strait-laced managers, rigid technologists, and quick-buck salesmen. No two human groups have been more deeply divided by a common language, but for the United States and Indian defense bureaucracies, close competitors for the paralyzing incompatibility prize.

That is why even now the Indian armed forces—which have accumulated decades of anguished dissatisfaction with the infinite delays of India's state-owned industries,[15] and just as many decades of impotent fury at the obdurate refusal of Soviet and now Russian aviation and military industries to supply replacement parts in timely fashion (or even a year after that), and almost as many decades of resentment over the very high costs of actually operating beautiful French fighters—have been unable to equip themselves with the U.S. aircraft and weapons they know and crave, except in a few cases, after agonizingly difficult negotiations. The institutional barriers are formidably resistant. Though there have been some important transactions, no principal or critical weapon system in Indian service is of American origin as yet, as opposed to a mass of Soviet/Russian platforms, some European-designed aircraft, and Israeli avionics and missiles.

But that is not how the U.S.-India arms supply relationship is seen—or at least depicted—in Beijing. This is the version of the steadfastly "leftist" (national-militarist) *Global Times:*

US President Barack Obama's visit to New Delhi in November [2010] may secure $5 billion worth of arms sales. . . . [This] . . . would make the US replace Russia as India's biggest arms supplier . . . [and ] help India curb China's rise. India's shortlist includes *Patriot* defense systems, Boeing mid-air refueling tankers and certain types of howitzers, and the total cost . . . may exceed $10 billion [a 100 percent increase in one paragraph].

. . . [T]alks are underway between Indian and US officials over . . . 10 Boeing C-17 military transports.

> Wang Mingzhi, a military strategist at the PLA Air Force Command College, [said that] . . . Those arms sales will improve ties between Washington and New Delhi, and, intentionally or not, will have the effect of containing China's influence in the region . . . For example, once India gets the C-17 transport aircraft, the mobility of its forces stationed along the border with China will be improved.[16]

Given that the energetic coalition-building of the U.S. State Department—whatever its subjective aims—objectively connects its own "string of pearls" from Japan to India via the Philippines, Indonesia, Vietnam, and Singapore, in a manner that could easily interdict that other reputed "string of pearls" from the harbors of southern China to Port Sudan,[17] it is easy to understand Chinese complaint that U.S. State Department policy is basically unfriendly, that it seeks to "encircle" China, and even acquire the means to cut it off from imports of oil, gas, and other raw materials.

That is, of course, an impossibility, because the United States does not have much influence over China's inland neighbors: the Russian Federation, Mongolia, Kazakhstan, Kyrgyzstan, Tajikistan, and Uzbekistan. These are countries replete with raw material and energy resources, actually or potentially available. And routes through Turkmenistan could in addition provide access to China's sometime quasi ally Iran, and thus to the entire Persian Gulf with its uniquely large hydrocarbon resources. What is true is that the U.S. State Department certainly tries to reinforce the abilities and also the resolve of the countries that have recently been threatened by China, not only verbally but also by way of harassing maneuvers and intrusive patrols, including Japan, the Philippines, Laos, and Vietnam. India, which does not ask for U.S. military reassurance or diplomatic support, also has come under Chinese pressure because of the development of logistic infrastructures in Tibet, the qualitative enhancement of its garrisons, and a great deal of aggressive patrolling of the Indian-held border of Arunachal Pradesh, which the Chinese claim as "South Tibet" (Zàngnán).

Moreover, while the U.S. Treasury criticizes China only in the mildest and most inoffensive terms, and only when China's misconduct is most blatant (as in government procurement protectionism), under Secretary Clinton especially the U.S. State Department has been forthright in criticizing Chinese practices that offend American values. For example, at the very time when Treasury Secretary Geithner was even more effusive than usual, and she was set to meet her Chinese counterparts for the aforementioned U.S.-China strategic and economic dialogue of 2011, Clinton stated in an interview:[18]

> We do business with a lot of countries whose economic systems or political systems are not ones we would design. . . . But we don't walk away from dealing with

China because we think they have a deplorable human rights record.

Interviewer Jeffrey Goldberg: And (the Chinese) are acting very scared right now, in fact.

Clinton: Well, they are. They're worried, and they are trying to stop history, which is a fool's errand. They cannot do it. But they're going to hold it off as long as possible.

The U.S. State Department policy for China has therefore combined three diverse lines of conduct in a manner that reconciles a broad range of U.S. interests:

- cooperation, of which there is a great deal between U.S. and Chinese governmental organizations for a great variety of purposes, from the harmonization of obscure technical regulations to multilateral counterproliferation initiatives—so much so that some in the State Department would prefer to emphasize the cooperative aspect almost exclusively;

- containment, achieved by the prompt and persuasive reassurance of China's neighbors—whether they are treaty allies or not—when they come under pressure, to enable them to withstand Chinese demands; and

- mostly polite but insistent ideological warfare against the CCP regime, by the frequent invocation of human rights, of political rights on occasion, and of the cultural-

233

THE THREE CHINA POLICIES OF THE UNITED STATES

religious if not national rights of the Tibetans, and in some degree of the Uyghurs also (the Mongols of Inner Mongolia may be next); and by intermittent demands for the liberation of high-profile imprisoned dissidents.

By the end of 2011, however, there was a perceptible and very deliberate hardening in the State Department's China policy, which was described and explained in considerable detail by Secretary Clinton in a programmatic article under the revealing title "America's Pacific Century," better understood if the first word is read in italics.[19] The key word, however, was "pivot," as in America's turning away from costly and arguably futile warfare in the nullity of Afghanistan and the stagnant Middle East, to the dynamic world of Asia that starts just east of it in India. Inevitably, the speech attracted much attention in Beijing, and also much criticism of course, not only there but also from American skeptics, who noted the reluctance to abandon Afghanistan to its inevitable fate sooner rather than later.

Although there was much in the article about U.S.-Chinese cooperation, as indeed there is in reality and in very many fields, those in Beijing who read the article as introducing a sharper policy focus on China's expansive tendencies were quite right. That was made perfectly evident by its inclusion of a passage that welcomed "progress on the Trans-Pacific Partnership (TPP), which will bring together economies from across the Pacific—developed and developing alike—into a single trading community"—the point being that China is not part of the TPP. Had it not been accompanied by President Obama's announcement of the new U.S. base in Darwin, Australia—he was there to inaugurate it in person by November 17, 2011—Clinton's "pivot" statement might have been less resonant; indeed, it might even have been discounted as mere political posturing by a secretary of state who still has a political future. As it was, a policy of containment was made official for the first time, but that is not the same thing as a policy of confrontation, for it is purely reactive, not active, and indeed passive if China itself does not act in a destabilizing manner. Unfortunately, rapid military growth is destabilizing in itself.

It is a measure of the remaining U.S. advantage in the overall balance of power as most broadly defined that the U.S. State Department and indeed the U.S. government as a whole can still pursue simultaneously both policies of cooperation and policies of containment. If China were in a stronger position—as indeed it already is in many other bilateral relationships, not only with mendicants but also with South Korea, for example—the United States would be forced to choose between cooperation and containment, between cooperation and the affirmation of its values.

A ready measure of Chinese progress in imposing its own preferences in the matter of values is the list of countries that refuse entry to the "Dalai," as the Chinese call him to deny him priestly status—a rather long list that includes devoutly Buddhist (albeit not Tantric) Thailand, as well as South Korea. Another measure of Chinese progress in imposing its own conception of CCP-directed harmony upon the world emerged from the December 2010 Liu Xiaobo Nobel Peace Prize award ceremony struggle already mentioned. And it definitely was a real struggle for the Chinese Foreign Ministry, whose diplomats were forced to work overtime in dozens of capitals around the world. As mentioned, out of sixty-five resident ambassadors or deputy chiefs of mission in Oslo (nonresident envoys are not invited), China scored itself, Russia, Kazakhstan, Tunisia (as then governed), Saudi Arabia, Pakistan (U.S.-funded but never with the United States if it can help it), Iraq (unpunished by the United States), Iran, Vietnam (VCP-CCP solidarity), Afghanistan (unpunished), Venezuela, Egypt (another unpunished aid recipient), Sudan, Cuba, and Morocco (an accurate reflection of its dictatorial reality behind the monarchical claptrap). On the other hand, Liu Xiaobo and the cause of human rights at all costs scored forty-six rather more important countries, including Argentina, Bosnia and Herzegovina, Brazil, Chile, Colombia, Costa Rica, Guatemala, India, Indonesia, Israel, Japan, Republic of Korea, Philippines, Serbia, South Africa, Sri Lanka, Thailand, Turkey, and the Ukraine, in addition to all European Union members.

The altogether greater Chinese objective, however, is not to intimidate the likes of Sri Lanka or to bribe Guatemala over an Oslo ceremony but rather to induce the United States to accept a genuine "G-2" parity that would include "mutual respect," whereby neither side would criticize the political system of the other, or provide aid or comfort for local dissidents.

To be sure, any U.S.-China parity would be an interim condition on the way to China's superiority in all things, when unreciprocated respect would be demanded, in addition to more tangible bounties, no doubt.

A G-2 complete with parity in values is certainly recognized as a very long-term objective by CCP leaders, but for a tantalizing season it seemed very near, indeed almost achieved. During the worst "free fall" phase of the 2009 financial crisis, when the newly installed Obama administration was urgently soliciting Chinese cooperation in increasing aggregate demand by spending money as quickly as possible on public works (successfully: I myself saw many thousands at work on new Yunnan roads a few months later), there was a definite desistance on the issue of human rights. In a 2009 "Strategic and Economic Dialogue" press briefing, when Secretary Clinton was pressed on the subject, she responded in a manner revealingly oblique: "We obviously had some very good exchanges between ourselves and the Chinese about their perspective and ours, but it was certainly a matter of great interest and focus."[20]

The moment passed, but not without consequences in the interim: it was the 2008–2009 financial crisis that unleashed China's triumphalism with its assertions of imminent or at least inevitable superiority, and also intensified its territorial assertiveness in word and deed.

As it turned out, it was all counterproductively premature for China, for it revealed the menace behind the irenic mask of

"Peaceful Rise," inducing reactions as diverse as Japan's retreat from the Ozawa flirtation with Beijing, Australian coalition-building, Indian bilateral initiatives with several of China's neighbors starting with the Russian Federation (via military joint ventures inter alia), Vietnam's convergence with the United States as well as India, the Philippine reversal on U.S. military visitations, and most strikingly, Myanmar's opening to democracy and the West, in preference to China's embrace.

But this process will not suffice if there is no interruption in China's uniquely high growth rates. A China that can grow at 9 percent per year for a few more decades, and which can also keep allocating a steady portion of its resources to the accumulation of power in all its forms, would no longer need to be aggressive, or even assertive, to impose its will on almost all the countries around it, thereby magnifying its own power still more.

*The Third U.S. China Policy: The Department of Defense.* As already mentioned in particular cases in regard to naval visits especially, the U.S. Department of Defense as a whole and the armed forces severally have been very effective since 2010 in supporting the increasingly explicit "containment" dimension of the State Department's overall China policy.

Whether through the low-key comings and goings of the International Military Education and Training (IMET) program of the Defense Cooperation Agency, the scarcely more visible Air Force joint exercises such as the annual "Commando

Sling" with the Republic of Singapore Air Force at Paya Lebar air force base (which, incidentally, serves year-round for USAF bed-down when needed), or the spectacular apparitions of aircraft carriers with their panoply of escorting warships—the U.S. armed forces complement the occasional statements and encounters of American diplomacy with their much more continuous connections: IMET, which often creates lifelong bonds, regular annual exercises, the ship visits, and permanent basing in some cases.

None of this is of much help with countries captive to a thoroughly hostile ideology (as with Pakistan's virulent forms of Islam), but the U.S. armed forces otherwise serve to put the substance of security guarantees into alliance relationships. And in the absence of formal alliance arrangements, their practiced habits of liaison and cooperation with local armed forces can almost suffice to replace them, if there is a political entente as well. That allows very satisfactory cooperation with such valuable "non-allies" as Vietnam and Indonesia.

Even aside from the actualities of containment in Asia, which are in any case localized and may also be transitory, for the Defense Department as a whole and for the U.S. Air Force and Navy more decidedly, China has unambiguously become the prospective "Main Enemy," at least for planning and procurement purposes. While the "global war on terror" inevitably sinks below the horizon because the vast number of prospective enemies—anyone, anywhere, inflamed by jihad— is offset by their impotence but for rare exceptions, China's military aggrandizement is by far the greater and entirely more consequential phenomenon.

Accordingly, the acquisition of major new U.S. weapons is increasingly justified by China-oriented missions or, much more often, simply as a competitive response to the anticipated, if not actual, development of Chinese weapons. Hence, for example, the U.S. Air Force already makes much of the arrival of the *Chengdu J-20 Jiān èr shí* ("Annihilator Twenty") even though it remains uncertain if it is a true prototype that could soon be produced in numbers or just a technology demonstrator for a future heavyweight, long-range, stealthy fighter-bomber of the *F-22* class that might still be ten or fifteen years away from the *start* of production, let alone an initial operational capability. For one thing, there is no evidence that the Shenyang Aero-Engine Research Institute can develop reasonably efficient and reasonably reliable engines powerful enough for a 70,000- to 80,000-pound aircraft such as the *J-20* (though that might change with the innovations brought to China by the General Electric and Pratt & Whitney engine-making joint ventures already mentioned).

Unsurprisingly, U.S. military services under severe budget pressures are inclined to anticipate Chinese capabilities that might not be deployed for a very long time, and to exaggerate greatly the strength of the PLA's forces already in being. For one thing, they still do not have a joint forces command above the military region level, that is, no unity of command at the national level, no instantaneous ability to concentrate the forces of different military regions, or even to coordinate their actions. That makes no sense at all operationally, but it is a very sensible arrangement for the unelected leaders of the CCP, who want to command the soldiers instead of being dominated by them.

Yet the U.S. military are right to take China if not today's PLA very seriously, just as the Air Force is fundamentally right to take the *J-20* seriously, and the Navy too is right in taking seriously the Chinese navy's submarine and aircraft-carrier ambitions. With the economy providing rapidly increasing resources, China's entire scientific and technological superstructure is growing both quantitatively and qualitatively, and that in turn is providing an expanding base for military innovation in *every* sector and even in every subsector. For it is a defining aspect of the quasi-anarchical and internally highly competitive Chinese system that every branch of every service, and every paramilitary force too, vigorously seeks more resources for its own advancement and expansion, duly obtaining them in most cases. The result is an expanding torrent of more and technologically more advanced weapons and platforms.

In addition to their active role in supporting the containment of low-intensity Chinese threats against the maritime possessions of American allies, quasi allies, and new or renewed friends, the U.S. armed forces have long had, and of course still have, the mission of deterring high-intensity Chinese military threats. Of these, the least improbable is, of course, the peri- odically renewed threat to invade Taiwan or otherwise subject it by force—"unification," in PRC parlance.

*Taiwan.* For a long time now, it has been thoroughly under- stood within the higher leadership of the CCP that the overt use of force against Taiwan could trigger not merely a U.S. military response that would carry its own dangers of escala- tion, even to the nuclear level just possibly, but also something altogether more frightening because it would be so much more probable: the interruption of trade with the United States, Japan, and other like-minded countries. Such an interruption could be imposed almost instantaneously, but it might be fully lifted only after a long interval (the July 1989 interruption of military trade still remains in effect). Worse still for China, if there were stiff resistance in Taiwan with serious combat and many civilian deaths, import restrictions or prohibitions could be supplemented by the denial of raw material shipments to China, including oil (Australian raw material shipments would certainly stop immediately).

That is why the CCP leaders limited themselves to menac- ing missile deployments, some edgy aerial patrolling, and a great many verbal threats even when the Taiwan government was headed by the declaredly separatist President Chen Shui- bian, now inmate 1020 in the Taipei prison in Gueishan, Taoyuan County. The present role of Taiwan in CCP policy in general, and in military policy specifically, is precisely defined in "China's National Defense in 2010" issued March 2011 by the Information Office of the State Council.[21]

Section I, "The Security Situation," reads:

> The two sides of the Taiwan Strait are destined to ultimate reunification in the course of the great rejuvenation of the Chinese nation. It is the *responsibility of the Chinese people on both sides* of the Straits to work hand in hand to end the history of hostility, and to avoid repeating the history of armed conflict between fellow countrymen. The two sides should take a positive attitude toward the future, and strive to create favorable conditions *to gradually resolve, through consultation on an equal footing*, both issues inherited from the past and new ones that emerge in the development of cross-Strait relations. The two sides may discuss political relations in the special situation that China is not yet reunified in a pragmatic manner. *The two sides* can hold contacts and exchanges on military issues at an appropriate time *and talk about a military security mechanism of mutual trust*, in a bid to act together to adopt measures to *further stabilize* cross-Strait relations and ease concerns regarding military security. *The two sides* should hold consultations on the basis of upholding the one-China principle to formally end hostilities and reach a *peace agreement*. [Italics added]

All this refers back to the KMT-CCP civil war—the two sides must negotiate an end to fratricidal conflict. Moreover, with

Han on both sides a fundamental equality obtains that over-rides the balance of power. Given the need to "hold consultations" to prepare the opportunity to "talk about a military security mechanism of mutual trust" in order to "gradually resolve . . . ," there is no great urgency either. Further, given that the two sides are now "on an equal footing," as between the KMT and CCP, that is (not with Taiwan's native Minnanhua-speaking southern barbarians), it is natural that there are armed forces on both sides, which therefore remain unmentioned.

For the time being, it seems that the U.S. military mission of deterring and, if need be, repelling an attack on Taiwan, howsoever demanding, is not likely to be tested. More broadly, although today's China is similar to post-1890 Germany, insofar as it is advancing successfully in all peaceful endeavors yet is bent on pointless military aggrandizement accentuated by aggressive claims over inconsequential islets and shoals,[22] there is no 1914 end to the story in war, destruction, and defeat, as already noted. Instead of a slide toward war, there is only the self-defeating process whereby China is uniting powers large and small against it, explicitly to contain its future strength. There is no such endgame for an excessively successful China as there was for excessively successful Germany, because that would require large-scale, sustained warfare, which is simply impossible in the presence of nuclear weapons—the irremovably extant court of appeal against an adverse verdict in the lower court of non-nuclear warfare. Because nuclear weapons cannot reliably inhibit any and all armed conflict between nuclear-armed powers—incidents could take place, and they could escalate into localized combat—military strength retains its importance between nuclear powers. But it can only ensure a local escalation dominance, not the strategic outcome.

Moreover, there is no "Star Wars" solution, either—China cannot be undone by overstressing its technological capacity. Whatever else the U.S. Defense Department might achieve by acquiring weapons expressly to compete with Chinese weapons, or more accurately, to greatly exceed them in capacity, it cannot possibly achieve the great result that was achieved by competing technologically with the Soviet Union in the later 1970s and 1980s. In attempting to keep up with American military innovation, the Soviet Union allocated to that purpose an ever greater proportion of the scarce high-technology resources of an increasingly stagnant economy. As they were palpably falling behind more and more, Soviet leaders under Gorbachev finally attempted the economic restructuring launched as Perestroika, which instead resulted in the disintegration of the planned economy, which in turn undid the entire Soviet system.

By contrast, in the present competition it is not the Chinese economy that is relatively stagnant but rather the U.S. economy, for its highest sustainable growth rate cannot exceed 4 percent or so, while the Chinese economy is set to grow at least twice as fast for many years ahead, aside from temporary disruptions.

Hence, there is nothing within the jurisdiction of the Department of Defense—neither its necessary but insufficient support of containment, nor devastation by war, or a "Star

Wars" technological offensive—that can stop the processes that even now are eroding the material base of American hegemony and adding to the material base of China's power. To put it crudely, that task is above its pay grade. That is true in spades of the recently introduced "Air-Sea Battle" concept, which is mostly about achieving even more "jointness," especially between the U.S. Navy and the U.S. Air Force to allow them to combine their forces in combat more synergistically. That makes this a tactical or at most an operational-level concept, that is, a set of desired modalities for fighting battles more effectively with both aircraft and warships, and all their diverse sensors and weapons. Yet a special office under a three-star officer has been established to promote the concept, and simply because it is specifying a theater of war of vast dimensions, and huge distances, that is, the Pacific rather than the Atlantic, the function of this new Air-Sea Battle Office has been elevated to the strategic level, or at least the theater-strategic level, one notch below national strategy but much above mere operations or tactics. Moreover, there is a great deal of emphasis on power-multiplying ultra-advanced technologies, ultra-long-range forces, unmanned systems of global range, and so on.

All this is rather unfortunate, because when allies old and new are briefed by the new office they are more alarmed than reassured. First, they worry that "long-range" might mean that U.S. forces will be pulled back to Guam or even Australia, leaving them exposed without the U.S. garrisons now in place, in Japan notably. Second, they fear that talk of the "Air-Sea

Battle" implies a readiness to escalate in response to Chinese intrusions, or worse, an inability to contain them without escalating the confrontation into an outright battle. Third, less advanced but still very willing allies under Chinese maritime pressure do not see how they could contribute usefully to "Air-Sea Battle" forces that are so terribly high-tech; and yet, in defending against naval intrusions amid shoals, reefs, and rocks, small boats and even coastal artillery might be very effective.

Mostly the Air-Sea Battle talk is unfortunate because it is a very long way from geo-economic containment, all the more effective when costly military efforts are minimized rather than maximized.

# CHAPTER TWENTY-TWO

# Conclusions and Predictions

*The entire argument* here presented rests on certain assumed continuities. But if China's economy stops growing rapidly, there will be no global adversarial reaction to China geo-economically. And if the CCP abandons the pursuit of military aggrandizement, or if its power wanes, there will be no geo-political reaction, even if China's growth remains rapid.

The first assumption is that China's economy will continue to grow very rapidly, temporary disruptions aside—that is, at an annual rate of 8 percent or more. That is, very much less than the rate recorded in the last pre-crisis year (2007), but still twice as high as the highest sustainable growth rate for the U.S. economy, let alone the lower rates of recent years.

The Chinese economy, however, could slow down for any number of reasons, including, for example, the inordinate accumulation of local government debt (40 percent of China's gross domestic product, or perhaps 50 percent). Its growth cannot simply continue, and once it is slowed down, that will necessarily depress the construction and infrastructure sectors, significantly reducing overall growth, other things being equal. Accelerating inflation could be another impediment, for it would force the People's Bank of China to restrict commercial lending, reducing domestic demand, and therefore growth.

More generally, in the natural evolution of originally backward economies that take off, acceleration toward very fast growth is eventually followed by a gradual deceleration, typically because the supply of previously unemployed and underemployed labor from the countryside diminishes. As of now, semi-skilled and even unskilled labor shortages in heavily industrialized areas are causing wage-push inflation and impeding the continuation of rapid growth.

More simply, insofar as China's growth continues to derive disproportionately from exports—because of very high savings rates that restrict domestic consumer demand—9 percent annual rates cannot long persist if the major export markets are growing much more slowly, or not at all.

China's rapid growth can also be impeded by the environmental dysfunctions generated by that very growth. These include extremes of air pollution that can be sufficiently intolerable to prevent the further expansion of especially polluting industries in metropolitan areas, or even to force the closure of specific processes or entire plants. When the authorities do not intervene, popular protests can erupt, occasionally on a sufficient scale and with sufficient intensity to force the closing of especially polluting plants, given the diminishing propensity of the regime to suppress Han agitations with unrestrained force (the protests of ethnic minorities, by contrast, are still repressed with much brutality). That is what happened in the relatively high-income, rather pleasant, and relatively unpolluted port city of Dalian, which incorporates what is left of both historic Port Arthur and Japanese Dairen, in August 2011. Mass protests by more than 10,000 demonstrators who were demanding the removal of a smelly petrochemical plant for P-xylene, an aromatic believed to be carcinogenic, were initially contained with standard riot-control tactics. But when the number of demonstrators increased to as many as 50,000 or even more, the authorities had to choose between violent, even lethal tactics or capitulation, and preferred the latter.[1] Dalian is no doubt better off for it, but the relocation of the P-xylene plant has an inevitable opportunity cost that diminishes China's overall economic capacity. More important, the episode—a distinct humiliation for the authorities—no doubt taught other local and provincial officials in urban areas across China to be more restrictive when it comes to visibly polluting industries, and that too has its opportunity costs that are bound to become much larger in the long run. Where there is muck there is money, while clean skies can slow growth.

Air that is at least breathable without immediate injury, if not more than that, is one ineluctable necessity, and a minimally adequate supply of drinkable water is another. Its supply too is becoming increasingly expensive, as more accessible natural sources are locally exhausted because of urban population growth compounded by the increasing consumption rates that come with rising living (and bathing) standards, as well as industrial demand. To cite a current example, the city of Tianjin, a vast metropolitan area, must increasingly rely on water from the sea, for which purpose a combined coal-fired generating and desalinization plant imported from Israel was completed in October 2011 at a cost of some 26 billion yuan, US$4 billion.[2] It is a very large plant by world standards, but except in the Persian Gulf where natural gas, if not oil, is still virtually a free good, desalinization is still too expensive for public supply to any but relatively small, relatively high-income populations, in such places as Caribbean tourist destinations and Israel. But the Tianjin conurbation has 13 million people, yet its authorities have no choice but to supply desalinated water that costs twice what it sells for at the current city tariff (which itself cannot be increased without risking protests). Moreover, in addition to prior natural supplies and the extensive use of recycled water, Tianjin will need several more desalinization plants for a cost of more than US$20 billion.

Such expenditures do not depress the gross national product; indeed, they increase it. But when cheap natural water is replaced by expensively desalinated water, there is again a real opportunity cost, which is paid for by giving up something else, such as private saving or consumption, or perhaps productive investment, if not the government's military expenditure. Even without the thousands of well-funded environmental groups that pursue yet more funding by loudly opposing any and all forms of extractive, industrial, or infrastructural activity across the Western world, it is certain that environmental impediments of one sort or another will increasingly constrain China's growth as well. In any case, slow growth would invalidate the basic premise, for a slow-growing China would not evoke resistance from its neighbors and global peers.

The central political assumption on which this book is based is also fallible: the presumption that the CCP will remain in firm control of China, notwithstanding all manner of threats to the stability of the regime, large, small, and of unknown dimensions, whether old, new, or barely formed. There is absolutely no point in speculating as to the probabilities of each: threats deemed probable are more likely to be successfully anticipated and energetically repressed, so that it is the unexpected, improbable threats that are more dangerous for dictatorships. One example suffices: the Tunisian dictatorship of Zayn al-'Ābidīn bin 'Alī that for some twenty-three years efficiently repressed all attempts at organized opposition, was overthrown in less than a month between December 16, 2010, and January 14, 2011, by wholly spontaneous riots sparked by a street fruit seller who set himself on fire to protest his harassment by a female municipal official and her minions. (Ironically, his family deemed it appropriate to explain that his act was prompted by the humiliation of being ill-treated by a mere female—a reflection of common Muslim views about the advancement of women that was energetically promoted by the bin 'Alī regime, one of its saving graces in Western eyes.)

It is such unpredictable turns of fate that are the bane of even the seemingly most solid and well-structured dictatorships, which are indeed more apt to finally fall because of their few virtues rather than their many defects, as with land reform in the shah's Iran that mortally antagonized landowning clerics, or Gorbachev's attempt to modernize the Soviet Communist Party's gerontocracy, which might well have lasted for decades longer under a less energetic, less intelligent, and especially less innovative chief.

Without, therefore, any attempt at ranking them, one can only enumerate the most obvious threats to the persistence of the CCP regime. No doubt there are many more, and perhaps it is a threat now not even imaginable that might prove to be the most dangerous:

- The increasing social tensions generated by ever-more extreme income and wealth inequalities in a country that is inconveniently stuck with an egalitarian official ideology.
- The frequent riots against local government authorities, provoked by land expropriations above all, among other varieties of official misconduct. That they number in the hundreds every day, that some are violent enough to feature the burning of police cars, are things less significant than the inherent potential of any one riot to energize many more rioters nearby or even far away, because its repression was too harsh, or because it was

not harsh enough, or merely because of happenstance.
In a contrary vein, there are even protests against
police actions aimed at locally popular or influential
criminal gangs.[3]

- Ethnic unrest with a definitely national and therefore
political character, now also manifest at times in the
Inner Mongolian Autonomous Region, as well as in the
Xinjiang Uyghur Autonomous Region, the Tibetan
Autonomous Region, and the Tibetan-inhabited parts
of Qinghai and Sichuan, if not yet Yunnan; and the
possible unrest of the Muslim Hui, now seemingly
tranquil but with a very violent past of harsh repression
that evoked widespread and very destructive rebellions
in parts of Qinghai, Gansu, Shaanxi, and Yunnan in
1862–1877 and again in 1885–1886.

- The much broader threat to the morale and cohesion of
the CCP itself, that arises from the ideological bank-
ruptcy of a nominally Communist regime very largely
dedicated to the advancement of Capitalism. The loss
of a once powerfully motivating ideology was highlighted rather than diminished by now abandoned
attempts to replace the ideological legitimacy lost by
the regime with the décor and props of Maoism, by way
of flag-waving processions, mass choral singing of
Party hymns, and tiresome commemoration ceremo-
nies. None could finally persuade anyone to serve the

CCP without businesslike recompense. (Bo Xilai, Politburo member, former Minister and former Party boss of the Chongqing metropolis of some 28 million people, gained fame as the purveyor of such futile spectacles, before his downfall in scandal.)[4] In the absence of a motivating ideology, it must be personal ambitions that power the CCP, as with any other nonideological organization. Its problem is the prevalence of material rather than purely power-seeking political ambitions, and the resulting corruption that erodes the party's legitimacy, as also its cohesion.

- Then there is the broadest of all forces acting against the regime: the ever-increasing disaffection of the better educated in the population, who aspire to the freedoms of their global peers made familiar by new and old forms of communication. The Internet can be filtered automatically at little cost, or simply shut down, but even conscientiously watchful and indefatigable censors cannot preserve Chinese readers from the ideological contamination of books. They can work to exclude the books of identified dissidents and declared opponents from bookshops, they can censor books that address politics directly, but they cannot possibly keep out the ultimately more deeply subversive novels of Conrad, Dickens, or Manzoni to name a few, nor ostensibly apolitical Chinese novels such as the recent

best-seller *Láng Túténg* (Englished as "Wolf Totem")
by Lü Jiamin writing under the pseudonym Jiang Rong,
whose patriotic final paean cannot undo what goes
before—a picturesque demolition set in Inner Mongolia
of the herdlike collectivism favored by the CCP that is
contrasted to the teamwork that individualism allows.
Visiting the Xidan bookshop that occupies its own large
building on Chang'an Avenue in the heart of Beijing,
one sees many "objectively" subversive books on the
shelves, whose impact is less immediate but certainly
far more profound than tweets, or mini-blogs.

China's rulers and their security officials are themselves
far from confident in the stability of their rule, judging by
their hysterical overreaction to the faint threat of a social-
media "Jasmine revolution" in the spring of 2011. Perhaps they
are just being prudently overcautious, but perhaps they are
better informed about the fragility of their rule than outside
observers.

Finally, this book assumes that, for whatever reason, the
CCP leadership will continue to increase overall military and
related expenditures[5] during the years ahead, in step with China's economic growth, which is itself assumed to remain very
rapid. For the time being, all available information confirms
this assumption as well, but then all the available information
is either retroactive or declaratory. It is theoretically possible

that the proportion of public funds allocated to military and related expenditures will be greatly reduced—for example, to implement announced plans for publicly funded health care and minimum retirement pensions.

*Conclusions.* It is from these possibly fragile assumptions that this book proceeds to its findings.

The first is that because of its inherent magnitude, quite independently of China's conduct on the regional and international scene, the very rapid growth in its economic capacity and military investment must evoke adversarial reactions, in accordance with the logic of strategy.

Other things being equal, when a state of China's magnitude pursues rapid military growth, unless the resulting shift in the power-balance passes the culminating point of resistance inducing the acceptance of some form of subjection, it causes a general realignment of forces against it, as former allies retreat into a watchful neutrality, former neutrals become adversaries, and adversaries old and new coalesce in formal or informal alliances against the excessively risen power.

The governments of nearby states that fear for their very independence, the governments of more secure states that are nevertheless unwilling to accept the rising international authority of a China that remains authoritarian in its own governance (as in the case of Australia, for example), and the governments of the United States, the Russian Federation, and

India—that seek to resist the long-term emergence of a global Chinese hegemony—are all now reacting to the rise of China with self-strengthening measures, including some increase in relevant military capabilities, but mostly by coalescing against China in various pairings and combinations. (The American and Russian governments are not converging to be sure, but each is definitely converging with India, a functional substitute in some degree.)

These reactions, which express the very logic of strategy, ensure in themselves that China cannot *concurrently* increase its military strength and also its diplomatic or, more broadly, its political influence, as we have seen. Unless and until the rise in China's relative power as compared to each of its weaker neighbors passes beyond the relevant tipping point, to impose the acceptance of subjection in some form, increases in China's relative military strength must continue to increase resistance to its political influence and thus reduce it, as its potential targets find allies and form coalitions.

These inevitable reactions to the objective reality of rapidly increasing power have been greatly augmented, since 2008 especially, by the variously arrogant, provocative, or even threatening words and deeds that have emanated from the many different components of the Chinese state that operate internationally in some way. They range from the very summit of power, the Foreign Affairs Leading Small Group of the CCP, Zhōngyāng Wàishì Gōngzuò Lǐngdǎo Xiǎozǔ, which supervises the Foreign Ministry, among other things, down to the China Maritime Surveillance (CMS) organization, Zhongguo Haijian of the State Oceanic Administration, which operates perhaps the most actively provocative of China's paramilitary fleets, with numerous other ministries, armed forces, and state-owned enterprises in between.

Individually, each component of the Chinese state that operates internationally is purposeful enough in pursuing its own institutional objectives, but the overall effect is frequently contradictory and damaging to China's overall interests, by evoking hostile reactions,[6] as in the cases briefly discussed above of Japan, Vietnam, Mongolia, Indonesia, and the Philippines.

Aside from all the countries threatened by China's maximalist maritime claims, and India, whose land borders are contested, Chinese influence has also diminished elsewhere in the world, in spite of the steadily rising importance of the Chinese economy and its very real benefits, as countries as varied as Australia and Myanmar have acted to resist Chinese pressures, often by seeking closer relations with the United States, but also with the Russian Federation. Only in South Korea has Chinese influence increased instead of declining, not least because of a South Korean cultural predisposition to servility toward China and the Chinese. In this, as noted, South Korea is the polar opposite of Vietnam, whose own political culture is especially refractory to Chinese influence, notwithstanding the sometimes effusive interparty relations of their respective communist parties.

China's diplomatic setbacks in the region that should be its primary sphere of influence are especially remarkable because of the ever-rising importance of its trade, including imports as well as exports, investment, and, lately, tourism, on an ever larger scale globally to be sure, but more especially in Asia. It has been argued above that this failure is not due to chance errors or individual failures, but instead derives from a deeply rooted strategic culture that is both intellectually seductive and truly dysfunctional. Its harmful consequences have marked the historical experiences of the Han nation, supremely accomplished in generating wealth and culture from earth and water by hard work and wonderful skill, but exceptionally autistic in relating to the non-Han, and therefore unsuccessful in contending with them whether by diplomacy or by force. Nor is this culture at all appropriate for the fluid conduct of interstate relations among formal equals, as opposed to the management of a China-centered tributary system.

These disabilities are compounded by delusions of supreme strategic wisdom vouchsafed by ancient texts—delusions that are sometimes reinforced by innocent or meretricious foreigners,[7] and that are remarkably resistant to the historical record. For two-thirds of the last thousand years and more, the text-possessing Han were ruled by small numbers of materially much less advanced non-Han who defeated and conquered them, because their intracultural little stratagems were swept aside by synergistic combinations of force and diplomacy—the very thing absent in recent Chinese conduct as well.

*Predictions.* Even when its current and reputedly weak leader changes, if the CCP's power base remains the same, the Chinese state will continue to pursue military aggrandizement at a rate comparable to the country's economic growth, or very rapidly at any rate, while concurrently trying to advance its vast maritime claims in a threatening manner. It will also engage in periodic acts of repression that will remind the world that China is ruled by a self-appointed authoritarian party elite, not subject to any rule of law.

The resulting adversarial reactions, which express the logic of strategy by way of self-strengthening or coalescence, are already depriving China's government of much of the prestige and influence that should naturally derive from its great economic accomplishments, as well as its control of vast foreign-currency reserves, of access to rapidly expanding Chinese markets. Even the countries most dependent on China's economy are nevertheless openly acting against its desires, with only a few exceptions, of which South Korea is the most important.

The measure of China's strategic failure is the risen influence of the United States across East Asia and beyond it, as interrupted or eroding alliances have been revived with the Philippines and Japan notably, and embryonic alliance-like connections have emerged with India to some extent, Indonesia, and Vietnam, with which a formal military cooperation memorandum of understanding was signed on September 19, 2011.[8] With the addition of Australia and Singapore, with which the solidity of the alliance was never in question, those countries alone are a substantial counterpoise to China's current and imminent military strength. Certainly only China's military growth and threatening conduct explain the slow, difficult, contested, yet relentlessly advancing strategic cooperation between the United States and India.

It is remarkable how ineffective the Chinese have been in countering the territorial-security anxieties that prevent a rapprochement with India. In January 2012, the fifteenth round of talks was held at the highest subpolitical level ("Special Representative"), with China represented by Dai Bingguo, in charge of foreign affairs for the State Council, and as such the highest governmental authority on the subject, outranking the foreign minister. In one more initiative to reduce border tensions, a "Working Mechanism for Consultation and Coordination on India-China Border Affairs" was established to link in real time the two foreign ministries in responding to reported intrusions across the "Line of Actual Control"—which is itself in dispute, however. But hard-won progress in the inter-diplomatic dialogue, in which officials on both sides were sincerely engaged by all accounts, was nullified by an *increase* in Indian-reported Chinese intrusions, from some 200 in the year 2010 to some 300 in the year 2011—and the upward trend seemingly continues still.[9] The concrete results are manifest, not in India's de-

clared foreign policy, which continues to favor improved relations with China, but in its defense policy, now characterized
by ever-increasing spending on both domestic and imported
armaments increasingly aimed at China rather than Pakistan.
Objectively, this impacts on the overall correlation of forces
faced by China.

Moreover, the coalescence under way to respond to China's
rising strength is also unfolding bilaterally even without the
United States at either end—yet still in ways inherently beneficial for U.S. security interests. For example, while Vietnam is
seeking antisubmarine patrol aircraft from the West, and is
now choosing between American and European-made mod-
els,[10] it has also ordered six Russian Project 636 *Varshavyanka*
(or "Kilo class") diesel-electric antisubmarine submarines—
China's own largest submarine base is in Hainan Island, less
than 200 miles off Vietnam's nearest coast. These will be Vietnam's first full-scale submarines, hence the training needed to
work up the boats will have to start from zero. In another new
pairing, on September 16, 2011, an Indian delegation led by
Defense Secretary Shashikant Sharma agreed to provide slots
for Vietnamese officers at the Indian Navy's *INS Satavahana*
submarine training establishment in Vishakapatnam.[11] This is
a service that the United States could not possibly have provided, because the U.S. Navy operates no diesel-electric submarines at all, whereas the Indians by contrast have Soviet
Kilo-class boats of their own. In partial exchange, among other

mutual favors, the Indian Navy will have the use of berthing facilities in Vietnamese naval ports.

The parallel emergence of strategic cooperation between the Philippines and Vietnam, furthered by regular intermin- isterial meetings,[12] has a very limited scope militarily, because the Philippine armed forces lack even basic combat capabilities; but it is of diplomatic significance, because it resolves the po- tential problem of overlapping claims on the Spratly archipel- ago that could have opened the way for Chinese wedge tactics.

Further anti-China pairings are emerging between the many parties involved from Central Asia to Japan. None but the U.S.-Japan and the U.S.-Australia alliances can be described as solid compacts between strong parties, yet all serve in their to- tality to Gulliverize China. The resulting benefits to the United States may be unintended and may even be unwanted (as, for instance, with Russia's supply of combat aircraft to Vietnam), but they are very real all the same.

For that reason also, and more specifically because of base facilities provided by allies old and new, the threat potential generated by China's military aggrandizement in the medium term will continue to be offset relatively easily by U.S. military strength. There has been a distinct tendency to overestimate Chinese military strength of late, or at least to anticipate liber- ally its expected future growth. Imminent U.S. military budget cuts are enhancing this tendency to exaggerate Chinese mili- tary strength, in contrast to an expected U.S. military decline. But the gap is very large—the 11-to-1 ratio in the number of aircraft carriers on each side is the crudest possible measure, yet not wildly misleading. Ruin may be ahead, but there is still a lot of ruination left in American military strength, decades of it, not years. Moreover, one may hope that U.S. military spending cuts will be offset in the near term by much less spending on the enormously costly military malpractice of "counterinsurgency" applied to entire countries, as opposed to very cheap counterterrorism focused on individual miscreants.

While China's economic capacity and resulting military potential have grown enormously in the last three decades, it remains true that just three of the countries its policies have increasingly antagonized since 2008—India, Japan, and Vietnam—conjointly match or exceed China in population, gross domestic product, and overall technological capacity. Because the three countries are not, or not yet, cohesive and coordinated allies, their power potential cannot be validly added up to reach a meaningful total, but each cooperates strategically with the United States, and it too has its own population, gross domestic product, and technology to place in the balance.

It is important to recognize in that regard that perceptions of the United States as a declining power increase rather than reduce its "alliance-value" for India, the most ambitious of its emerging coalition partners, and potentially for the Russia Federation, loudly antagonistic so far, and certainly the most ambiguous of its possible future coalition partners. India would not be so ready to cooperate with a rising United States on its way to an even more expansive superpower capacity, while for

Russia the United States is much too powerful at present, and it is only the expectation of its decline that could perhaps make it into an acceptable strategic partner. In proper paradoxical fashion, weakness can thus generate strength—India was certainly very disinclined to collaborate with the United States when the latter's strength was still at its post–Cold War peak. That will continue to be true in the future as well—unless one day a tipping point of overall coalition inferiority to China were to be reached.

In the longer term, however, should China's economic capacity continue to grow much faster than that of its principal antagonists in combination, the latter would no longer be able to match its military investment, while coalescence might also reach its political limits. For example, for internal political reasons alone, the Russian Federation might long remain in its present equipoise between China and the emerging anti-China coalition. At that point, with their relative power still eroding, the United States and its allies could no longer limit themselves to military cooperation to negate potential Chinese military threats, and diplomatic coordination to restrict Chinese influence.

The only remaining means of resistance would then be "geo-economic," to apply the logic of strategy in the grammar of commerce,[13] by restricting Chinese exports into their markets, denying raw materials to China insofar as possible,[14] and stopping whatever technology transfers China would still need in that future. It is obvious that if China's military growth can no longer be effectively negated, the only remaining alternative to subjection would be to impede China's economic growth, and in sufficient degree to preserve a tolerable balance of power.

As it is, China's sustained military growth and more recent propensity for threatening conduct have already begun to prejudice the highly favorable trading atmosphere that allowed its very rapid export-led economic growth. Chinese exports to certain markets are already encountering signs of consumer antipathy, notably in Japan, the United States, and Vietnam. Because of sundry food and toy scandals, but also because of declining goodwill for China in general, private demand for some categories of Chinese goods has declined in many more markets. These are matters of consumer choice, necessarily uneven and perhaps of slight significance overall. But explicit political choices are involved when it comes to purchases by central or local authorities. In the United States, as in some other countries, authorities are now less likely than in the past to purchase high-visibility Chinese-made public goods, such as steel bridges.[15]

It would require much more to impede China's economic growth to any significant extent, but a future of more purposeful restrictions is perhaps presaged by a scattering of recently enacted measures:

- the tacit prohibition of telecomm switchgear imports by the United States, in the name of communication security;

- the prohibition of certain categories of government procurement from China, and all Defense Department procurement;
- the prohibitions of land sales to Chinese buyers recently enacted in Argentina and Brazil (neither prohibited such sales when the buyers were American or European); and the informal but effective prohibition of Chinese acquisitions of Australian mines and natural-gas fields.

In that long-term future, U.S. military strength would still be necessary to contain China's, but it alone could not preserve the ability of the United States to pursue containment in the future as well. In those circumstances, only an adequate geo-economic response could deny a regional, if not global, hegemony to a still-authoritarian China. It is possible, of course, that the United States might wait too long before acting—that it might wait past the tipping point marking the advent of China's *economic* hegemony. In that case, Chinese economic retaliation could inflict sufficient pain to leave the United States bereft of allies, if not to force its own economic capitulation.

On the other hand, if geo-economic action were to begin in good time, its limited aim of impeding China's economic growth to some degree—say from 8 percent per annum to 4 percent per annum—rather than stopping it or reversing it (not a desirable aim in any case), would in turn severely limit the retaliatory options of the Chinese government. Against a devastating attack, all available means can be employed to retaliate regardless of cost, but that is not true when the attack inflicts only limited damage and the costs of retaliation must be finely calculated.

Besides, if China were to continue to hold large amounts of U.S. debt—unlikely but possible—its retaliatory options would be even more restricted, because borrowers can benefit by damaging lenders, but no lender can benefit by damaging the borrower. It is also very unlikely that China would respond with force to geo-economic action, for that would stop economic relations altogether.

*Envoi.* The logic of strategy is not self-executing, but over time its imperatives tend to prevail over political hesitations, cultural impediments, and ideological fixations, just as they prevail over older enmities when alliances become strategically necessary. At this time, the rising threat emanates from an authoritarian, increasingly assertive China empowered by very rapid economic growth. The logic of strategy evokes corresponding reactions, which are diplomatic in the main but may still be warlike even in our nuclear era, though they can no longer achieve purposeful aims by actual warfare, except on the small scale allowed by escalation risks at each remove. Hence, if the economic disparity between China and the anti-China coalition were one day to reach proportions that no longer allow a tolerable military balance to be maintained, the reaction must assume economic forms, even if it is wholly strategic in content. Only a fully democratic China could advance unimpeded to global hegemony, but then the governments of a fully democratic China would undoubtedly seek to pursue quite other aims, to maximize the happiness of the population rather than their own power. In the meantime, the strategic aim of the United States and other like-minded powers cannot be to outmaneuver and defeat China, but rather to dissuade its own self-defeating pursuit of military aggrandizement in the best interests of the peoples of the world, and China's first of all.

.......................................

APPENDIX

NOTES

GLOSSARY

INDEX

·······································

# *The Rise and Fall of "Peaceful Rise"*

The slogan "Peaceful Rise," 中国和平崛起 *Zhōngguó hépíng juéqǐ*, was first given international currency by Zheng Bijian, Hu Jintao's senior advisor, a former vice principal of the Central Party School, and at present also a Ministry of Public Security advisor, with his own elegantly housed institute. The occasion was the 2004 session of the China-Australasia Bo'ao Forum, which meets annually in Hainan. Subsequently, Zheng Bijian published a widely noticed article in *Foreign Affairs* (Sept.–Oct. 2005) that presented the concept more fully as "China's Peaceful Rise to Great-Power Status."

中国和平崛起 *Zhōngguó hépíng juéqǐ* was very well received, but by the time the *Foreign Affairs* article was published, it had been replaced in Chinese official parlance by 中国和平发展 *Zhōngguó hépíng fāzhǎn*, "China's Peaceful Development," to remove the challenging undertone of "rise," and further dissuade adversarial reactions.

In essence, it conveyed the promise (Zheng Bijian's advisory role was made explicit) that China would employ the ever-increasing resources generated by rapid economic growth for its continued internal development rather than military aggrandizement, and that it would join, rather than seek to disrupt or supersede, the comity of the principal nations, the United States, the European Union, and Japan, while being mindful of the needs of the Global South.

The success of the grand strategy thus ably presented was manifest in what did *not* happen: even as China's economic growth accelerated, no anti-Chinese military alliance emerged among China's neighbors all around, and there was no move to impose trade barriers specifically meant to slow its economic growth. (It is true that there was and there is always some "protectionism"—specific trade barriers—but their aim is to protect favored sectors, usually for domestic political reasons, and not to hurt China's economic growth for strategic reasons; claims to the contrary are common, but without any evidence to support them.)

Under either name, this declared grand strategy was characterized not by what it included—that could be determined only in the future—but by the threatening possibilities it ruled out. Over the years, successive Chinese leaders made those exclusions perfectly clear. Each was a guarantee not to do something that rising economic capacity and its military potential could have made possible:

Guarantee 1: Peacefully rising China would not seek to create its own world system but would rather join in the existing world system; it would be "rule-taking" in Chinese terms, not "rule-making."

Guarantee 2: Peacefully rising China would not seek regional, let alone global, hegemony, hence its military forces would not threaten or deliberately intimidate other countries.

Guarantee 3: Peacefully rising China would not try to use force over territorial and maritime disputes but would resolve them by diplomatic means only, including bilateral or multilateral negotiations, and possibly international adjudication and arbitration (though the latter was not explicitly stated).

Guarantee 4: Peacefully rising China would not use its rapidly increasing economy to maximize its accumulation of military strength as the Soviet Union had done in the last thirty years of its existence (with a final outcome that did not inspire imitation).

Guarantee 5: Peacefully rising China would not disrupt the economies of other countries while seeking to expand its own. For example, it would not condone, but instead would seek to repress, the theft of intellectual property, while respecting the common rules of international trade that would later be specified by the WTO.

Guarantee 6: Peacefully rising China would peacefully reabsorb Hong Kong and Macao; moreover, so long as Taiwan's identity as a province of China was not challenged, no force would be used against the island.

Because these reassuring promises were presented by successive Chinese leaders in credible ways, and—more important—because actual Chinese conduct kept faith with these promises in the years 2005–2008, there was no "natural" reaction to China's extremely rapid rise: no elements, even tacit, of any anti-Chinese alliance emerged on its periphery, and there was not even any speculation about any attempt to deliberately slow China's economic growth.

Until 2009 the credibility of the Peaceful Rise grand strategy was reaffirmed by actual Chinese conduct. But that is no longer true of course. Guarantees 4, 5, and 6 have been respected so far, but not the first three guarantees.

........................................

# *Notes*

## *1. The Fallacy of Unresisted Aggrandizement*

1. For fiscal year 2011, the Department of Defense *requested* a total of $708.3 billion, a 1.3 percent increase over FY 2010, including $159.3 billion for operations in Afghanistan and Iraq.

2. But military friends, e.g., MG Huang Xing, then (2010) director of the Research Guidance Department of the Academy of Military Science, bitterly complained that civilian officials could augment official salaries with "corruption"; and also that in some cases ranks were filled by accepting low achievers. It seems, however, that the PLA can still recruit into its academies talented youths too poor to enroll in civilian universities. In addition, the PLA can be welcoming to the well educated; e.g., by offering instant *Shao Xiao* 少校 rank (equivalent to a U.S. major OF-3) to a returning Ph.D. with no previous military experience.

3. Minnie Chan, "PLA Delegates Go into Battle against Improper Spending," *South China Morning Post*, March 10, 2011. Extract: "The auditing programme that checked nearly 10,000 military officials in 126,700 units from 2006 to last year [2010] found nearly 2.8 billion yuan of inappropriate funding on construction projects, and 1.5 billion yuan was overspent on purchasing equipment"; http://www.ftchinese.com/story/001039153/en. But these are small numbers and refer to errors, not fraud. A June 17, 2011, Bank of China report included the estimate that 17,000 party cadres, police, judicial officers, and state-owned enterprise executives had fled the country (up to 2008) taking an estimated 8 billion renminbi (RMB) (US$123.6

billion) with them. PLA personnel are not listed, but small-scale misappropriation is common. The 2006 US$15 million Vice-Admiral Wang Shouye case (he was one of five deputy navy chiefs) is atypical.

4. Not only on the part of the malevolently tendentious, such as Martin Jacques, *When China Rules the World: The End of the Western World and the Birth of a New Global Order* (London: Penguin, 2010). Long a British Communist militant, Jacques assuages his bitter disappointment at the Soviet collapse by gleefully anticipating the downfall of the West as well.

5. See Edward N. Luttwak, *Strategy: The Logic of War and Peace*, rev. ed. (Cambridge, Mass.: Harvard University Press, 2002).

6. Admittedly one did occur in March 2011: the most powerful earthquake in Japan's history, which happened to come at a time when the public was already demoralized by prolonged economic stagnation and the perceived lack of adequate political leadership.

## 2.  *Premature Assertiveness*

1. Malcolm Moore, "China's 'Next Leader' in Hardline Rant: Xi Jinping, the Man Earmarked to Become China's Next President, Has Roundly Attacked His Country's Critics while Giving a Speech in Mexico," *The Telegraph*, March 31, 2012, http://www.telegraph.co.uk/news/worldnews/asia/china/4637039/Chinas-next-leader-in-hardline-rant.html.

2. The Banyan blog, "The Law in China: A Spear Not a Shield," *The Economist*, April 4, 2011, http://www.economist.com/blogs/banyan/2011/04/law_china.

3. *Wall Street Journal*, Asia, July 26, 2010.

4. See Appendix, "The Rise and Fall of 'Peaceful Rise.'"

5. Dai Bingguo, "Adhere to the Path of Peaceful Development," official Xinhua News Agency translation of "Janchi zou heping fazhan zhi lu," *Waijiaobu wangzhan*, December 6, 2010.

6. Zheng Bijian, interview with Francesco Sisci, "Ordine, riforme e apertura all'Occidente: Il teorico di Hú Jǐntāo ci spiega la nuova ideologia della Cina," *Il Sole, 24 Ore*, March 31, 2011.

7. So long as China's population outnumbers India's. But the Han will not be outnumbered by any nation.

### 3. Great-State Autism Defined

1. The revival of the Chinese territorial claim for what is now the Indian state of Arunachal Pradesh (see below), the de-recognition of Indian control over Jammu-Kashmir by the refusal to stamp visas on the Indian passports of Kashmir-born applicants, and China's supply of a nuclear reactor to Pakistan are not unreasonably viewed as "reckless" by Indian senior officials (private communication).

2. M. Taylor Fravel, *Strong Borders, Secure Nation: Cooperation and Conflict in China's Territorial Disputes* (Princeton: Princeton University Press, 2008), passim, summary, table 1.3, pp. 46–47.

3. Unlike the addition of Goa, Daman, Diu, Dadra, and Nagar Haveli, all seized from the Portuguese by 1961, and of Sikkim, taken from its ruler in 1975.

4. As a co-signatory of the Susan Eisenhower/Roald Sagdeev anti-enlargement declarations, I was much exposed to the Russian literature on the subject. Interviews in 2011 in Moscow, at the June St. Petersburg presidential conference and the September Yaroslav presidential conference, revealed no change in interpretations of NATO's expansion.

5. On this day, June 30, 2011, for example, it was announced that average pork prices had reached 25 yuan/kg, a 70 percent increase in 12 months; the average price of pigs sold for slaughter reached 19.26 yuan/kg, an 85 percent increase. When food budgets are squeezed, income inequalities acquire added political significance *(South China Morning Post)*. Concurrently, ethnic riots continue in the Inner Mongolian Autonomous Region: the killing of a traditional herder has opened a wider contention over Mongol control of Mongol lands. (Southern Mongolian Information Center, "Herders take to the streets, four arrested," http://smhric.org/news_378.htm).

6. Black: ordinary local police of the Ministry of Public Security *Gōng ān Bù* 公安部, normally armed with 9-mm pistols only.

Green: the paramilitary China People's Armed Police Force (PAP) *Zhōngguó Rénmín Wǔzhuāng Jǐngchá Bùduì* 中国人民武装警察部, normally armed with assault rifles. White: Ministry of State Security *Anquan Bu* 安全部 operatives, invariably with concealed pistols only.

### *4. Historical Residues in Chinese Conduct*

1. See the critical survey in Zhang Feng, "Rethinking the 'Tribute System': Broadening the Conceptual Horizon of Historical East Asian Politics," *Chinese Journal of International Politics* 2 (2009): 545–574.

2. Possibly the ancestors of the Huns; they are described in a military report in book 88 of the *Hòu hàn shu* (Book of the Later Han) attributed to Fan Ye. John E. Hill, http://depts.washington.edu/silkroad /texts/hhshu/hou_han_shu.html.

3. Predecessor of *Khagan* or *Qagan*, chief (khan, *qan*) of chiefs. For the subjection, see Nicola di Cosmo, *Ancient China and Its Enemies: The Rise of Nomadic Power in East Asian History* (Cambridge: Cambridge University Press, 2002), 206ff. If it is true that the Huns emerged from them, as some evidence indicates, the Xiongnú had a formative impact on both world empires.

4. Ibid., 193–194.

5. From the *Shiji* 史记, *The Records of the Grand Historian* (or *Grand Scribe*) *of Sima Qian* (Ssu-ma Ch'ien), 司馬遷, vol. 99, cols. 2144 and 2179. Increasingly available in English translations, referenced under several different author transliterations.

6. The current U.S. secretary of the treasury is the former China specialist of Kissinger Associates, much of whose income has derived directly or indirectly from its access to CCP leaders, gained by deference to their priorities. Kissinger himself has propagated their views, most recently at book length in his *On China* (New York: Penguin, 2011).

7. Allen Carlson, "Moving beyond Sovereignty? A Brief Consideration of Recent Changes in China's Approach to International Or-

der and the Emergence of the *Tianxia* Concept," *Journal of Contemporary China* 20, no. 68 (2011).

8. Katie Cantle, "Chinese Carriers Order up to 35 Embraer 190s," *Air Transport World*, April 13, 2011.

9. Ghana news agency release, "Xinhua Opens Photo Gallery in Accra," Accra, April 8, 2011, http://www.modernghana.com/news/323877/1/xinhua-opens-photo-gallery-in-accra.html.

10. At that same meeting, Yang Jiechi reportedly told his Singaporean counterpart, George Yeo, minister for foreign affairs, that "China is a big country and other countries are small countries, and that's just a fact." One trusts that Yeo was grateful for the information that China is larger than Singapore; http://online.wsj.com/article/SB10001424052748704483004575523710432896610.html.

11. The brochure closes with: "The workshop is co-sponsored by the Confucius Institute, the Department of East Asian Languages and Cultures, the Center for East Asian Studies, and the School of Humanities and Sciences. Major funding is provided by Stanford's Presidential Fund for Innovation in the Humanities." It is odd yet unsurprising to encounter such infantile fecklessness in such a place.

### 5. The Coming Geo-Economic Resistance to the Rise of China

1. For the concept, see Edward N. Luttwak, "From Geopolitics to Geo-Economics," *The National Interest* (Summer 1990): 17–23.

2. "Mongolia's Rail Choice Seen as Breaking China's Grip," http://www.bcmongolia.org/news/1126-mongolias-rail-choice-seen-as-breaking-chinas-grip (the source is Bloomberg.com, April 27, 2011); and *Mongol News*, August 8, 2011, http://ubpost.mongolnews.mn/index.php?option=com_content&task=view&id=5094&Itemid=36.

3. Http://www.huffingtonpost.com/2011/06/28/romney-us-cut-off-trade-with-china_n_886008.html.

### 6. China's Aggrandizement and Global Reactions

1. In Japan, notably Nakasone Yasuhiro, prime minister from 1982 to 1987.

2. See the discussion in Chapter 16 on the Republic of Korea as a consumer rather than a producer of security.

3. Globescan public opinion survey data, BBC, March 27, 2011. http://www.globescan.com/news_archives/bbc2011_china/bbc_2011 _China_global_rls.pdf.

4. Ibid.

5. Qin Yaqing, "A Chinese School of International Relations Theory: Possibility and Inevitability," *Shijie jingji yu zhengzhi* (World Economics and Politics), no. 3 (2006): 7–13. Translated for the author.

6. Information Office of the State Council, *China's National Defense in 2010*, issued in March 2011. (Xinhua, English.news, http://news.xinhuanet.com/english2010/china/2011-03-31/c_13806851 .htm, March 31, 2011.)

### 7. The Inevitable Analogy

1. Hence, surprise is the greatest of boons, for it grants a nonreacting other, a mere object against which straightforward action does achieve straightforward results. But in warfare, with all guarding against it, surprise is rare; in the competitive peacetime acquisition of major weapons, it rarely lasts long enough to matter; while the stately processes of shipbuilding and aircraft-making deny any hope of surprising competitors.

2. Which would be very useful for today's China as well—it would exclude full-scale aircraft carriers, for example, to provide instead asymmetric forces to absorb, deflect, or block enemy attacks with *operationally* defensive methods, minimizing strategically offensive capabilities and maximizing defensive capabilities in a very secure yet nonthreatening overall posture.

### 8. Could China Adopt a Successful Grand Strategy?

1. Hence, the logic of Carl von Clausewitz and that of Sunzi *are necessarily identical, and equally paradoxical.*

2. Zhu Shanshan, "We Want a Carrier," *Global Times*, May 5, 2011, http://military.globaltimes.cn/china/2011-05/651642.html.

### 9. The Strategic Unwisdom of the Ancients

1. Ralph D. Sawyer and Mei Mei-chün Sawyer, trans., *The Seven Military Classics of Ancient China* (Boulder: Westview Press, 1993).

2. (Sawyer title: "Six Secret Teachings") 六韬 *Liù Tāo* of 姜子牙, Jiāng Zǐyá; (The Methods of the Ssu-ma) 司马法 *Sīmǎ Fǎ;* (Sun Tzu's *The Art of War*) 孙子兵法 *Sūnzǐ Bīngfǎ;* (Wu Qi's *Wuzi*) 吴子 *Wúzǐ* of 吴起: *Wú Qǐ;* (Wei Liaozi) 尉缭子 *Wèi Liáozi;* (The Three Strategies of Huang Shigong) 黄石公三略; *Huáng Shígōng Sān Lüè;* (Questions and Replies between Tang Taizong and Li Weigong) 唐太宗李卫公 *Táng Tàizōng Lǐ Wèi Gōng Wèn Duì.*

3. In addition to cameo appearances in sundry historical films, he was the protagonist of Kuan Hui's 1981 feature film *Sun Bin xia shan dou pang juan (Art of War* by Sun Tzu). Hollywood citations include Star Wars; see http://www.artofwarsuntzu.com/suntzuandhollywood.htm.

4. When a French edition by the Jesuit Jean Joseph Marie Amiot was published. A Beijing resident, Amiot paraphrased a Manchu translation and commentary for his version. The first edition was successful enough to be reprinted a few years later.

5. The corpus extends much beyond the seven texts of the Song dynasty canon; one text, *The Art of War* of *Sūn Bìn* (孙膑兵法), of ancient fame, was rediscovered only in 1972, in the form of excavated bamboo strips.

6. Practitioners of course rarely recognize the ritualistic element in what they do, but it can be discerned by straightforward bureaucratic analysis.

7. A spectacular policy error, given China's own dependence on uninterrupted raw material imports, and strong evidence of strategic incompetence.

8. "China Denies Visa to IAS Officer," Cable News Network–Indian Broadcasting Network (CNN-IBN), May 25, 2007.

9. "A Thaw? China Lets Arunachalee Visit," Times News Network, December 9, 2007, http://articles.timesofindia.indiatimes.com/2007-12-09/india/27989328_1_marpe-sora-chinese-visa-arunachalee.

10. Henry Kissinger, *On China* (New York: Penguin, 2011), prologue, p. 4.

11. Among many examples of Henry A. Kissinger's propensity to admire CCP leaders uncritically, the most widely known is his worshipful report of Zhou Enlai's famous response, "Too early to say," when asked about the impact of the French Revolution. But Zhou was referring to the then very recent 1968 uprising and not to 1789, according to the only U.S. Mandarin-speaker present, the later ambassador Chas Freeman. FT.Com. Richard McGregor, June 10, 2011.

12. "Hero," http://www.youtube.com/watch?v=WTIrIGI-lvc&feature=youtube_gdata_player.

13. In the opening section. See, more broadly, Ralph D. Sawyer, with the collaboration of Mei-chun Lee Sawyer, *The Tao of Deception: Unorthodox Warfare in Historic and Modern China* (Cambridge, Mass.: Basic Books, 2007).

14. Translated in Burton Watson, *Records of the Historian* (New York: Columbia University Press, 1969), 175ff. More broadly, see Ralph D. Sawyer, with the collaboration of Mei-chun Lee Sawyer, *The Tao of Spycraft: Intelligence Theory and Practice in Traditional China* (Boulder: Westview Press, 2004), 249–285.

15. Unsigned editorial, "Don't Take Peaceful Approach for Granted," *Global Times*, October 25, 2011, http://www.globaltimes.cn/NEWS/tabid/99/ID/680694/Dont-take-peaceful-approach-for-granted.aspx.

16. *The Charlie Rose Show*, PBS, May 11, 2011.

### 10. Strategic Competence

1. Henry A. Kissinger's *On China* (New York: Penguin, 2011) starts with a fawning dithyramb to the farsighted strategic wisdom of the Han, personified by Mao Zedong, and conceptualized by the inevitable Sunzi (p. 25, as Sun Tzu).

2. Actually *Aisin Gioro* (Golden clan) was also a new invention; Giovanni Stary, "The Meaning of the Word 'Manchu': A New Solution to an Old Problem," *Central Asiatic Journal* 34, nos. 1–2 (1990): 109–119.

3. Jonathan Karam Skaff, "Tang Military Culture and Its Inner Asian Influences," in *Military Culture in Imperial China*, ed. Nicola di Cosmo (Cambridge, Mass.: Harvard University Press, 2009), pp. 165–191; see more fully the same author's "Straddling Steppe and Town: Tang China's Relations with the Nomads of Inner Asia (640–756)," Ph.D. diss., University of Michigan, 1998.

### 11. The Inevitability of Mounting Resistance

1. Information Office of the State Council, *China's National Defense in 2010*, issued in March 2011; and State Councilor Dai Bingguo, "Adhere to the Path of Peaceful Development," *Jianchi zou heping fazhan zhi lu*, released December 6, 2010.

### 12. Why Current Policies Will Persist

1. *China Daily*, December 24, 2010 (http://www.china.org.cn /environment/2010-12/24/content_21609300.htm), "China Fisheries Get More Protection," based on Ministry of Agriculture posted announcement of December 26, 2010.

### 13. Australia

1. The phenomenon is most obvious in Latin America, with its abundance of de jure restrictions on foreigners (including fellow Latin Americans), which coincides with de facto pliancy.

2. Australian Government, Department of Defence, "The Defence White Paper 2009," released May 2, 2009, http://www.defence.gov.au/whitepaper/.

3. Notably the acquisition of Boeing 737 NG Wedgetail AEW&C aircraft. Wide-area ocean monitoring is useful for Australia itself, and more so to aid its prospective allies, only one of which, Japan, can provide that capability for itself.

4. Australian Government, Department of Foreign Affairs and Trade, "Australia–Viet Nam Comprehensive Partnership," http://www.dfat.gov.au/geo/vietnam/comprehensive_partnership_vietnam.html.

5. Vietnamese Embassy in Australia, "Vietnam Marks Army Day in Australia," September 12, 2009; see http://members.webone.com.au/~vembassy/News/News%20on%20the%20relationship.htm#40.

6. Vietnamese Embassy in Australia, "The First Strategic Dialogue between Vietnam and Australia," February 21, 2012; see http://members.webone.com.au/~vembassy/News/News%20on%20the%20relationship.htm#63.

7. Australian Treaty Series 1971, No. 21, Department of Foreign Affairs, Canberra, "Five Power Defence Arrangements"; see http://www.austlii.edu.au/au/other/dfat/treaties/1971/21.html.

8. The Hon. Stephen Smith, MP, Australian Minister of Foreign Affairs and Trade, "Singapore-Australia Joint Ministerial Committee," July 26, 2009; see http://www.foreignminister.gov.au/releases/2009/fa-s090726.html.

9. Caren Bohan and James Grubel, "Obama Boosts U.S. Military in Australia, Reassures China," Canberra, November 16, 2011, 2:26 pm EST. Reuters US Edition, http://www.reuters.com/article/2011/11/16/us-usa-australia-idUSTRE7AF0F220111116.

10. Others in Japanese politics may be equally dubious, but not in regard to accusations of Chinese bribery, and subsequent blackmail.

11. Prime Minister of Australia, the Hon. Julia Gillard, MP, "Keynote Address to the Japan National Press Club," Friday, April

22, 2011, http://www.pm.gov.au/press-office/keynote-address-japan
-national-press-club-tokyo.

## *14. Japan*

1. What follows is based on a prolonged conversation with Nakasone Yasuhiro in his Tokyo office on March 3, 2011.

2. The Xinhua News Agency's release of December 11, 2009,
with accompanying photographs is revealing: "Hu meets secretary
general of Japanese DPJ: Ruling parties of China and Japan on
Thursday pledged to deepen trust and work together for a stronger
strategic relationship of mutual benefit between the two countries." See
http://www.china.org.cn/world/2009-12/11/content_19046400.htm.

3. "Ozawa Expresses Concern over China's Military Buildup,"
*Japan Today*, December 16, 2009.

4. March 2011 interviews with (a) *Gaimusho* officials, Rui Matsu-
kawa, 2nd Div. Koji Tsuruoka, Director-General of Policy Planning;
Kimihiro Ishikane Deputy Director-General, Asian and Oceanian
Affairs; Akira Muto Director of the Policy Planning Division; (b)
Diet members, including: Shinzo Abe (LDP), Akihisa Nagashima
(DPJ), Takakane Kiuchi (LDP), Motohisa Furukawa (LDP), Ms.
Noriko Miyagawa (LDP), Jin Matsubara (DJP), Koki Kobayashi
(DJP), Shozo Azuma (DJP), Katsutoshi Ono (DJP); and (c) outside
experts, including: Motohiro Kondo; Seiichio Takagi; Masahiro Mi-
yazaki; Masa Okuda; Tomohiro Taniguchi, Isamu Ishikawa; Keiichi,
Kawanaka Tomoko Suzuki; Shinichi Kitaoka; Yasuhiro Nakasone;
Kunihiko Miyake Hisahiko Okazaki; Shotaro Yachi; Shinichi Kita-
oka, Tomoko Suzuki, Jun Osawa, Hitoshi Tanaka.

5. Ministry of Foreign Affairs of the People's Republic of China,
"Joint Press Communiqué between the Defense Ministries of China
and Japan," Beijing, March 20, 2009. See http://www.fmprc.gov.cn
/eng/zxxx/t558002.htm.

6. See the comprehensive and detailed review in *Defense of Japan
2011*, Ministry of Defense, 2012, pp. 81–84.

7. *Yomiuri Shinbun*, English edition, online, April 30, 2011.

8. Confirmed in the *Global Times*, April 14, 2011, under the misleading title "Beijing Refutes Carrier Claims" (= it is not a carrier, it is just a training vessel).

9. Helicopters from 33rd Rescue Squadron, 18th Wing, Kadena Air Base, and even SH-60 antisubmarine helicopters from Naval Air Facility Atsugi, also flew relief missions.

10. Http://ajapaneseossan.blogspot.com/2011/04/jsdf-jmsdf-pics -of-fukushima-daiichi.html.

11. Reuters (from *Yomiuri*, Japanese edition), May 7, 2011.

12. Yoichi Funabashi, "Tokyo Has No Option but to Cleave to China," *Financial Times*, May 17, 2011. "Japan's triple disaster holds a magnifying glass to my country's vulnerabilities. . . . In these trying times there are . . . many reasons for Japanese despair."

13. E.g., sailors of the perilous convoys to Murmansk were treated as dangerous spies—they were kept under continuous surveillance and denied contact with the local population.

14. Most recently, May 16, 2010, Kyodo: Foreign Minister Takeaki Matsumoto "summoned . . . Russian Ambassador . . . Mikhail Bely . . . and told him that he regrets the trip to the islands of Etorofu and Kunashiri [by Russian Deputy Prime Minister Sergei Ivanov and four other Cabinet ministers] . . . as it . . . hurts the feelings of the Japanese people." No sanctions were even mentioned.

## 15. Defiant Vietnam

1. It is their refusal to accept the balance of power that has made successive Palestinian leaders the objects rather than the subjects of regional politics.

2. Andrew Scobell, *China's Use of Military Force: Beyond the Great Wall and the Long March* (New York: Columbia University Press, 2003), 119–123. (I owe the citation to an anonymous reviewer for Harvard University Press.)

3. See the detailed summary by Colonel G. D. Bakshi, VSM, "The Sino-Vietnam War—1979: Case Studies in Limited Wars," *Bharat Rakshak Monitor*, November–December 2000.

4. The conventional periodization does not include periods in which Vietnam was not occupied but acknowledged imperial suzerainty: First Chinese domination, 111 BCE–39 CE; Second, 43–544; Third, 602–905; Fourth, 1407–1427.

5. Bruce Elleman, "Sino-Soviet Relations and the February 1979 Sino-Vietnamese Conflict," 1996 Vietnam Symposium, Texas Tech University, April 20, 1996. See http://www.vietnam.ttu.edu/events/1996_Symposium/96papers/elleviet.htm.

6. M. Taylor Fravel, *Strong Borders, Secure Nation: Cooperation and Conflict in China's Territorial Disputes* (Princeton: Princeton University Press, 2008), 146.

7. Ibid. Hence, the old vineyards of Cizhong village, Dêqên County 德钦县, Yunnan.

8. Ibid., 148. In my own communications with PLA officers, I heard expressions of real hostility only against Indians ("real snakes") and Vietnamese (words amounting to "vainglorious upstarts"); resentment persists because of the humiliations of the 1979 fighting.

9. He Sheng, "Building a Border of Friendship: The China–Viet Nam land border demarcation is a breakthrough for bilateral relations," *Beijing Review*, http://www.bjreview.com.cn/world/txt/2009-03/31/content_188764.htm. It is interesting to note that the simulation of friendship was wholly persuasive for an unwitting European observer: "Last Stone Laid to Mark Border between China and Vietnam," Asia News It, http://www.asianews.it/news-en/Last-stone-laid-to-mark-border-between-China-and-Vietnam-14568.html.

10. Carlyle A. Thayer, "The Tyranny of Geography: Vietnamese Strategies to Constrain China in the South China Sea," paper to the International Studies Association Convention, Montreal, March 16–19, 2011.

11. "Vietnam Opposes China's Fishing Ban in East Sea," *Vov News*, May 14, 2011, http://english.vovnews.vn/Home/Vietnam-opposes-Chinas-fishing-ban-in-East-Sea/20115/126608.vov.

12. Thayer, "The Tyranny of Geography," abstract.

13. Officially described in U.S. Department of State, "Lower Mekong Initiative." See press releases: http://www.state.gov/p/eap /mekong/c34260.htm; summary in http://www.state.gov/p/eap/me kong/index.htm.

14. Public affairs release on joint activities by the U.S. 7th Fleet and the Vietnam navy: "Seventh Fleet Kicks Off Vietnam Naval Engagement Activities," U.S. 7th Fleet Public Affairs, August 9, 2010, story no. NNS100809-01.

15. Kao Wei-min: "The United States and Vietnam Must Not Behave Unscrupulously in the South China Sea," *Ta Kung Pao (Dàgōng Bào)*, August 13, 2010, BBC monitoring service translation.

## 16. South Korea

1. Public opinion polls commonly show 75+ percent approval ratings for the United States, among the highest in the world. Among the educated elite, on the other hand, anti-Americanism is common and can reach the extremes exemplified by the unprintable Yoon Min-suk protest song (http://www.robpongi.com/pages/combo FUCKINGUSAHI.html).

2. F. L. Olmstead, "Korean Folklore and Attitudes towards China," *Journal of American Folklore*, 68, no. 267 (January–March 1955).

3. Ronald Storrs, *The Memoirs of Sir Ronald Storrs* (New York: Putnam, 1937), 95.

4. Robert Hathaway, "The Making of 'Anti-American' Sentiment in Korea and Japan," Woodrow Wilson International Center for Scholars, May 6, 2003, http://www.wilsoncenter.org/event/the -making-anti-american-sentiment-korea-and-japan.

5. Lee Myung-bak, since February 25, 2008. At the April 2, 2009, G-20 London meeting, Presidents Obama and Lee agreed on a "stern" response" to a threatened North Korean satellite launch. On April 5, the North Koreans launched a *Taepodong-2* IRBM. There was no South Korean response, stern or otherwise.

6. Chang Se-jeong, "China's No to Kim's Request: North Leader Asked for 30 Bomber Jets," *Choson Ilbo*, May 9, 2011.

7. Xian JH-7; NATO: *Flounder* or FBC-1, "Flying Leopard" two-seat, twin-engine fighter-bomber; IOC from 1998 with the PLAAF; 2002 with the PLANAF.

8. "Kim Jong-il Demands Fighter Jets from China," *Choson Ilbo*, June 17, 2010.

9. Naresh Kumar Sharma, "South Korea Denies Visa to Dalai Lama," *The Times of India*, May 27, 2006.

10. Office of His Holiness the Dalai Lama, News, June 27, 2010, "Dalai Lama Meets Korean Buddhists in Tokyo," http://www.dalailama.com/news/post/560-dalai-lama-meets-korean-buddhists-in-tokyo.

11. Choe Sang-Hun, "Chinese Fisherman Kills South Korean Coast Guardsman," *New York Times*, December 12, 2011.

12. "Statue of 'Comfort Woman' Erected outside Japanese Embassy in Seoul," *Japan Times* online from Kyodo, December 15, 2011, http://www.japantimes.co.jp/text/nn20111215a5.html.

## 17. *Mongolia*

1. An advantage that the Chinese are determined to keep. The website of the Inner Mongolia University (http://ndnews.imu.edu.cn/english/) is marked "copyright The Propaganda Department." The Mongol version is in Mongol script, of course.

2. Ministry of Foreign Affairs of Japan, Regional Affairs, March 2012, Japan-Mongolia Relations, http://www.mofa.go.jp/region/asia-paci/mongolia/index.html.

3. *Mongolian Views*, "South Korean Ambassador in Ulaanbaatar Fathered a Child with a . . . Teen . . . Refused to Pay Child Support," March 11, 2011. See http://www.mongolianviews.com/2011/03/south-korean-ambassador-in-ulaanbaatar.html. ("Most [South Koreans] are like their ambassador . . . not interested in anything except money and sex. . . . Maybe, Japanese military should come back and teach them right or wrong.")

4. *UB Post*, "Mongolia Coal Railway Will Link with Russia," http://ubpost.mongolnews.mn/index.php?option=com_content& task=view&id=5094&Itemid=36.

5. Mongolia Business Council, press release, April 27, 2011, citing the Bloomberg News Service, "Mongolia's Rail Choice Seen as Breaking China's Grip," http://www.bcmongolia.org/news/1126 -mongolias-rail-choice-seen-as-breaking-chinas-grip.

## 18.  *Indonesia*

1. Douglas Johnson, "Drawn into the Fray: Indonesia's Natuna Islands Meet China's Long Gaze South," *Asian Affairs: An American Review*, September 22, 1997.

2. See, inter alia, Wikipedia, "Legislation on Chinese Indonesians," http://en.wikipedia.org/wiki/Legislation_on_Chinese_Indone sians.

3. In the last mass outburst, in May 1998, several hundred were killed and hundreds more were raped. See http://en.wikipedia.org /wiki/Jakarta_Riots_of_May_1998.

4. Huayang Jiao or Wang Huayang to the Chinese, Nguyen Chau Vien in Vietnamese, Felipe Calderon de la Cruz for the Filipinos. The Chinese have built a large fortress-like structure over the reef.

5. NajmiMaulana World Press, July 1, 2008, "China Denies Island Dispute, Seeks Talks." See http://najmimaulana.wordpress.com /2008/07/01/china-denies-island-dispute-seeks-talks/.

6. Li Jinming and Li Dexia, "The Dotted Line on the Chinese Map of the South China Sea: A Note," *Ocean Development and International Law* 34 (2003): 287–295.

7. Simon Sinaga, "No Problem with China over Natuna Isles, Says Matas," *Straits Times*, June 27, 1995. Cited in Johnson, "Drawn into the Fray," n. 97.

8. By David S. Cloud. "U.S. to Resume Aid to Kopassus, Indonesia's Controversial Military Forces," *Los Angeles Times*, July 23, 2010.

9. Australian Government, Department of Foreign Affairs and Trade, "Agreement between the Republic of Indonesia and Australia

on the Framework for Security Cooperation." See http://www.dfat
.gov.au/geo/indonesia/ind-aus-seco6.html.

10. "China Asks Indonesia to Free Fishermen," *Jakarta Globe*,
June 26, 2009.

11. U.S. Navy, Commander Surface Forces Pacific, Eric J. Cut-
right (USN, PA), "Indonesia Welcomes Task Group for Naval Engagement Activity," May 26, 2010. See http://www.public.navy.mil
/surfor/cds31/Pages/IndonesiaWelcomesTaskGroup.aspx#.T3wO9
zH2ZWN.

### 19. The Philippines

1. Charles P. Wallace, "Manila Senate Rejects U.S. Pact: Philippines: The 12–11 Vote Would Bar American Use of Subic Bay Naval
Base," *Los Angeles Times*, September 16, 1991, http://articles.latimes
.com/1991-09-16/news/mn-1690_1_subic-bay-naval-base.

2. For both Notes Verbales, see http://www.un.org/Depts/los
/clcs_new/submissions_files/submission_vnm_37_2009.htm.

3. Li Jinming and Li Dexia, "The Dotted Line on the Chinese
Map of the South China Sea: A Note," *Ocean Development and International Law* 34 (2003): 287–295.

4. Philippine Mission to the United Nations, Letter, April 5,
2011. See http://www.un.org/Depts/los/clcs_new/submissions_files
/vnm37_09/phl_re_chn_2011.pdf.

5. See UN Commission on the Limits of the Continental Shelf
(CLCS), Outer Limits of the Continental Shelf beyond 200 Nautical
Miles from the Baselines: Submissions to the Commission: China: 14
April 2011. See http://www.un.org/Depts/los/clcs_new/submissions
_files/vnm37_09/chn_2011_re_phl_e.pdf.

6. Joyce Pangco Pañares, "Aquino Pushes for United Stand on
South China Sea," *Manila Standard Today*, May 10, 2011.

7. "Coast Guard to Secure Oil Exploration in Kalayaan Island
Group," *GMA News*, April 19, 2011: "Recognizing the sensitivity of the
disputed Kalayaan Island Group, President . . . Aquino on Tuesday
instructed the Philippine Coast Guard (PCG) to provide the security

needed for exploration activities in the area. . . . The PCG [was des-
ignated] in order not to be provocative . . . [with] the support of
the . . . Philippine Navy."

8. Pia Lee-Brago, Jaime Laude, and Jose Katigbak, http://www
.philstar.com/Article.aspx?articleId=686194&publicationSubCate
goryId=63.

9. Cheng Guangjin, "Washington's Intervention Bringing East
Asia to a Boil," *China Daily, Global Research*, August 18, 2010.

10. BBC Worldwide Monitoring—Asia Pacific—Political, Friday, August 13, 2010,

11. "US Advises PHL: Settle Spratlys Row with China Peacefully," *GMA News*, March 15, 2011.

12. Jaime Laude, "Chinese Jets Buzz PAF Patrol Planes," *Philippine Star*, May 20, 2011, http://www.philstar.com/Article.aspx?article
Id=687844&publicationSubCategoryId=63.

13. U.S. Department of State, Secretary of State Hillary Rodham
Clinton, Remarks with Philippines Foreign Secretary Albert del Rosario after Their Meeting, June 23, 2011, http://www.state.gov/secretary
/rm/2011/06/166868.htm.

### 20. Norway

1. Bjoern H. Amland, "Norway Feels Sting of China's Nobel
Anger," Association Press, May 6, 2011, http://www.forbes.com/feeds
/ap/2011/05/06/general-industrials-eu-norway-china-nobel-backlash
_8453124.html.

2. Joachim Dagenborg and Victoria Klesty, "Orkla Sells Elkem to
China's BlueStar," Reuters, January 11, 2011, http://www.reuters.com
/article/2011/01/11/us-orkla-idUSTRE70A13Q20110111 ; "Orkla Metal
Unit in $70m China JV with Chinalco," *China Daily*, April 12, 2011,
http://usa.chinadaily.com.cn/business/2011-04/12/content_12312596
.htm; and "Norway Feels Sting of China's Nobel Anger," Associated
Press, Oslo, May 6, 2011, http://abcnews.go.com/Business/wireStory
?id=13543959&page=2#.T3zVSjH2ZWM.

3. Bjoern H. Amland, "Norway Feels Sting of China's Anger after Liu Xiaobo Nobel Prize Win," *Huffington Post*, May 6, 2011, http://www.huffingtonpost.com/2011/05/06/norway-china-liu-xiaobo-peace-prize_n_858506.html.

4. Nina Berglund, "Pressure Grows on Nobel Committee," *Views and News from Norway*, February 28, 2011, http://www.newsinenglish.no/2011/02/28/pressure-grows-on-nobel-committee/.


### 21. *The Three China Policies of the United States*

1. The latter cannot intervene directly with the U.S. Treasury because they are not its clients, bureaucratically speaking, and they are sociologically alien as well: they can offer no fit employment for former Treasury officials, and the latter were not recruited from the manufacturing sector, let alone from trade unions.

2. Rachelle Younglai and Doug Palmer, "The United States is becoming more competitive with China as more companies see fewer benefits of moving their investments offshore, U.S. Treasury Secretary Timothy Geithner said on Wednesday," Reuters, Washington, March 28, 2012, http://www.reuters.com/article/2012/03/28/us-usa-china-geithner-idUSBRE82R16U20120328.

3. Paul Eckert, "Analysis: China Trade Deal Follow-Up Critical," Reuters, Washington, D.C., May 11, 2011.

4. No. 332-519 US, ITC Publication 4226, May 2011.

5. See below regarding collateral penetration and recruitment.

6. Michael Mecham and Joseph C. Anselmo, "Aviation 'Learnaholics': China Has the Size, Money and Interest to Engage and Challenge Western Companies," *Aviation Week and Space Technology*, April 25, 2011, pp. 43–67.

7. Security precautions are of course standard in corporate aerospace activities, with additional precautions likely in Chinese joint ventures. But cost-conscious commercial entities that value conviviality are unlikely to rigidly resist normal processes of habituation and the consequent relaxation of vigilance.

8. U.S. aerospace companies frequently rely on U.S. citizens of ethnic Chinese origin for assignments in China. Especially if they have local relatives, they are more vulnerable to blackmail, or merely family pressures.

9. The continuation of which, year after year, decade after decade, has been viewed with joyous incredulity, as China was relatively enriched much more than the United States. Leninists would not have been surprised.

10. "Pakistan, China Agree to Set Up Media University," Pakistan World News, May 18, 2011, http://www.pakistanworldnews.com/pakistan-china-agree-to-set-up-media-university.html.

11. "Chinese to Pay for Spy Centre," staff report, *The Zimbabwean*, May 15, 2011.

12. He joined Wang Qishan (王岐山), vice-premier in charge of economic, energy, and financial affairs, in a prolonged TV discussion in conjunction with the 2011 "strategic and economic dialogue." Wang Qishan was tactless, but Geithner was fawning. It would be distressing if after he leaves public life, Secretary Geithner were to serve Chinese clients. His father, Peter Geithner, is (in 2011) a member of the board of the National Committee on United States–China Relations.

13. The outcome of a July 23, 2009, meeting between Secretary Clinton and the foreign ministers of Lower Mekong Initiative members: U.S. Department of State, Office of the Spokesperson, Washington, D.C., July 22, 2011, http://www.state.gov/p/eap/mekong/index.htm.

14. Section 123 of the U.S. Atomic Energy Act of 1954 establishes an agreement for cooperation as a prerequisite for nuclear transactions between the United States and any other country.

15. It has been twenty-eight years since program initiation for the urgently needed *Tejas* light fighter; it now flies, but only because of its imported ("interim") subsystems.

16. "Huge U.S.-India Arms Deal to Contain China, India; US to Ink Huge Military Deal: Report," *Global Times in Global Research*, July 13, 2010, http://globalresearch.ca/index.php?context=va&aid=20116.

17. From Hong Kong, Strait of Malacca, Strait of Lombok, Strait of Hormuz, Strait of Mandab, to Port Sudan, alongside Pakistan, Sri Lanka, Bangladesh, Maldives, and Somalia. Christopher J. Pehrson, "String of Pearls: Meeting the Challenge of China's Rising Power across the Asian Littoral," U.S. Army, Strategic Studies Institute, July 2006, http://www.strategicstudiesinstitute.army.mil/pdffiles/PUB721.pdf.

18. Jeffrey Goldberg, "Hillary Clinton: Chinese System Is Doomed, Leaders on a 'Fool's Errand,'" *The Atlantic*, May 10, 2011, http://www.theatlantic.com/jeffrey-goldberg/.

19. Hillary Clinton, "America's Pacific Century," *Foreign Policy*, November 11, 2011, http://www.foreignpolicy.com/articles/2011/10/11/americas_pacific_century?page=ful.

20. Secretary of State Clinton Joint Press Availability with Secretary of the Treasury Timothy Geithner, Eisenhower Executive Office Building, Washington, D.C., July 28, 2009, http://www.trackpads.com/forum/us-state-department/913569-sos-clinton-joint-press-availability-secretary-treasury-timothy-geithner.html.

21. "China's National Defense in 2010," Xinhua, English, Official translation of State Council Information Office, March 31, 2011, http://news.xinhuanet.com/english2010/china/2011-03/31/c_13806851.htm.

22. Even the highest estimates of the hydrocarbon and fishing value of the entire South China Sea (proven producible reserves are unimpressive) are dwarfed by the dimensions of the Chinese economy.

## 22. Conclusions and Predictions

1. A Trotskyite citation is irresistible: Vincent Kolo, "Mass Demonstration against Pollution in Dalian," *Chinaworker.info*, August 14, 2011, http://chinaworker.info/en/content/news/1542/.

2. Michael Wines, "China Takes a Loss to Get Ahead in the Business of Fresh Water," *New York Times*, October 25, 2011, http://www.nytimes.com/2011/10/26/world/asia/china-takes-loss-to-get-ahead-in-desalination-industry.html?ref=world&pagewanted=print.

3. Fear of unrest was the explanation given to the present writer for the failure to repress Zhuang gangs that prey on the tourist trade of much-visited Yangshuo County of Guilin Prefecture in the Guangxi Zhuang Autonomous Region.

4. Some observers have disagreed with this dismissive appraisal. See, e.g., John Garnaut, "Profound Shift as China Marches Back to Mao," *Sydney Morning Herald*, October 9, 2011, http://www.smh.com.au/world/profound-shift-as-china-marches-back-to-mao-20111008-1lewz.html#ixzz1c13mQlqh.

5. For the PLA, paramilitary forces of international significance, military space and foreign intelligence activities, and the supporting R&D and industrial base.

6. I have encountered no theory that explains this conduct as advantageous for China.

7. Including Henry A. Kissinger, judging by the opening pages of his *On China* (New York: Penguin, 2011).

8. Signed by Deputy Defense Minister Nguyen Chi Vinh and U.S. Deputy Assistant Secretary of Defense Robert Sher. It provides for a regular high-ranking strategic dialogue and for practical forms of "mutual support" at sea. Ship-to-ship communication provisions are implied. The official Vietnamese announcement stated that the memorandum of understanding proved Vietnam's "self-reliance" (!). "Vietnam, US Ink Deal to Boost Defense Ties," *Thanh Nien News*, September 25, 2011, http://www.lookatvietnam.com/2011/09/vietnam-us-ink-deal-to-boost-defense-ties.html.

9. Jabin T. Jacob, "China-India Special Representatives Talks: Moving beyond the Boundary Dispute," RSIS Commentaries No. 029/2012, dated February 20, 2012, S. Rajaratnam School of International Studies, Nanyang Technological University.

10. Lockheed P-3Cs and Airbus Military (CASA) C295s. Leithen Francis, "Turbulent Waters," *Aviation Week and Space Technology*, October 17, 2011, p. 54, col. 2.

11. Rajat Pandit, "India to Help Train Vietnam in Submarine Operations," *The Times of India*, September 15, 2011, http://articles

.timesofindia.indiatimes.com/2011-09-15/india/30159288_1_bilateral
-defence-cooperation-submarine-vietnamese-navy.

12. See "PHL, Vietnam Agree to Enhance Cooperation at Hanoi Talks," Official Gazette, Office of the President of the Philippines, October 8, 2011, http://www.gov.ph/2011/10/08/phl-vietnam-agree -to-enhance-cooperation-at-hanoi-talks/.

13. "From Geopolitics to Geo-Economics," *The National Interest*, Summer 1990, 17–23.

14. For which the Chinese authorities themselves set a precedent in 2010, by stopping shipments of rare earths to Japan, an extreme case of strategic incompetence on their part.

15. The public reaction to the actual arrival of the San Francisco Bay Bridge replacement segment from China in June 2011 suggests that few highly visible items are likely to be imported by other U.S. public authorities in the future—unless China's overall image were to change.

# *Glossary*

*Key:*

S = simplified characters
T = traditional characters

People's Liberation Army (PLA)
*Rénmín Jiěfàngjūn*
S = 人民解放军
T = 人民解放軍

People's Liberation Army Ground Force (PLAGF)
*Zhōngguó Rénmín Jiěfàngjūn Lùjūn*
S = 中国人民解放军陆军
T = 中國人民解放軍陸軍

People's Liberation Army Navy (PLAN)
*Zhōngguó Rénmín Jiěfàngjūn Hǎijūn*
S = 中国人民解放军海军
T = 中國人民解放軍海軍

People's Liberation Army Air Force (PLAAF)
*Zhōngguó Rénmín Jiěfàngjūn Kōngjūn*
S = 中国人民解放军空军
T = 中國人民解放軍空軍

People's Armed Police Force (PAP)
*Zhōngguó Rénmín Wǔzhuāng Jǐngchá Bùduì*
S = 中国人民武装警察部队
T = 中國人民武裝警察部隊

Ministry of State Security
*Guójiā Ānquán Bù*, abbrev. *Guóānbù*
S = 国家安全部
T = 國家安全部

National Office for Teaching Chinese as a Foreign
Language
*Hanban* S: 汉办

CCP (or CPC): Communist Party of China
*Zhōngguó Gòngchǎndǎng*
S = 中国共产党
T = 中國共產黨

Hu Jintao (Hú Jǐntāo)
S = 胡锦涛
T = 胡錦濤

General Secretary of the Communist Party of China
*Zhōngguó Gòngchǎndǎng Zhōngyāng Wěiyuánhuì Zǒngshūjì*
S = 中国共产党中央委员会总书记
T = 中國共產黨中央委員會總書記

President of the People's Republic of China
*Zhōnghuá Rénmín Gònghéguó Zhǔxí*
S = 中华人民共和国主席
T = 中華人民共和國主席

Chairman *(Zhuxi)* of the Central Military Commission (CMC)
*Zhōngyāng Jūnshì Wěiyuánhuì*
S = 中央军事委员会
T = 中央軍事委員會

The state body thereof: the CMC of the People's Republic of
China
S = 中华人民共和国中央军事委员会
T = 中華人民共和國中央軍事委員會

The party body: the CMC of the CCP
S＝中国共产党中央军事委员会
T＝中國共產黨中央軍事委員會
(The membership of the Party CMC and the State CMC is the same, but the last two former chairmen of the party CMC lingered one more year as chairmen of the state CMC.)

Xi Jinping, Hu Jintao's designated successor (2011)
S＝习近平
T＝習近平

Premier Wen Jiabao (Wēn Jiābāo)
S＝温家宝
T＝溫家寶

State Councilor Dai Bingguo
S＝戴秉国
T＝戴秉國

The Foreign Affairs Leading Small Group of the Communist Party of China
*Zhōngyāng Wàishì Gōngzuò Lǐngdǎo Xiǎozǔ* (currently chaired by Hu Jintao; Dai Bingguo is a member)
S: 中央外事工作领导小组
T: 中央外事工作領導小組

Foreign Minister Yang Jiechi
S＝杨洁篪
T＝楊潔篪

Vice Foreign Minister Fu Ying
S＝傅莹
T＝傅瑩

The Ministry of Foreign Affairs of the People's Republic of China
*Zhōnghuá Rénmín Gònghéguó Wàijiāobù*
S＝中和国外交部
T＝中華人民和國外交部

Senkaku Islands
*Senkaku Shotō* or *Senkaku-guntō*
尖閣諸島

Pinnacle Islands in British charts; called Diaoyutai by the Chinese
S = 钓鱼岛及其附属岛屿
T = 钓鱼台群岛

"South Tibet"
*Zàngnán*
藏南
(Chinese designation of territory mostly within the state of
Arunachal Pradesh, northeast India)

Administration Office for Xisha [Paracel] Islands, Zhongsha Islands
and Nansha [Spratly] Islands, county level, Hainan Province
S = 西沙群岛、南沙群岛、中沙群岛办事处
T = 西沙群島、南沙群島、中沙群島辦事處

Xinjiang
*Shinjang*
新疆

Xinjiang Uyghur Autonomous Region
新疆维吾尔自治区

*Tianxia*, "under heaven"
天下
(the emperor-centered world)

Tāo guāng yǎng huì
韬光养晦
("Hide brightness, nourish obscurity," or less literally, "Hide one's
capacities and bide one's time")

"Warring States" period (conventionally: 475–221 BCE)
*Zhànguó Shídà*
S = 战国时代
T = 戰國時代

*Art of War*
*Sūnzǐ Bīngfa* [lit.: Sun Tzu's Military Principles]
S = 孙子兵法
T = 孫子兵法

The author is most commonly known as:
Sun Tzu or Sunzi
S = 孙子
T = 孫子

or Sun Wu
S = 孙武
T = 孫武

The Records of the Grand Historian (or Scribe) *Shiji*
S = 史記
T = 史记

The author is known as Sima Qian or Ssu-ma Ch'ien
S = 司马迁
T = 司馬遷

Volume 86 contains the biographies of the assassins 刺客列傳
Including Jing Ke 荊軻

Qing (Qīng) dynasty
S = 大清帝国
T = 大清帝國

Beijing's Wángfǔjǐng 王府井

Zhongnanhai 中南海

Fǎlún Dàfǎ 法轮大法 movement

Fǎlún Gōng 法轮功 organization

yuan 元 primary unit of the Renminbi (RMB), "people's currency"

# Index

Fu Ying, 9
Futenma base polemic, 132

Gates, Robert M., 155
Geithner, Timothy F., 213, 216,
    217, 226, 232, 295n2, 296n12
Geo-economics, 40–42
German imperialism, 56ff.
Gillard, Julia, 120–123, 137
Ginowan city, 136
*Global Times*, 84
"Great East Japan earthquake"
    (March 11, 2011), 133
"Great-state autism," 13, 17, 24,
    30, 54, 71, 89, 100

Hainan Province Paracels,
    Spratlys, and Zhongsha
    Islands Authority, 81, 89, 100
Hamada Yazukazu, 129–131
Han and non-Han, 260
Han Xuandi, 26
Hanban, 35, 36
Hoa, 151
Hoag Sa (Paracel Islands), 155,
    157
Hōppo Ryōdo, 139, 144
Hu Jintao, 9, 10, 11, 12, 22, 29,
    127

India, 11, 13–17, 44, 48, 265,
    279n1, 298nn9,11
Indonesia, 50, 186–196
Inner Mongolia Autonomous
    Region, 181, 185, 254, 279n5

International Military Educa-
    tion and Training Program
    (IMET), 192

Japan, 8, 49, 52, 61, 73, 120,
    125–144, 155, 182, 242, 259,
    261, 264, 287n2, 290nn4,14
"Jasmine revolution," 256
Jiang Zemin, 149, 150
Jin dynasty, 91
Jing Ke, 83, 84
Johnson South Reef, 189
Jurchen, 89, 91, 92

Kalayan Island Group (Spratly
    Islands), 200
Khitans, Kitans. *See* Qidans
Kim Jong-il, 175–176, 291nn6,8
Kissinger, Henry, 79, 80, 81,
    226, 280n6, 284n11, 285n1,
    298n7
Kopassus, 192
Korea. *See* North Korea; South
    Korea

*Láng Túténg* (Wolf Totem),
    256
Law Enforcement Command of
    the Administration of Fishery
    and Fishing Harbor Supervi-
    sion, 102, 103, 156
Lee Myung-Bak, 177, 290n5
Levitin, Igor, 185
Liang Guanglie, 129, 131, 135,
    207